'The field of Queer Criminology is evolving quickly, as our knowledge about the nuance and complexity of gender and sexuality continues to grow. Research in this area has exploded since the publication of the first edition of *Queer Criminology*, and the second edition provides an important update to our knowledge as we continue to "queer" criminology and embark upon the process of centering a field that was once marginalized.'

Christina DeJong, *Associate Professor of Criminal Justice, Michigan State University*

'*Queer Criminology* broke new ground by providing an accessible introduction to the field; it quickly became a foundational text. The authors bring a crucial focus on intersectionality in this second edition as they engage with recent scholarship to present contemporary debates in the discipline and deepen their analysis and recommendations.'

Aimee Wodda, *Assistant Professor of Criminal Justice, Law and Society, Pacific University*

'The world changed quickly and Buist and Lenning responded with this exceptionally approachable and timely new edition that is sure to remain a cornerstone text. *Queer Criminology* expands its intersectional scope and brings in the latest on queer victimization and offending, newly emerging political contexts, and developments in theory and practice.'

Xavier Guadalupe-Diaz, *Associate Professor of Sociology, Framingham State University*

D0869622

QUEER CRIMINOLOGY

This book surveys the growing field of Queer Criminology. It reflects on its origins, reviews its foundational research and scholarship and offers suggestions for future directions. Moreover, this book emphasizes the importance of Queer Criminology in the field and the need to move LGBTQ+ issues from the margins to the center of criminological research. Core content includes:

- Contested definitions of and conceptual frameworks for Queer Criminology
- The criminalization of queerness and gender identity in historical and contemporary context
- The relationship between LGBTQ+ communities and law enforcement
- The impact of legislation and court decisions on LGBTQ+ communities
- The experiences of queer victims and offenders under correctional supervision

This revised and updated edition includes new developments in theory and research, further coverage of international issues and a new chapter on victimization and offending. It is essential reading for those engaged with queer, critical, and feminist criminologies, gender studies, diversity, and criminal justice.

Carrie L. Buist is Associate Professor at Grand Valley State University's School of Criminology, Criminal Justice, and Legal Studies. Dr. Buist has been published in several notable journals such as *Critical Criminology*, *University of Richmond Law Review*, *Crime and Justice*, and *Culture, Health, and Sexuality*. Dr. Buist, along with *Queer Criminology*, has edited, with Lindsay K. Semprevivo, *Queering Criminology in Theory and Praxis: Re-imagining Justice in the Criminal Legal System and Beyond*. Dr. Buist has been recognized for her contributions to the discipline with multiple awards in research, teaching, and mentoring.

Emily Lenning is Professor of Criminal Justice at Fayetteville State University. Her publications cover a diverse range of topics, from state-sanctioned violence against women to queer experiences in the criminal legal system to creative advances in pedagogy. Her accomplishments in and out of the classroom have been recognized by several awards, including the 2017–2018 UNC Board of Governors Award for Excellence in Teaching and the 2016 Book Award from the American Society of Criminology's Division on Critical Criminology & Social Justice, for the first edition of this book.

NEW DIRECTIONS IN CRITICAL CRIMINOLOGY

This series presents new cutting-edge critical criminological empirical, theoretical, and policy work on a broad range of social problems, including drug policy, rural crime and social control, policing and the media, ecocide, intersectionality, and the gendered nature of crime. It aims to highlight the most up-to-date authoritative essays written by new and established scholars in the field. Rather than offering a survey of the literature, each book takes a strong position on topics of major concern to those interested in seeking new ways of thinking critically about crime.

Edited by Walter S. DeKeseredy, West Virginia University, USA

From Social Harm to Zemiology
A Critical Introduction
Victoria Canning and Steve Tombs

Queer Criminology Second Edition
Carrie L. Buist and Emily Lenning

For more information about this series, please visit: www.routledge.com/New-Directions-in-Critical-Criminology/book-series/NDCC

QUEER CRIMINOLOGY

Second Edition

Carrie L. Buist and Emily Lenning

Routledge
Taylor & Francis Group

LONDON AND NEW YORK

Cover image: Nelson Antoine

Second edition published 2023
by Routledge
4 Park Square, Milton Park, Abingdon, Oxon OX14 4RN

and by Routledge
605 Third Avenue, New York, NY 10158

Routledge is an imprint of the Taylor & Francis Group, an informa business

First edition published by Routledge 2015

British Library Cataloguing-in-Publication Data
A catalogue record for this book is available from the British Library

Library of Congress Cataloging-in-Publication Data
Names: Buist, Carrie L., author. | Lenning, Emily, author.
Title: Queer criminology / Carrie L. Buist and Emily Lenning.
Description: 2nd edition. | Milton Park, Abingdon,
Oxon ; New York, NY : Routledge, 2022. |
Includes bibliographical references and index.
Identifiers: LCCN 2022007114 | ISBN 9780367760229 (hardback) |
ISBN 9780367760236 (paperback) | ISBN 9781003165163 (ebook)
Subjects: LCSH: Sexual minorities. | Criminology. |
Criminal justice, Administration of.
Classification: LCC HQ73 .B85 2022 |
DDC 306.76–dc23/eng/20220303
LC record available at https://lccn.loc.gov/2022007114

ISBN: 978-0-367-76022-9 (hbk)
ISBN: 978-0-367-76023-6 (pbk)
ISBN: 978-1-003-16516-3 (ebk)

DOI: 10.4324/9781003165163

Typeset in Bembo
by Newgen Publishing UK

We dedicate this book to all of the Queer people who continue to confront and experience injustice around the globe. We applaud all those who have fought for and continue to fight for equality, and we challenge our students and colleagues to advocate for a more just criminal legal system.

CONTENTS

PREFACE

The fact that there is interest in a second edition of this book gives us great pride and hope. It reflects the steady, perhaps even rapid, growth of queer criminology, driven by a dedicated and impressive cadre of critical queer scholars. In the handful of years since the first edition of *Queer Criminology* was released, the field has grown by leaps and bounds. What began with a few conference panels and special journal issues has catapulted into an impressive subfield within the broader discipline, bolstered by ground-breaking scholarship, cutting-edge research, public activism and feverish organizing, as evidenced by the establishment of the American Society of Criminology's Division on Queer Criminology. The speed with which queer criminology has grown, while long in the making, has no doubt been propelled by a series of tragic events including, but not limited to, the Trump Administration's assault on LGBTQ+ rights in the United States and abroad, the Pulse nightclub shooting, the effects of which were felt the world over, and the COVID-19 pandemic, which has forced all of us to reflect on the impact that we have on others. Whatever the impetus, we are in awe of the tenacity shown by the scholars forging this field, and consider ourselves lucky to have a seat at the table.

Our intent with the first edition of this book, and still with the second, is to provide an accessible text that is concise and easy to consume. Our intended audience is not, as some might assume, those already engaging in queer criminological scholarship, though we hope queer scholars will continue to consider this manuscript a useful learning tool in their classrooms and, when they grow weary, a reminder of why the work they do is so vital. Conversely, it is readers with little to no understanding of, or even interest in, queer criminology that we are hoping to reach. Our wish is that an undergraduate student picks up this book and that one of the stories within in it will inspire them to continue engaging in queer scholarship, or that a criminal justice practitioner seeking greater understanding of LGBTQ+ people is inspired by this book to become a change agent in their field.

As such, this book is intentionally limited in scope. It is not our goal to cover all of what constitutes or characterizes queer criminology, despite the title of the book. It is meant to be an introduction to the field – an invitation of sorts. This is why some queer criminologists may find our limited coverage of theory to be disappointing, but also why (we hope) newcomers won't walk away feeling overwhelmed or perplexed. More advanced students will find that there is a growing body of theoretical literature that will quench their thirst for highly complex epistemological discussions, and we are hopeful that this book will motivate them to seek out that work.

Similarly, some may criticize this work for not covering enough of any one geographic region, while others will say we have addressed too many regions without offering great enough coverage of the social, cultural and political landscapes that differentiate them. However, discussing two or more staunchly different countries in the span of a few pages is not meant to undermine cultural differences or ignore cultural context. It is done to provide a breadth of examples without exhausting and therefore losing our audience or, more importantly, the point – which is that, sadly, examples of injustice against Queer people are found the globe over. Understanding that basic truth is where this book invites readers to begin and, if our efforts are not futile, will foster in them a desire to seek a deeper and more nuanced understanding of the Queer experience. Thank you, for choosing to join us on this most important journey.

ACKNOWLEDGEMENTS

We would first like to thank Walter DeKeseredy for believing in the importance of a queer criminology and the contributions that it has made and will continue to make in the field of critical criminology. Next, we want to thank our team at Routledge. We would like to thank Thomas Sutton for his support, constant guidance and dedication to the project. This book benefited from the thoughtful critique of reviewers and we appreciate the time they took to share with us their thoughts and suggestions. This book would not have been possible without the support of our colleagues at Grand Valley State University and Fayetteville State University. We acknowledge Matthew Ball, Christina DeJong, Angela Dwyer, Xavier Guadalupe-Diaz, Adam Messinger, Vanessa Panfil, Lindsay Kahle Semprevivo, Jace Valcore, Allyn Walker, Aimee Wodda, Jordan Blair Woods, Meredith Worthen, and all of the scholars, practitioners and students who are working and living queer criminology every day. We would also like to thank Human Rights Watch for their permission to reproduce previously published material in this book. We also wish to recognize the members of the Division on Queer Criminology of the American Society of Criminology whom we consider mentors, colleagues, friends, and a constant source of inspiration and encouragement. And finally, we would like to recognize countless scholar-allies and accomplices who have supported our work throughout the years – we are lucky to have had the support of far too many people to list here, but your love has not gone unnoticed.

Carrie

First, I would like to thank my wife, Cherie Dale Bryant-Buist, for making my world complete, for making every day with you the best day of my life, and for being an example of love in action. I am deeply grateful to the mentors I have been lucky enough to have along the way and the support of colleagues, students, and friends. I would like to spotlight the support and mentorship of Paul Leighton who has been a valued teacher, mentor, confidant, and friend. Sincere thanks to my first unapologetic feminist teacher, mentor, and friend, Marilyn Corsianos; to Angie Moe for waffles, Susan Carlson for her heart and Ron Kramer for his baseball knowledge. Walter DeKeseredy, you have been a friend and mentor since day one and for you I'll always be grateful. I'd also like to thank all my former graduate school peers, colleagues, and queer criminology scholars whose work and courage inspires me. I am also honored to have worked with some amazing students in the last decade or so: Regina Cline, Tyler McCarty, Christina Ledezma, Alyssa McCord, and Kayla Bates should be recognized for their work on iterations of this book. I would be nothing and nowhere without the love and support of strong women in my life: Sherry Buist, Mary Buist, Regenia Tongate Barnes, Angela Bryant, Sarah Scott, Jes Edel, Jenn Vanderminden, Kay Gugala, and Susan Mellor. I'd also like to recognize the awesome young people who have enriched my life more than they know: Charley Scott, Ethan Fagan, Skyler Fagan, Maia Edel Harrelson, Avi Edel Harrelson, and Asher Wrenn Vanderminden, I hope that everyone, even those folks whose names aren't mentioned here, will understand that it doesn't mean you aren't loved and that I am not thankful for you. I am, indeed, eternally grateful to everyone in my life no matter what role or purpose you served. I continue to wish that we may all, to quote my friend Amanda Burgess-Proctor, "Live boldly, love deeply, and give thanks always." Finally, thank you, Emily Lenning for your lasting friendship, patience, support, and dogged determination.

Emily

First and foremost, I would like to recognize and thank my wife. Shay, you are my greatest inspiration and source of support, and I am a better person because of you. The last 25 years with you has been an incredible journey, and I can't wait to see what the next 25 years hold for us. Next, I must acknowledge that I would not be where I am today if not for the constant encouragement of my family, especially my parents, Nancy and Pete Grendze, Bob Lenning, and Jim McClatchy. Thank you for always telling me that there was nothing I couldn't do, for pushing me to reach for the stars, and for teaching me to be proud of who I am. I am a better person because of the unconventional family that I have been blessed with, to include my sister and confidante Cindy Willson, my brother Brandon (B) Lee Grendze, whose memory motivates me to live every moment to the fullest, and my partner-in-crime, Heather Grendze. To my BFF Sara Brightman, I owe you a debt of gratitude. Thank you for bringing me joy when I am sad, for celebrating every accomplishment (no matter how small), for being a strong woman that I can look up to and strive to be like, and for blessing me with the type of friendship that most people spend their entire lives searching for. To Walter DeKeseredy, your mentorship helped guide me to where I am in my career today, but your friendship has helped guide me through life. Whether we are chatting about cheesy shark movies or discussing the serious problems of the world, every conversation we have had has been an important part of my life's script. To Michael DeValve, know that it is you who has taught me the true meaning of love, and that I will always strive to care for the wellbeing of others without qualification, even when it is difficult to do so. To Angie D. Gordon, thank you for challenging and renewing my faith in redemption, and for reminding me that even when I think no one is listening, they are. So many friends have supported me throughout this project and my entire career, and to those who are not named here – please know that your assistance and support does not go unnoticed. To my Fayetteville State family, past and present – especially Brent Lewis, Rob Taber, Jeremy Fiebig, and every member of the Criminal Justice department – thank you for being amazing colleagues and friends. Last, but certainly not least, thank you to Carrie Buist for your friendship, for taking on this daunting project, for always putting up with me, and for believing in not just me, but in us.

1

QUEER(ING) CRIMINOLOGY

Queer criminology is a theoretical and practical approach that seeks to highlight and draw attention to the stigmatization, the criminalization, and in many ways, the rejection of the Queer community, which is to say the LGBTQ+ (lesbian, gay, bisexual, transgender, and queer +) population, as both victims and offenders, by academe and the criminal legal system. Further, queer criminology examines the experiences of LGBTQ+ people as victims, as offenders and as professionals who work within the criminal legal system and its ancillary areas of "justice" (Ball 2014a; Ball 2016; Buist & Semprevivo 2022; Buist & Stone 2014; Dwyer, Ball, & Crofts 2016; Groombridge 1998; Peterson & Panfil 2014a, Tomsen 1997; Woods 2014). Although there is no question that persons who identify as part of the Queer community have been included in research samples, "their sexual and/or gender identities are not interrogate[d] as salient characteristics, as these are likely not recognized at all" (Peterson & Panfil 2014b: 3). Thus, queer criminology seeks both to move LGBTQ+ people, to borrow from bell hooks, from the margins to the center of criminological inquiry, and to investigate and challenge the ways that the criminal legal system has been used as a tool of oppression against Queer people.

DOI: 10.4324/9781003165163-1

Since the first edition of *Queer Criminology* was released, the field has expanded to include a variety of new topics. These topics include but are not limited to: gay gang affiliation (Panfil 2017), sex-positive criminology (Wodda & Panfil 2021), queer theory and criminology (see Dwyer, Ball, & Crofts 2016; Ball 2016), stigma (see Worthen 2020), queer criminology and activism (see Ball 2016; Buist 2019), new PREA updates (see Malkin & DeJong 2019), intimate partner violence (see Guadalupe-Diaz 2019; Messinger 2017), queer criminality (see Asquith, Dwyer, & Simpson 2017), merging theory and practice (see Buist & Semprevivo 2022), and of course ongoing policy and practice discussion and implementation from a variety of sources, such as the Human Rights Campaign, the National Center for Transgender Equality, Transgender Europe, and the Williams Institute. Further, even as we write this book, legislation continues to evolve across the United States and abroad.

As the field continues to grow, new approaches in applying queer criminology have been developed and will no doubt continue to develop and, while queer criminology has gained some momentum, criminological research and the criminal legal system often ignore the experiences of Queer people in any real, substantive way. The exception to this is a focus on sexual proclivities as deviant – a presumption that was posited by early criminologists, such as Cesare Lombroso in the 1800s, and subsequently influenced much of criminological and sociological research on gay, lesbian, bisexual, transgender, and Queer people (Woods 2014). Further, Jordan Blair Woods has posited in the formation of his homosexual deviancy theory that the ways in which Queer people were treated within early criminological theory influenced how "baseless stereotypes and social biases shaped definitions of 'criminal behavior' and 'criminal populations'" (Woods 2015: 133). Woods's theory consists of two major components. The first component, *the deviance-centered element*, notes that, until the 1970s, any focus within criminological theory and research that was given to Queer populations was couched within the assumption that Queer people were deviant. He goes on to remind us that, during this time, there were

dominant external legal, political, and societal mechanisms of social control that defined Queer populations as deviants in different ways ... criminal anti-sodomy laws, medical conceptions of homosexuality as mental illness, and sociological conceptions of homosexuality as products of failed socialization patterns.

Woods 2015: 133

The second component of Woods's (2015) theory contains the *invisibility element*, which posits that research on Queer people and on sexual orientation and gender identity essentially disappears from the criminological landscape, particularly after the 1970s. According to Woods (2015: 135), this invisibility led to "changing attitudes about sexual deviance." Regardless of the disappearance or the change in focus about sexual deviance, Woods reminds us that, historically, sexual orientation and/or gender identity have been researched and theorized within a deviancy framework. Although changes have taken place, these historical and cultural presumptions about Queer people and the Queer community continue to influence the ways in which Queer folks are treated in the field.

Woods's theory draws attention to the historical roots of homophobia within criminology as a discipline, while also bringing to light the present concerns within the field based on the lack of research conducted on Queer people and their experiences within the criminal legal system and within criminology in general. This *invisibility* breeds complacency within the field and allows us to further ignore the experiences of Queer people. In this book, we offer examples of the plethora of experiences that Queer folks have within the criminal legal system in an effort to bring this population from the margins to the center of focus.

While we offer you a definition of queer criminology, it would be remiss of us to assume that this is the *only* definition. Queer criminology continues to be a developing subdiscipline within criminology broadly and, as many believe, critical criminology more specifically. In fact, *all* of what might characterize the field has not yet come to fruition, though the examples of how the field has expanded since the first edition of this book speak to the different directions queer criminology can go and the variety of scholars working in the area. This book, regardless of the edition, may always reflect where the field is in this moment, while never fully being able to address all that has happened, is happening, or will happen. As the work continues, we should welcome new scholars, new research trajectories, and more broadly, a variety of perspectives about the many queer-focused issues in criminological research and theory meant to spark and advance an important conversation. So, while some have demanded that queer criminology have a narrow, rigid definition – we could not disagree more. We believe that the definition of queer criminology should be broad and dynamic and remain so in order to reflect the fluidity of Queer identities and therefore allow for a variety of contributions theoretically, empirically, and via practical application in the field. For instance, our definition of queer criminology is a practical definition that is specific to individual and group experiences in the system itself while also supporting a theoretical foundation. However, we cannot take for granted the need to *queer* (see Ball 2016) and disrupt criminology. This is an important suggestion, especially since mainstream criminology has failed in any real way to add to the research on LGBTQ+ experiences.

Queer criminology continues to move forward, incorporating the application of intersectionality, cultural competency, trauma-informed care, victim advocacy and more. This research has extended, contributed to, or created new dialog in any number of disciplines including sociology, psychology, social work, gender studies, and sexuality studies, including a growing interest from practitioners and other professionals working in the criminal legal system and similar fields. However, there continues to be pushback, often from mainstream scholars in a variety of disciplines. Indeed, even with the support of critical criminology, at least one well-known and respected academic journal, *Feminist Criminology*, has opted to publish what many queer criminologists and critical criminologists, along with feminist criminologists, believe to be anti-transgender rhetoric (see Burt 2020 and Valcore, Fradella, Guadalupe-Diaz, Ball, Dwyer, DeJong, Walker, Wodda, & Worthen 2021). When this happens, as it has and will most likely continue to, it proves a need for queer criminology, but also reminds us that queer criminology may look different to different individuals, and one such example of this difference can be found in language.[1]

Language

Throughout this book, we use the word Q(q)ueer as an umbrella term to capture lesbian, gay, bisexual, transgender, and intersex[2] folks, and any others who fall outside cisgender heteronormative binaries. We recognize that not everyone who identifies as lesbian, gay, bisexual, or transgender also identifies as Queer. We further recognize that the reasons why some individuals may or may not identify with or even agree with the use of Queer vary, and that those reasons are often deep-seated at the cultural level – for example, experiences of rejection, violence, and overall negative encounters are, for some, immediately attached to the word "queer." This is especially true for older generations of LGBTQ+ identifying individuals. In August of 2019, NPR (National Public Radio) explored the use of queer in popular culture and communication, including various news outlets. While many young folks embrace the importance of reclaiming the word *queer*, contributors to the NPR piece argue that the reclamation of queer actually began decades ago, with one participant noting that they remember queer being used without contempt during the AIDS crisis, typically considered to have begun in the early to mid-1980s. The report continues by highlighting those generational differences – some younger folks appreciating the fluidity of the word with one participant noting, "I like saying that I am queer because I am. I don't fall on society's ideas of a traditional sexuality or a traditional gender identity. And I'm OK with being queer" (Mallory Yu, as cited in Rocheleau 2019: n.p.). Language and meanings evolve – so, although queer may have been a word reclaimed and used proudly decades ago, there are still older members of the community who experienced hate and violence attached to it, while younger generations have only known it as empowering.

While some may embrace the word queer, others will never feel comfortable with its use and in this sense, even language that is meant to be inclusive has the potential to divide. We want to make clear that we do not use this word to offend or bother – we do this understanding the power of language and how it can be either inclusive or exclusionary. We use it with the intention of the former rather than the latter, and even though we, as mentioned, understand that some may disagree, we remind you that the use of the word *queer* and its general definition have evolved over time. Language will always be evolving, interpreted, understood, and experienced differently based on any number of reasons including, time, space, and location.

As we move forward, some things are worth noting regarding the use of language and our language choices. First, it should be noted that where we have used an acronym (e.g., LGBT) in lieu of queer, it is because the authors and researchers we are citing have used that acronym and we want to accurately reflect their research population and respect that they likely have legitimate reasons for focusing on specific identities. We will also occasionally use acronyms in lieu of queer because they may be more specific to what we are discussing. Additionally, the use of "homosexual" is used as sparingly as possible and only applied for the same reasons as stated earlier – that is, in order to maintain research integrity. We, however, strongly suggest that the use of "homosexual" to define one's sexuality is medicalized language used as an antiquated diagnosis of psychopathology and more (see Goorens & Gijs 2015; Drescher 2010; Ross 1988), and is therefore potentially dangerous and stigmatizing. We do not recommend its use and avoid it as best we can throughout the book.

Queer is also a word offered for your consideration to mean *something that differs from the norm* and we suggest that queer criminology is and can be an amalgamation of theory, research, and/or praxis that falls outside the norms of orthodox criminological research. As mentioned, while criminologists have been theorizing about and researching the experiences of the Queer community for much of the last century (although the amount of research is still scant and the focus of the research is myopic), it is not "out of the norm" to do so. What is historically out of the norm is to do so from *a position of critique* – for example, recognizing and highlighting the *construction* of Queer identities as deviant and criminal, questioning the state's role in criminalizing sexual orientation and/or gender identity, or exploring the role of the criminal legal system as a mechanism for the social control of Queer identities. A truly queer criminology moves beyond the traditional deviance framework and shifts the spotlight from the rule breakers to the rule makers (see Ball 2014b; Woods 2014).

Language and identity

First and foremost, we must point out that sex and gender are two different things. As indicated by Lenning (2009), sex describes the DNA and sex organs that we are born with, while gender is distinguished by our actions and thus should be recognized as a verb. In other words, gender is a social construction characterized by outward presentation of masculinity, femininity, or anything in between. Sex is a biological fact determined by genetic codes and physical anatomy and, like gender, it is fluid and not binary. Further, neither gender nor sex are inextricably linked to one's sexual orientation, meaning that your sex or gender does not determine who you are emotionally, relationally, and sexually attracted to.

At this point in history, one can find literally hundreds of words used to describe various sexual and gender identities, and the list continues to grow. Though most commonly used to represent the Queer community, the "LGBT" acronym is simply not representative of all members of the Queer community. As Lenning (2009) found in her study that included 249 trans-identified individuals, participants used no less than 23 terms to describe their own gender identity. Even their romantic partners, most of whom were presumably cisgender, used a dozen terms to describe their own gender identity. When asked to identify their sexual orientation, the answers were just as varied. What Lenning (2009) concluded, at least in regards to gender identity, is that, at the very least, researchers need to identify an individual's gender orientation *and* gender presentation in order to even begin to understand trans experiences. More recently, non-binary identities, perspectives, and language have been recognized in news and media outlets – with artists such as Sam Smith, Janelle Monae, Jonathan Van Ness, Halsey, and Nico Tortorello, among others, who have come out publicly as either using they/them pronouns and/or identifying as gender nonconforming or non-binary. The latter, Tortorello, commented, "We are ALL multidimensional dynamic creatures and as much as I understand the spectrum, the less I believe in the binary of gender, the more liberated I myself am becoming" (as quoted in Ahlgrim 2021: n.p.).

Language and identity go hand in hand as we define who we are and traverse our worlds, although what we see may not be what society sees. Jack Halberstam (2018) examines "unbuilding gender" as related to art, "anarchitecture," and the work of artist Gordon Matta-Clark. The ideas shared by Halberstam in their essay highlight identity language and the non-binary. Halberstam notes that indeed the social system in and of itself is problematic and the need is to "dismantle the system that metes out rightness and wrongness according to the dictates of various social orders" (Halberstam 2018: n.p.). The author continues by highlighting gender as related to intersectionality when noting:

> Trans* bodies, in other words, function not simply to provide an image of the non-normative against which normative bodies can be discerned, but rather as bodies that are fragmentary and internally contradictory; bodies that remap gender and its relations to race, place, class, and sexuality ...
>
> Halberstam 2018: n.p.

Although Halberstam is not a criminologist, the points they make allow us to take stock of how research is conducted in the field. As we continue to challenge the status quo in criminology we also see what Halberstam's essay speaks to – the materials used to build art as related to our materials used to "build and unbuild" the body. The metaphor can be applied to queer criminology, in that it works towards building and unbuilding criminology and the criminal legal system. One example of this is unpacked by Valcore and Pfeffer (2018) as they examine the difficulty in measuring gender in criminological research. Not unlike Lenning's (2009) findings, individual definitions of who trans and non-binary people are, how they identify or recognize gender, or not, and how they construct or deconstruct identity is a very personal decision, and in turn it complicates research. For instance, Valcore and Pfeffer (2018) found that gender is often conceived in research as binary (male/female) when we know this is wholly problematic. The authors indicate previous reports that estimate 1.4 million transgender and non-binary people are living in the United States and, with disproportionate contact with the criminal legal system, these numbers alone support the need for inclusive research. As noted, "[m]ainstream research published in top CCJ journals privileges and maintains cisgenderism by continuing to treat gender as a binary category determinable by sex assigned at birth ..." (Valcore & Pfeffer 2018: 334), thus ignoring the myriad gender constructions that go well beyond "male" and "female." Building and unbuilding is also an example of construction and deconstruction – both concepts of importance when discussing queer theory and queer criminology.

In the most general sense, we reject essentialist attitudes because they fail to fully recognize sexual and gender identity and its fluidity among some Queer individuals, especially trans folk. This is true in part for other Queer folks as well. If the bodies of Queer people are seen as "different," then those identifying as transgender are an embodiment of deconstruction which, according to the *Cornell Chronicle* (2008: n.p.) "has come to mean a critical dismantling of tradition and traditional modes of thought." This is not unlike our call to mainstream criminologies and critical criminologies to *queer* criminology. A necessary component of queer criminology is to queer methods as well. Not unlike the basic concepts behind feminist epistemology (ways of knowing), queer criminological research must focus on not only being inclusive but creating a new way to create and disseminate the production of knowledge. Further, as noted by Jagose (1996: 3), "queer theory's debunking of stable sexes, genders, and sexualities develops out of a specifically lesbian and gay reworking of the post structuralist figuring of identity as a constellation of multiple and unstable positions." Therefore, while sexual orientation and gender identity may be easily identifiable and definable for some, they are not for others, and there are a great many who do not require a definition. Further, and of great significance in the criminal legal system, an outsider looking in may need to define or identify another person and may be wholly inaccurate; therefore, it is important to understand the complexities of categorization. In short, it is always problematic when we make assumptions regarding another's sexuality and/or gender.

There are, of course, the biological arguments and considerations regarding sexual orientation – which posit that an individual does not choose who they are sexually, emotionally, and relationally attracted to. Conversely, there are the socialization-centered arguments that one's sexual orientation and/or gender identity are constructed in the formal and informal, cultural, institutional, and structural elements within society that influence one's personal decisions regarding who they choose to be or be sexually, emotionally, and relationally attracted to. There are indeed pros and cons to each of these arguments, and, quite frankly, instead of making broad and sweeping generalizations about sexual orientation and/or gender identity, we contend that it does not really matter. What matters is that we do have a significant percentage of the world's population who identify as gay, lesbian, bisexual, transgender, and queer, and the community has continued to experience differential and disproportionately negative encounters and treatment within the criminal legal system from all aspects of the system – as offenders, victims, practitioners and state agents, and within academe.

Further, in general, there is no debate over whether or not heterosexual people are born that way or have chosen that identity because we live in a world where heterosexuality is normative and compulsory. We ask those of you who continue to debate the sexual orientation and/or gender identities of others to look inward and think about your own. But more so, we challenge you to understand that, regardless of these debates, what is known, what is a social fact that we are addressing here, is that Queer people continue to have fewer human rights and liberties than heterosexual and gender-conforming people, and that, based solely on sexual orientation and/or gender identity, people continue to face discrimination, harassment, victimization, torture, and even death. If for no other reason, this is why there needs to be a queer criminology.

Within a developing field of study, the ongoing debate regarding how a queer criminology should look can be problematic. Language, symbols, personal identity and more are integral for communication, but language looks different and feels different between groups and geographical location. Language also has the ability to change at varying speeds and without a doubt language that we have used in the first edition may have been, to some, inaccurate. Language we use in this second edition will most likely be imperfect as well. As mentioned, language can change at a rapid rate or move along like an exhausted sloth. This is true for fields of study as well, because although queer criminology has found some allies along the way there are still lessons to be learned and changes to be made. Perhaps the greatest ally thus far has been critical criminology and other areas defined as critical criminologies but that are just as strong standing on their own as well, most prominently feminist criminology.

Queer criminology's allies, advocates, and frenemies

Critical criminology developed in the 1960s and continues to have a major impact and influence in the criminological world. Critical criminology is rooted in understanding, explaining, and exposing power structures and, as a discipline, continues to be the home of numerous criminological inquiries including race, class, the environment, corporations, political crime, state crime, and even gender and sexuality. However, critical criminology was slow to include, for one example, cis-girls and cis-women at the center of the research. Therefore, feminist criminology developed – first to focus on those experiences and later expanded to include research on cis-boys and cis-men, recognizing that gender is not limited to one sex. At the core of feminist criminology is a belief that gender is and should be a primary concern of criminological research. Early feminist criminology leaned towards the liberal feminist ideals of inclusion in mainstream criminological research and development of feminist theoretical approaches that included the hotly debated emancipation/liberation theories of Adler (1975) and Simon (1975). These theories posited that greater equality and independence for women would lead to their increased criminality. However, these theories, among others, were problematic – much like the liberal feminist agenda within the women's movement. Other theories that explored the influence of family structure on girls and boys, such as Hagan, Simpson, and Gillis's (1987) study, examined power-control theory in the household, which also explored class structure. Feminist criminology argued, rightly so, that girls and women were ignored in the existing research but the assumption at the time was that theories that were developed from research conducted on males could yield the same findings for women. This "add women and stir" (Chesney-Lind 1988) approach, as we came to learn, would simply not suffice. Neither will "add Queer and stir" (Ball 2014a) approaches sufficiently explain Queer experiences in the criminal legal system. Highlighting the fact that there are multiple feminist theories and new approaches that are still developing is important to note. For instance, some feminist criminology is inclusive, or takes into account the experiences of marginalized women, while other strands continue to privilege the voices and experiences of cisgender white women. Evidence suggests that a more intersectional framework and ways of knowing is integral not only in queer criminology but in criminology as a whole. The importance of intersectionality cannot be understated when looking at the experiences of people of color, queer folks, and more.

One example of expanding existing research to queer people would be feminist pathways, which highlights life events and experiences that often influence and contribute to female offending such as race, class, history of abuse, drug use, mental illness, and so on. The impact of these factors plays a unique role in their experiences within the criminal legal system, and attention to the cycle of violence and the impact that victimization has on female offenders are key tenets of the approach (Belknap & Holsinger 1998; Belknap & Holsinger 2006; Brennan, Breitenbach, & Dieterich 2010; Daly 1992; Mallicoat 2015). Queer folks also experience unique pathways to offending (see Asquith, Dwyer, & Simpson 2017; Winters 2022) that in many ways relate specifically to their sexual orientation and/or gender identity. For example, as the forthcoming chapters will show, as young Queer boys and girls come out to their families, they are often kicked out of their homes by disapproving family members. Queer youth also experience disproportionate levels of bullying in school that can lead to suspension or expulsion. Further, they Queer youth are more likely to attempt suicide than their heterosexual and cisgender peers. These experiences can lead to arrest and/or criminal labels and further stigmatization unique to Queer young people, especially Queer Black, Indigenous, and People of Color (BIPOC) youth. These experiences not only speak to pathways theory, but highlight the importance of implementing trauma-informed practices in the criminal legal system and its derivative branches.

As mentioned earlier, both critical criminology and feminist criminology helped clear a path for queer criminology to follow, and none are without their flaws. For instance, almost exclusively, feminist research has privileged the voices and experiences of cisgender women and girls, meaning women and girls who were assigned female at birth. Not only has feminist criminology privileged the experiences of cisgender women and girls over transgender women and girls, it has also at times been outright dismissive of the transgender community. Therefore, let it serve as an important reminder that there is no one feminist perspective and that people who identify as feminists often disagree on any number of topics. The term TERF (trans-exclusionary radical feminist), perhaps currently most associated with JK Rowling of Harry Potter fame, in brief means feminists who believe that only people assigned female at birth are women, who would themselves identify as radical, and who are "unwilling to recognise trans women as sisters …" (Smythe 2018 n.p.). This brief definition is from Viv Smythe, who has been credited with coining the term back in 2008. Smythe is also quoted as stating *"marginalising trans women at actual risk from regularly documented abuse /violence in favour of protecting hypothetical cis-women from purely hypothetical abuse /violence from trans women in women-only safe-spaces strikes me as horribly unethical as well as repellently callous."* (Smythe 2018: n.p. emphasis on the original).

Exclusionary practices have a long and sordid history in the United States, and these practices can contribute to excluding Queer people, especially transgender individuals. In an article criticizing the U.S. Equality Act of 2019, Burt (2020: 373) notes, "… under the Equality Act, any male can gain unchallengeable access to female provisions or spaces simply by self-declaration, whether that reflects their feelings or they just want to enter the space for some predatory reason." We strongly disagree with Burt's stance. It is also insulting to note (as Burt does) that transwomen are a vulnerable group, yet dedicate so much time and energy into questioning their personhood. Additionally, multiple research studies as well as popular news outlets have reported no such danger of predatory transgender individuals creeping around public restrooms or other "female" spaces (see Deliso 2021; Crocket 2015; Hasenbush, Flores, & Herman 2019; The National Center for Transgender Equality 2016). Moreover, Sheffer and McCord (2021: 38) have noted the importance of considering how sex has been determined in the higher courts and argue that "there is no justifiable reason or argument that discrimination against individuals with other LGBTQ identities is not also sex-based discrimination."

There is certainly important advocacy and support that has come from more critical approaches to criminology but we still wait to see more work done in these realms – we continue to ask why critical criminology or areas such as cultural criminology, environmental crime, political crime, and more, often do not explore the experiences of LGBTQ+ people as related to their research areas. It seems a topic that should have been discussed in more detail in the last 30 years. Why has queer criminology just recently, within the last ten or so years, emerged onto the critical criminological landscape? Certainly, influential articles on the topic were first published in the late 1990s (Groombridge 1998; Tomsen 1997), but the first time we saw any real attention from critical criminology on queer issues was in 2014 when the journal *Critical Criminology* dedicated a special edition to Queer/ing Criminology. When the first edition of this book was published, a few other publications also focused on LGBT experiences within the criminal legal system, namely Mogul, Ritchie, and Whitlock's (2011) *Queer (In)Justice: The criminalization of LGBT people in the United States* and Peterson and Panfil's (2014a) edited monolithic *Handbook of LGBT communities, crime, and justice*. Now, as we write the second edition, we have a more impressive array of invaluable publications on queer or queering criminology, many of which were mentioned at the beginning of this chapter, such as Guadalupe-Diaz's (2019) *Transgressed: Intimate partner violence in transgender lives*; or Worthen's (2020) *Queer, bis, and straight lies: An intersectional examination of LGBTQ stigma*; there's also Dwyer, Ball, and Crofts's (2016) *Queering criminologies*; and *Sex-positive criminology* by Wodda and Panfil (2021) among others. As the research expands and new students and scholars as well as professionals working in the criminal legal field turn their focus to these concerns, we see more and more time spent on developing queer criminology as a discipline, including the creation of the Division on Queer Criminology within the American Society of Criminology, newly established in 2020.

Although there is always room for improvement and care, we are not implying that queer criminology has not had some support; if we had no advocates or allies you would not be reading this (especially as a second edition) today. Critical criminology developed from the radical criminological perspectives developed in the 1960s as a response to mainstream criminology's tendency to ignore the influence of the powerful (Buist & Stone 2014; Lynch & Michalowski 2000). Further, as noted by Leighton (2010: 16), "when you are the power you shape people's vision of the truth." These perspectives are integral to concepts within not only queer theory, which we will discuss in more detail below, but in the development of queer criminology as well. Questions often arise within the criminal legal system regarding who has the power and how those powerful people are the most politically influential. This in turn shapes policy, to include the implementation of policy that has for the most part worked to keep Queer people marginalized. Who has the power matters – whether politically or personally – and the lack of power matters. These concepts have been explored time and again within the social sciences and beyond. Soon, we will dedicate space to discuss the importance of intersectionality but first, it is important to explore queer theory's influence on queer criminology.

Queer theory's influence

Returning to the definition of queer criminology, while we are wholly concerned with highlighting and identifying the injustices that Queer people experience within the criminal legal system, and we are proponents of developing a queer criminology and supporting the myriad ways it looks, we are well aware of the prejudiced attitudes that are still alive in the United States and abroad regarding the Queer community. We also recognize that for some people, the word *queer* invokes a visceral and negative feeling. For those who reject the term, we are left with the hope that people will approach this work with a critical lens and recognize the existence of compulsory heterosexuality and the influence of heteronormativity on the criminal legal system. That regardless of personal politics, an educated person will concede that given the historical and current climates at the global level, Queer people are faced with certain injustices both within and outside of the criminal legal system that heterosexual and cisgender people do not experience because of their sexual orientation and/or gender identity. As mentioned, queer is something that has been considered outside of the norm, but it also represents the importance of fluidity and refusal to be labeled any one specific way. This approach relates to the influence that queer theory has had on the development of queer criminology.

Queer theory developed from a need to recognize that sexual and gender identities mattered – on both the micro and macro levels of research, and that the lived experiences of an individual identifying as queer was a part of a larger social structure that categorized and labeled that identity. Instead of keeping queer at the periphery of knowledge and research, queer theory called for specific attention to be paid to "sexuality and gender as subjects worthy of consideration in their own right" (Kirsch 2000: n.p.). Certainly, queer theory wanted focus to be turned to sexuality and gender as topics of inquiry, but there was a deeper need for these explorations. One major influence of queer theory on queer criminology is that it is distinctive because, rather than simply introducing sexuality and gender identity as a variable, queer criminological perspectives are/can be used as a lens through which to question the status quo. When we do this, we can begin to recognize that these identities have been used as structural mechanisms of social control. As noted by Rutter and Schwartz (2012: 27), "sexuality is never totally 'free' from its social context." Further, any discussion of labels, categories, or descriptives always have the possibility of influencing the ways in which we identify others, often times producing in and out groups, punishing others for behavior that is outside of the norm or, for purposes of queer theory and criminology, the hetero/binary norm (Ball 2014b; Rutter & Schwartz 2012).

As mentioned, we contend that queer criminology is also influenced by critical views in criminology. One of those topics includes, but is not limited to, power. Power with regard to sexuality is a topic that has been previously discussed in the literature. Indeed, Kirsch (2000) highlights the work of Foucault (among others) when discussing the importance of considering the influence of power on behavior. This is an important distinction to mention and it certainly supports our position that queer criminology is a critical criminology and should be thought of and respected as such. Radical criminologists predominately focused on class as the power differential that should be taken into account in criminological research. Sexual orientation and gender identity should also be viewed as identities that impact a power imbalance, especially when we are considering social capital. Topics such as equality and legal protections not only for victims, offenders, and practitioners within the criminal legal system but also regarding marriage, health care, employment, legal representation, harassment, and so on, speak to the inequities that Queer people face. When the law allows for heterosexuals and cisgender individuals to have protections, rights, and opportunities that are not equally afforded to nonheteronormative individuals, the imbalance and the lack of agency and capital for the Queer community is undeniable.

As noted by Foucault (1980) and reiterated by Kirsch (2000), the oppressive nature of power inhibits the freedom of others. Recognition of this oppression certainly contributed to events such as the Stonewall Riots that took place on June 29, 1969. Briefly, the riots took place as police officers raided a local gay bar and, instead of peacefully disbanding, the gay and transgender patrons of the Stonewall Inn fought back against the police, and, subsequently, this event became the symbol for the gay liberation movement (Jagose 1996). Although this one event is heralded as the defining moment within the movement and the reason why LGBTQ+ pride is celebrated every June, we must not let this single event overshadow the cumulative efforts for equality and freedom prior to the riots, during that time, and thereafter.

For instance, during the 1960s and 1970s, there were two gay liberation movements that were beginning to take shape and influenced the cause. Jagose (1996: 30) details the differences in the two major movements within the gay community – first beginning in the 1960s in what was referred to as homophile organizations, which sought to slowly gain acceptance within heteronormative society, the main goals of the organizations were to eventually gain "legal and social recognition on the same terms as heterosexuals." While the riots at Stonewall Inn became known as the genesis of the gay liberation movement, the event was more of a coincidence rather than what spawned the movement. In contrast to the homophile movement, the gay liberation movement of the 1970s and 1980s was focused on achieving equality not through passivity and patience, but through demands and urgency. Here we see some similarity with the feminist movement both on the larger scale and within criminology as well. They began, as noted above, with the more liberal feminist approach that focused on equality and recognition within society and the discipline, and then moved to the more critical approaches such as socialist, radical, lesbian, and Black feminist theoretical approaches that focused on several different factors and variables related to inequality beyond legislation, such as capitalism, patriarchy, heterosexism, and race.

In many ways, this is where we stand today with regard to Queer rights and, in turn, this is where we stand with queer criminology. We assure you that as we are writing this book, we are the minority. At conferences, we are looked upon quizzingly when we discuss this field of research. Professionals in the field question if this is even a required area of research, teaching, or study. We are puzzled by this confusion but not surprised. That is why we make this call for a queer-focused criminology, because, as previously argued, the inequities within the United States and around the world between the heteronormative/cisgender population and the Queer population are not only experienced through loss of social capital, but also experienced through the ways in which society, especially the criminal legal system, act in an effort to control the Queer population.

Even still, while queer theory was couched within the deconstruction of categories as Sedgwick (1990) contends, the binary categories that are used to describe homo and hetero identities are problematic, and people often do not exist within those binaries. Further, when we have these categorical distinctions grouped in those binaries, often times one of those categories is viewed as lesser than the other (Sedgwick 1990). We recognize the importance of deconstructing categories and worry, as Ball (2014a: 532) points out, that queer criminology does not specifically focus on deconstruction, which can be limiting in addressing injustice. Conversely, however, for some, categories can be empowering. They can bring people and groups together who experience similar inequalities and obstacles and breed new social movements. Certainly, deconstruction does matter, as even the language we use here may be problematic and deconstructing categories allows for a more organic way of knowing. However, as symbolic interactionism has taught us, we continue to construct meaning in our everyday lives in a variety of ways. Recall, as Green (2007) points out, that symbolic interactionists such as West and Zimmerman (1987) were "doing gender." And although Butler (1990) may be more identified as a queer theorist in her own right, her discussion of performativity is closely related to "doing gender" as we have now come to know it, but nevertheless examines the importance of discourse in understanding gender performance. This lends itself to the importance of language, as Sedgwick (1990: 17) indicates:

> ... terminological complication is closely responsive to real ambiguities and struggles of gay/lesbian politics and identities: e.g., there are women-loving-women who think of themselves as lesbians but not as gay, and others who think of themselves as gay women but not as lesbians.

In brief, we tend to agree with Woods's (2014) assertion that queer criminology should be both "identity-driven" and deconstructionist. While, as Woods points out, this may be a problematic position to take, we agree that it allows for a wider range of research and theorizing to take place. As he notes, because sexual orientation and gender identity can be central to so many people's lives, focusing on these can assist in understanding the Queer experience and how there are unique experiences that this population faces. This draws our attention back to earlier in the chapter and our discussion on building and unbuilding, construction and deconstruction, and the importance of including myriad identities in research in order to combat assumptions about gender which will ensure that the research more accurately depicts and, in turn, affects the Queer community. We believe that Woods's approach is one that seeks inclusivity within the research while understanding the problems that may arise. Woods contends that it is important to provide thoughtful and critical insight into this field of research in order to avoid further stigmatization (see Woods 2014).

Thus, while we recognize the possibility of examining whether there is a need to "forge connections between queer theory and criminology" (Ball 2014a: 533) we are not completely convinced that this is a make-it or break-it requirement within the field of research, and would rather cast a wider net, again, with inclusivity in mind. However, with that being said, Ball (2014a: 533) further notes that queer theory is a field with both academic and political underpinnings that has:

> ... focused on charting the various forms of regulation through which we are shaped as subjects, particularly with regard to sexuality and gender ... excavates the forms of (usually hetero) normativity that are embedded in social institutions and relations, and, drawing from post-structural thought, challenges essentialized notions of identity and identity politics ...
>
> *Ball 2014a: 533*

While gender and sexuality may be fluid for some, for others, it is absolutely fixed – therefore, while queer theory is influential in developing theoretical approaches to understanding and perhaps ultimately breaking down assumptive categories, we contend that it cannot be applied to queer criminology as a whole, because, quite simply, there are different ways of doing queer criminology just like there are different ways of doing critical criminology. For example, one might focus on the role of the state with regard to illegal dumping (Doyon 2014) or nuclear weapons (Kramer & Bradshaw 2011) or forced sterilization (Brightman, Lenning, & McElrath 2015) and although these topics differ, it does not make the research any less critical.

Deconstruction is also problematic because, quite frankly, we are probably never going to be in a world without categorical descriptions that are used in some way or another to provide an understanding of who people are. Is this beneficial? In some ways, of course not; in other ways, they are indeed beneficial. In a perfect world, we would not use categories, especially binary categories, but this world is far from perfect, and while one description, one label, one identity does not a person make, even without categories, we contend that there will always be meaning. We will continue to understand the world in which we live by constructing meaning and then giving significance to the people, the identities, the relationships, the knowledge, and so on, that we have come to know.

Ferrell (2013: 258–259) contends that we assign meaning to the

> ... contested social and cultural processes by which situations are defined, individuals and groups are categorized, and human

consequences are understood … made in many ways – but following the insights of symbolic interactionists, we know that one of the primary ways is through social interaction in the situations of everyday life.

Ferrell 2013: 258–259

We give meaning to our everyday worlds within every milieu as Ferrell (2013) points out, from casual interactions to criminality and deviant behavior. Therefore, while we are well aware that this will continue to be debated, we contend that while Queer may mean one thing to one person, it means something quite different to another. However, when taking everything into account, perhaps those categorical descriptions can allow for marginalized groups to understand their marginalization in new ways and draw support from each other, moving them to the center of knowledge construction.

A "queer/ed criminology" would not simply *repeat* these existing deconstructive approaches, but would expand them and develop them in new ways, doing what it could to ensure that the notion of "queer" is never put to rest, its critical potential never limited, and its productive power never foreclosed upon.

Matthew Ball 2014b: 33

When considering the deconstruction of categories, we come to understand that truth can be subjective, and, as pointed out earlier, truth can be molded to fit the needs of the powerful. It is our hope that by presenting the information we bring forth in this book, there is a collective understanding of the inequality that Queer folks face within the United States and abroad, particularly with and within the criminal legal system.

Intersectionality

Admittedly, while the first edition discussed intersectionality, or the idea that one's overlapping identities interconnect and impact our experiences with discrimination and oppression, there must be more said about this concept/theory/application and how we take it into consideration when examining queer criminology and, moreover, the lived experiences of LGBTQ+ folks in the system. The work on intersectionality and its application in criminology is not necessarily new – but we continue to see it ignored and lackadaisically implemented. First, there are indeed different ways of applying intersectionality depending on the discipline and depending on the interpretation of any one person or group. We will focus on the core concepts of intersectionality, the influence of feminism (namely Black feminism and postmodern feminism), how intersectionality and identity are related, and, finally, the call for an intersectional criminology (see Potter 2015) and how this all relates to queer criminology. While intersectionality will be briefly unpacked here, it will be discussed and applied in more detail throughout the entirety of the book.

First, Kimberle Crenshaw (1989) is regarded as the person to have coined the term, based on her experiences in law, and who argued that discrimination can and does take place towards individuals with multiple identities – that we should not be required to pick and choose which identity takes precedent. As we'll share examples throughout the book, to us, it is clear that an intersectional framework is required and should be applied (correctly and frequently) in criminology. In 2015, Hillary Potter released a book (in this series) on intersectional criminology, focusing on the experiential impact of multiple intersecting identities such as race, class, and more. Potter also takes care to highlight the impact of gender and sexuality, but the discussion is scant as a whole. This is but one example of why there is a need for a queer specific criminology that will also focus on intersectionality and its impact on the lived experience.

There are few, if any, topics that shouldn't highlight how one's multiple identities touch every part of an individuals' life. For instance, Potter (2013: 305) notes:

> Identities are socially constructed, fluid, and dynamic, and power – or the lack thereof – is situated differentially throughout the many social identities. Identities and power are relevant throughout all social aspects of human life, so they must also be considered within the contexts of criminality, victimization, and … responses to crime.

This is important to consider for many reasons; the first reason is because the influence of power is widely regarded as one of the major reasons for the development of critical criminology. Another reason is the impact of Black feminist theory on the development of intersectionality. Though lawyer Kimberlee' Crenshaw is credited with coining the term, and herself is considered a Black feminist, she has indicated that her work was inspired by many folks doing the work, and Potter (2013: 306, emphasis on the original) goes on to indicate that the "*conceptual foundations* of intersectionality had been in development long before Crenshaw's seminal articles." However, the overall influence of Black feminism cannot go unnoticed.

Recall that feminism in general was developed by white women for white women and that these women, while getting an awful lot right in their activism and scholarship, failed big time in assuming that all women's experiences were similar or the same because women experience the world similarly. Wrong. Black feminist theory, along with postmodern feminist theory, helped to center the lived experiences of women to include the influence of their multiple identities and how those identities affect the way in which individuals experience their lives. For this example, we turn to Collins' (1990) matrix of domination that highlighted the importance of multiplicative identities instead of additive identities. This work addresses several different levels of domination, including individual, cultural, and systems-level oppression. Collins (1990/2017) indicates that while "race, class, and gender" are representative of systems of oppression that act to oppress Black women, there is more to examine in addition to those intersecting identities.

> These systems and the economic, political, and ideological conditions that support them may not be the most fundamental oppressions, and they certainly affect many more groups than Black women. Other people of color, Jews, ... poor white women, and gays and lesbians have all had similar ideological justifications offered for their subordination.
>
> Patricia Hill Collins 1990/2017: n.p.

Patricia Hill Collins' (1990) work helps to identify additional issues that we will explore through a queer criminological lens. Once the concept/theory/application of intersectionality is understood, one can see how opportunity structure, legitimate resources, and histories of oppression can differentially impact certain folks. For example, the case infamously known as The New Jersey 4 – who stood trial for multiple counts of assault, and attempted murder, even though video footage of the event in question revealed that the women were harassed and aggressed on the street. The women, all Black lesbians from poor urban neighborhoods, some with histories of abuse, were convicted in the media before ever reaching the courtroom. This is also true of CeCe McDonald's case, a Black trans woman who was sent to prison for defending herself against a vicious assault. Both of these cases, among many others, will be discussed later in the book as examples of the impact of intersectionality. Collins and others have taught us that one identity does not necessarily outdo the others, but instead they are multiplicative in one body.

Looking ahead

In the chapters to come, we seek to highlight the experiences of Queer people as victims, offenders, and as criminal legal professionals. Each chapter highlights the experiences of Queer folks as related to the criminal legal system throughout the world, attempting to draw attention to the exposure to criminalization, victimization, offending, and more and make suggestions for changes that may improve the criminal legal system. We also seek to focus on the changes that must be made at structural and institutional levels in order to implement real, tangible change. Legislation continues to be passed that criminalizes or, at the very least, marginalizes Queer people based solely on their sexual orientation and/or gender identity. Once we accept and realize that these discriminatory practices are done most often on large-scale institutional levels, our hope is that there will be a clearer understanding for the need to not only understand the Queer experience in a practical sense but at the theoretical level as well. Finally, in recognizing these injustices, the need for a queer criminology comes to light (see Ball 2014b; Woods 2014).

Beginning with Chapter 2, "Criminalizing queerness," we examine the historical significance of sexual orientation and gender identity as related to the ways in which legislation has worked and continues to work to criminalize and therefore label and stigmatize Queer people, quite literally how "queerness" has been criminalized. For instance, it was not until the 2003 Supreme Court case, *Lawrence v. Texas*, that sodomy laws criminalizing homosexual sex were deemed unconstitutional in the United States. What's more, there are nearly 70 countries around the globe that currently have laws prohibiting consensual sex between members of the same sex, and some of those countries impose the penalty of death for such behavior. What we contend is that these laws represent a global culture of homophobia and transphobia that continues to persist regardless of common-sense opinions or how progressive current and future generations are and have become. What we mean by this is that as professors and researchers, we are well aware of the shifting opinions of many young people, especially in places like the United States, Canada, and the United Kingdom, regarding members of the Queer community and the rights that they should have. Further, because of this, it is often far too easy to assume that because opinion polls have indicated that most Americans, for example, support marriage equality that means there is little to no concern over equal rights for Queer people. This is as problematic as the assumption that racism in the United States has been eradicated because it elected its first Black president in 2008. While improved public opinion is certainly an important step in the right direction, we cannot be complacent to the injustices and terrors that Queer people face around the world every single day based solely on their sexual orientation and/or gender identity.

This chapter will identify the deep-seated homophobia that historically reflected colonial British values and continues to influence anti-gay sentiment and legislation throughout the world, such as in Africa where nearly 40 countries have criminalized homosexuality. We will offer examples of bribery, police brutality, humiliation, threats, and extreme violence in a variety of countries, including Uganda, Kenya, Nigeria, and Russia – all of which are the result of, or committed in the name of, compulsory heterosexuality.

In addition to the criminalization of sexuality, Chapter 2 highlights how gender nonconformity has been criminalized around the globe. Historically and presently, these laws have focused on individuals who are seen as "impersonating" the opposite sex, but more recently have shifted to challenging the rights of transgender people to access public accommodations such as bathrooms and locker rooms. Obviously, these regulations have significant impact on the transgender population, and, therefore, trans men and women suffer the most from the enforcement of these laws. To explore the criminalization of gender nonconformity, this chapter will highlight important cases where these laws have differentially impacted members of the Queer community who have been targeted for "imitating" the opposite sex or for "deception," or simply for participating in the normal functions of social life, and will highlight how Queer people are frequently blamed for their victimization based on their gender expression.

Chapter 3, "Queer criminology at the intersections: victimization and offending," turns our attention to the ways that Queer people become entangled in the criminal legal system, be it as victims or offenders, or both, and considers how one's intersecting identities can impact their likelihood to be the victim or perpetrator of crime(s). Beginning with victimization, we explore those crimes which Queer people are uniquely affected by, such as hate crimes and state negligence, and those crimes that they experience similarly to their cisgender and heterosexual peers, such as intimate partner violence and homicide. Within each type of victimization we will explore the social structures that make Queer people particularly vulnerable to these harmful actions, the unique ways they experience them personally and in their interactions with the criminal legal system, and the consequences that these harms impart on both individual victims and the broader Queer community. Real-life cases of interpersonal and state violence will be used to highlight these issues.

While little is known about queer offending, Chapter 3 explores why this is the case – why hesitance by queer criminologists and a dearth of useful data hinders our understanding of how and why Queer people commit crime. We consider the lens through which criminologists have historically viewed queer criminality, how media depictions shape our understanding of Queer criminals, and how both have distorted any meaningful knowledge that we may have gained about queer offending. We consider how these inaccurate conceptualizations of Queer offenders shape the public consciousness and perpetuate the stereotypes that lead to disproportionate and inexcusably severe involvement in correctional systems.

Lastly, Chapter 3 explores the intersection of victimization and offending. Queer people face pervasive forms of discrimination throughout their lives. From childhood to adulthood, Queer people experience rejection from their families, bullying and violence in school, repudiation from places of worship, and employment and housing discrimination, among other barriers. These hurdles can at times be insurmountable and have the potential to limit one's ability to simply support themselves. Consequently, some Queer people find themselves with no other choice than to engage in what are called survival crimes, like sex work and drug sales, in order to sustain their livelihood or cope in a world where the odds are stacked against them.

Chapter 4, "Queer criminology and law enforcement," turns our focus to how law enforcement fails in protecting and serving members of the adult and juvenile Queer population. This chapter draws attention to the lack of trust that Queer folks have of the police and the reasons why they feel suspicious and fearful of law enforcement officers and officials. We begin the chapter by calling attention to the tumultuous relationship between minority men and women and police officers and connote both the level of distrust that police officers have towards citizens and the level of distrust that citizens, more specifically marginalized populations, have towards law enforcement officials. Most recently, we have seen several newsworthy incidents involving police brutality towards young Black men and women that highlight the problems with policing on cultural and structural levels. We feel it is important to address race, class, and more, to include sexuality and gender, as they illuminate the impact of intersectionality and the effects on individuals from ongoing institutional and systemic prejudicial opinions and discriminatory practices that are pervasive within the criminal legal system. So, while we recognize these racist policing practices and note the influence of media campaigns such as #blacklivesmatter, we also bring to your attention the hashtag movement #blacktranslivesmatter. Although the latter is certainly far less known than the former, it is no less important. Transgender men and women, but especially trans women of color, experience physical and emotional abuse from police throughout the United States and abroad. While society knows much about the brutal murders of young men like George Floyd, Michael Brown, Eric Garner, and Tamir Rice, we still know little about how race, class, sexual orientation, and gender identity intersect and impact the Queer community with regards to their experiences with law enforcement.

Additionally, law enforcement officials who identify as LGBTQ+ have themselves experienced prejudice and discrimination on the job, although there is no evidence that indicates sexual orientation or gender identity has a negative impact on the ways in which officers perform their duties. Chapter 4 will discuss law enforcement from several different angles, first beginning with Queer civilian experiences with officers and officials, including police misconduct and brutality, followed by a discussion on the selective enforcement of Queer adults and juveniles. We highlight how police disproportionately target the Queer population, which in turn increases the level of distrust between officers and Queer people. As mentioned, we will detail the unique experiences of LGBTQ+ law enforcement agents and explore changes in departmental policy that may benefit officers and ultimately the Queer people they are supposed to protect and serve.

Finally, we will discuss these problems as they relate to the hypermasculine policing subculture that values machismo over compassion and has historically failed to implement effective policing strategies in ways that truly incorporate and encapsulate civilian concerns and partnerships between officers and citizens. In addition to these complexities, we will explore locations abroad that have worked successfully towards bridging the gap between Queer folks and officers and policy implementation that has worked in creating acceptance and understanding of Queer officers in their departments.

Moving forward, Chapter 5 follows the progression within the criminal legal system from policing to courts. In "Queer criminology and legal systems," we examine the myriad of ways in which the system has failed Queer folks regarding representation and equal protection under the law. As Chapter 2 explored the criminalization of queerness, this chapter will highlight how that criminalization and ultimately the denial of human rights, which significantly impacts agency and capital, are determined by overzealous prosecutors, inept defense attorneys, and biased judges. Legislation, which is ultimately decided upon in the court, can affect several different arenas in one's life, to include the legal recognition of one's existence, employment, marriage, and education, among others.

This chapter will provide a sampling of the civil rights (or lack thereof) afforded to Queer people in several parts of the world, as well as the backlash experienced by Queer people when these rights are granted.

Case studies used in this chapter will bring attention to discrimination including the exploitation of sexuality as fodder, hate speech from prosecutors who defile lesbian defendants based on gender stereotypes, and more. Research in this chapter also highlights court employees who have reported hearing derogatory comments about sexual orientation made by judges and lawyers. One of the major issues within the courtroom are cases involving what has come to be known as gay or trans panic defenses in which a defendant makes the claim that they harmed the victim because the victim made unsolicited sexual advances towards them. This relates to the discussion in Chapter 2 about the criminalization of queerness as related to "imitation" or "deception" and in turn often impacts transgender victims significantly.

In Chapter 6, "Queer criminology and corrections," we discuss what happens once Queer offenders are adjudicated, tried, and punished. This chapter examines the world of corrections and how that relates to punishment. We explore the ways in which correctional officers and institutions treat LGBTQ+ individuals within both adult and juvenile facilities and how that often-discriminatory treatment can have long-lasting effects. Again, we will examine issues within corrections both in the United States and abroad and detail the experiences that Queer people face beyond their initial sentences. For instance, we explore the additional punishments they are met with upon their incarceration, such as increased victimization, including rape, and the state's inability to assess their unique safety requirements beyond isolating Queer offenders: An action that can have long-lasting emotional and psychological effects, and that can be argued is a violation of the Eighth Amendment's cruel and unusual punishment provisions. This speaks to the problems associated with housing and classifying Queer incarcerated populations, including juveniles in youth facilities, who also face an increase of victimization. This chapter will also detail policy implementations and implications since the passing of the Prison Rape Elimination Act of 2003.

Transgender men and women have special needs when it comes to their physical and psychological well-being, and this should make no difference when it comes to incarcerated people. Therefore, this chapter will highlight medical provisions and the right to transition, housing and classification, in-take procedure, and more.

The final chapter, "Future directions in queer criminology," will explore the importance of developing and implementing a queer criminology and how this exploration and implementation is paramount when examining the criminal legal system as a means to control groups of people and individuals who identify outside of the heteronormative landscape.

Throughout this book, we argue that queer criminology is more than simply adding sexuality or gender identity as independent variables to research (i.e. the "add Queer and stir" approach). Instead, we provide our readers with an array of examples from the United States and beyond that highlight the ways in which sexuality and gender are used as weapons of the state to control the behavior of those who do not fit the societal norm. As you progress through this book, we ask you to consider these questions: What does a queer criminology look like to you? What would the theoretical constructions be? How can criminological methods be queered to capture the experiences of Queer people more accurately? What does queer epistemology look like? These are questions that may not have definitive answers as of today, though the debates surrounding them have advanced significantly in the short years since the first edition of this book was published. We are proud that this book has been a part of that important conversation, and hope that the changes and additions made to this edition inspire our readers to advance the field even further.

Activities and discussion questions

- Consider the use of the word "queer." What does this word mean to you? Can you think of other language that is changing or has changed in your location?
- Thinking about intersectionality: Take some time to write down your own identities[3] (student, friend, professor ...). Once you have several written down, think about what those identities mean to you and others you encounter. Do they have a positive or negative effect on your life?

- What are some ways you might consider being more inclusive in your research?

Notes

1 For a detailed glossary of terms please see PFLAG's National Glossary of Terms found online at https://pflag.org/glossary. While this is not an exhaustive list and definitions of terms may vary based on resource, we believe it is a superior collection. We would also note that language changes throughout the book based on a variety of reasons including research participants, the wording choices of other researchers, and more. We have worked to be up-to-date in language throughout and have made applicable notes about our choices when needed. It is likely that language has changed while writing not only the book, but this note.
2 To learn more about sex variations, visit www.isna.org
3 We recommend the 20 Statement Test found here: www.jstor.org/stable/2088175?seq=1#metadata_info_tab_contents

References

Adler, F. 1975. *Sisters in crime: The rise of the new female criminal*. New York, NY: McGraw-Hill.

Ahlgrim, C. 2021. 14 celebrities who don't identify as either male or female. *The Insider*, May 19. Accessed from www.insider.com/9-celebrities-who-identify-as-gender-non-binary-2019-6.

Asquith, N.L., Dwyer, A., & Simpson, P. 2017. A Queer Criminal Career. *Current Issues in Criminal Justice, 29*, (2): 167–180.

Ball, M. 2014a. *What's queer about queer criminology?* In D. Peterson & V. Panfil (eds.), *Handbook of LGBT Communities, Crime, and Justice* (pp. 531–555). New York, NY: Springer.

Ball, M. 2014b. Queer criminology, critique, and the "art of not being governed." *Critical Criminology, 22*, (1): 21–34.

Ball, M. 2016. *Criminology and queer theory: dangerous bedfellows?* New York, NY: Palgrave Macmillan.

Belknap, J. & Holsinger, K. 1998. *An overview of delinquent girls: How theory and practice failed and the need for innovative change*. In R. Zaplin (ed.), *Female crime and delinquency: Critical perspectives and effective interventions* (pp. 31–64). Gaithersburg, MD: Aspen.

Belknap, J. & Holsinger, K. 2006. The gendered nature of risk factors for delinquency. *Feminist Criminology, 1*, (1): 48–71.

Brennan, T., Breitenbach, M., & Dieterich, W. 2010. *Unraveling women's pathways to serious crime: New findings and links to feminist prior pathways.* American Probation and Parole Association.

Brightman, S., Lenning, E., & McElrath, K. 2015. State-directed sterilizations in North Carolina: Victim-centeredness and Reparations. *British Journal of Criminology, 55*, (3): 474–493.

Buist, C.L. 2019. LGBTQ Rights in the Fields of Criminal Law and Law Enforcement. *University of Richmond Law Review, 54*, (3), 877–900.

Buist, C.L. & Semprevivo, L.K. (eds.). 2022. *Queering criminology in theory and praxis: Re-imagining justice in the criminal legal system and beyond.* Bristol: Bristol University Press.

Buist, C.L. & Stone, C. 2014. Transgender victims and offenders: Failures of the United States criminal justice system and the necessity of queer criminology. *Critical Criminology, 22*, (1): 35–47.

Burt, C.H. 2020. Scrutinizing the U.S. Equality Act 2019: A feminist examination of definitional changes and sociolegal ramifications. *Feminist Criminology, 15*, (4): 363–409.

Butler, J. 1990. *Gender trouble.* New York, NY: Routledge.

Chesney-Lind, M. 1988. Doing feminist criminology. *The Criminologist, 13*, (4): 16–17.

Collins, Patricia Hill. 1990. *Black feminist thought: Knowledge, consciousness, and the politics of empowerment.* Boston: Unwin Hyman

Collins, P.H. 1990/2017. Black feminist thought in the matrix of domination. In C. Lemert (ed.), *Social theory: The multicultural, global, and classic readings (6th ed.).* New York: Routledge. doi.org/10.4324/9780429494635

Cornell Chronicle. January 24, 2008. Why deconstruction still matters: A conversation with Jonathan Culler. Accessed from https://news.cornell.edu/stories/2008/01/why-deconstruction-still-matters-according-jonathan-culler

Crenshaw, Kimberle. 1989. Demarginalizing the intersection of race and sex: A Black feminist critique of antidiscrimination doctrine, feminist theory and antiracist politics. *University of Chicago Legal Forum,* Vol. 1989, Article 8.

Crocket, E. 2015. The bizarre history of bathrooms getting in the way of equal rights. *Vox,* December 30. Accessed from www.vox.com/2015/12/30/10690802/bathrooms-equal-rights-lgbtq

Daly, K. 1992. Women's pathway to felony court: Feminist theories of lawbreaking and problems of representation. *Southern California Review of Law and Women's Studies, 2*: 11–52.

Deliso, M. 2021. 'Catastrophic' number of state bills target transgender youth, advocates say. The bills would limit access to school sports and gender-affirming health care. ABC News, March 7. Accessed from https://abcnews.go.com/US/catastrophic-number-state-bills-target-transgender-youth-advocates/story?id=76138305

Doyon, J.A. 2014. Corporate environmental crime in the electronic waste industry: The case of Executive Recycling, Inc. *Internet Journal of Criminology: Critical Perspectives on Green Criminology Series*: 68–89.

Drescher, J. Queer diagnoses: parallels and contrasts in the history of homosexuality, gender variance, and the diagnostic and statistical manual. *Archives of Sexual Behavior*, 2010 Apr;39(2):427-60. doi: 10.1007/s10508-009-9531-5. PMID: 19838785.

Dwyer, A., Ball, M., & Crofts, T. (eds.) 2016. *Queering criminology*. New York, NY: Palgrave MacMillan.

Ferrell, J. 2013. Cultural criminology and the politics of meaning. *Critical Criminology, 21*, (3): 257–271.

Foucault, M. 1980. *Power/knowledge: Selected interviews and other writings*. New York, NY: Pantheon Press.

Gooren, L. & Gijs, L. 2015. Medicalization of homosexuality. In A. Bolin & P. Whelehan (eds.), *The International Encyclopedia of Human Sexuality*, Wiley Publishers.

Green, A.I. 2007. Queer theory and sociology: Locating the subject and the self in sexuality studies. *Sociological Theory, 25*, (1): 26–45.

Groombridge, N. 1998. Perverse criminologies: The closet of Doctor Lombroso. *Social and Legal Studies, 8*, (4): 531–548.

Guadalupe-Diaz, X.L. 2019. *Transgressed: Intimate partner violence in transgender lives*. New York: New York University Press.

Hagan, J., Simpson, J., & Gillis, A.R. 1987. Class in the household: A power-control theory of gender and delinquency. *American Journal of Sociology, 92*, (4): 788–816.

Halberstam, Jack. 2018. Unbuilding Gender, *Places Journal*, October 2018. Accessed 05 Apr 2022 from https://placesjournal.org/article/unbuilding-gender/?cn-reloaded=1

Hasenbush, A., Flores, A.R., & Herman, J.L. 2019. Gender identity nondiscrimination laws in public accommodations: A review of evidence regarding safety and privacy in public restrooms, locker rooms, and changing rooms. *Sexuality, Research & Social Policy, 16*: 70–83.

Jagose, A. 1996. *Queer theory: An introduction*. New York, NY: New York University Press.

Kirsch, M.N. 2000. *Queer theory and social change*. New York, NY: Routledge.

Kramer, R.C. & Bradshaw, E.A. 2011. US state crimes related to nuclear weapons: Is there hope for change in the Obama administration? *International Journal of Comparative and Applied Criminal Justice, 35*, (3): 243–259.

Leighton, P. 2010. A professor of white collar crime reviews USA's White Collar series. *The Critical Criminologist, 19*, (4): 8–16.

Lenning, E. 2009. Beyond the binary: Exploring the dimensions of gender orientation and representation. *International Journal of Social Inquiry, 2* (2): 39–54.

Lynch, M.J. & Michalowski, R. 2000. *Primer in radical criminology: Critical perspectives on crime, power, and identity.* New York, NY: Criminal Justice Press.

Malkin, M.L. & DeJong, C. 2019. Protections for Transgender Inmates Under PREA: a Comparison of State Correctional Policies in the United States. *Sex Res Soc Policy 16,* 393–407. Accessed from https://doi.org/10.1007/s13178-018-0354-9

Mallicoat, S.L. 2015. *Women and crime.* Thousand Oaks, CA: Sage.

Messinger, A.M. 2017. *LGBTQ intimate partner violence: Lessons for policy, practice, and research.* Oakland: University of California Press.

Mogul, J.L., Ritchie, A., & Whitlock, K. 2011. *Queer (in)justice: The criminalization of LGBT people in the United States.* Boston, MA: Beacon Press.

National Center for Transgender Equality. 2016, July 10. Transgender people and bathroom access. Accessed from https://transequality.org/issues/resources/transgender-people-and-bathroom-access

Panfil, V.R. 2017. *The gang's all queer: The lives of gay gang members.* New York: New York University Press.

Peterson, D. & Panfil, V.R. (eds.) 2014a. *Handbook of LGBT communities, crime, and justice.* New York, NY: Springer.

Peterson, D. & Panfil, V.R. 2014b. *Introduction: Reducing the invisibility of sexual and gender identities in criminology and criminal justice.* In D. Peterson & V.R. Panfil (eds.), *Handbook of LGBT communities, crime, and justice* (pp. 3–14). New York, NY: Springer.

Potter, H. 2013. Intersectional criminology: Interrogating identity and power in criminological research and theory. *Critical Criminology,* 21, (3), 305–318.

Potter, H. 2015. *Intersectionality and criminology: Disrupting and revolutionizing studies of crime.* New York NY: Routledge.

Prison Rape Elimination Act of 2003. *PREA Public Law,* 108-79. Accessed from www.gpo.gov/fdsys/pkg/PLAW-108publ79/pdf/PLAW-108publ79.pdf.

Rocheleau, J. 2019. A former slur is reclaimed, and listeners have mixed emotions. *NPR,* August 21. Accessed from www.npr.org/sections/publiceditor/2019/08/21/752330316/a-former-slur-is-reclaimed-and-listeners-have-mixed-feelings

Ross, M.W. 1988. *The treatment of homosexuals with mental health disorders* (1st ed.). Routledge. Accessed from https://doi.org/10.4324/9781315804316 www.taylorfrancis.com/chapters/edit/10.4324/9781315804316-10/psychopathology-homosexuality-homophobia-jaime-smith-md?context=ubx&refId=a1acf0ae-adc2-466e-b652-64e13a3e5fa1

Rutter, V. & Schwartz, P. 2012. *The gender of sexuality: Exploring sexual possibilities.* Lanham, MD: Rowen & Littlefield.

Sedgwick, E. 1990. *Epistemology of the closet.* Berkeley, CA: University of California Press.

Sheffer, J.D. & McCord, A. 2021. Rounding the basis: Analyzing and applying Title IX's prohibition on sex-based discrimination to discrimination against individuals with LGBTQ identities. *The Legal Educator,* 35, (2), 24–41

Simon, R.J. 1975. *Women and crime.* Lexington, MA: Lexington Books.

Smythe, V. 2018. I'm credited with having coined the word "Terf." Here's how it happened. *The Guardian,* November 28. Accessed from www.theguard ian.com/commentisfree/2018/nov/29/im-credited-with-having-coined-the-acronym-terf-heres-how-it-happened

Tomsen, S. 1997. *Was Lombroso queer? Criminology, criminal justice, and the heterosexual imaginary.* Sydney, Australia: Hawkins Press, Australian Institute of Criminology.

Valcore, J., Fradella, H.F., Guadalupe-Diaz, X., Ball, M.J., Dwyer, A., DeJong, C., Walker, A., Wodda, A., & Worthen, M.G.F. 2021. Building and intersectional and trans-inclusive criminology: Responding to the emergence of 'gender critical' perspectives in feminist criminology. *Critical Criminology, online first.*

Valcore, J.L. & Pfeffer, R. 2018. Systemic error: measuring gender in criminological research. *Criminal Justice Studies,* 31, (4), 333–351.

West, C. & Zimmerman, D.H. 1987. Doing gender. *Gender & Society,* 1, (2): 125–151.

Winters, M.K. 2022. Queer Pathways. In Carrie L. Buist, & Lindsay Kahle Semprevivo, (eds.), *Queering criminology in theory and praxis: Reimagining justice in the criminal legal system and beyond.* Bristol: Bristol University Press.

Wodda, A. & Panfil, V.R. 2021. Sex-positive criminology: Possibilities for legal and social change. *Sociology Compass,* 15, (11). Accessed from https://doi. org/10.1111/soc4.12929.

Woods, J.B. 2014. Queer contestations and the future of a critical "queer" criminology. *Critical Criminology,* 22, (1): 5–19.

Woods, J.B. 2015. The birth of modern criminology and gendered constructions of the homosexual criminal identity. *Journal of Homosexuality,* 62: 131–166.

Worthen, M.G.F. 2020. *Queers, bis, and straight lies: an intersectional examination of LGBTQ stigma.* New York: Routledge. Accessed from https://doi.org/ 10.4324/9781315280332.

2

CRIMINALIZING QUEERNESS

Throughout history and across the globe, Queer people have had their bodies regulated, been arrested, and have faced punishment for no other reason than their sexual and gender identities. Quite literally, their "queerness" has been criminalized. While subsequent chapters will focus on specific instances of discrimination and violence against Queer people on an interpersonal level, by and within law enforcement, courts, and correctional institutions around the world, in this chapter, we focus on the much broader historical and contemporary context within which those acts are situated.

Today, billions of people live in countries where homosexual[1] sex and, in some cases, the mere mention of homosexuality is outlawed, and millions of people live in countries where gender nonconformity is policed, prosecuted, and punished. It is the pervasive proscription of queer bodies, behaviors, and rights that make criminal legal systems around the world the primary institutions through which queerness is socially controlled, thus demanding the attention of queer criminology.

DOI: 10.4324/9781003165163-2

Criminalizing homosexuality

More than a quarter (68) of the countries around the world have laws prohibiting the mere act of *consensual* sex between members of the same sex, at least six of which impose the punishment of death (Csete & Cohen 2010; Itaborahy & Zhu 2014; Mendos 2019; Ottosson 2008). Though these laws vary in terms of the language used to define illegal sex, the severity of punishment for violating them, and the degree to which they are enforced, they all *appear* to stem from and promote a global culture of homophobia and a forced value of compulsory heterosexuality. In truth, however, these laws (as pervasive as they may be) did not at the time of their implementation inherently or necessarily reflect a global culture. A significant portion of them reflected colonial British values and not necessarily the values of the countries now left to enforce them. Indeed, no less than 40 colonies and countries in Asia, the Pacific, and Africa have or had anti-sodomy laws imposed on them by British rulers seeking to "inculcate European morality into resistant masses" (Human Rights Watch 2008: 5). Ireland (2013) found that there was in fact a causal relationship between British colonialism and contemporary African anti-homosexuality laws, and that it was more significant than a country's religiosity or authoritarian political leadership. Combined, however, these variables are even more predictive; today, anti-homosexuality rhetoric and laws are often used to distract the religious public's attention from corrupt leadership (Ireland 2013; M'Baye 2013).

While it cannot be said that no homophobia existed in African countries prior to colonialism, it is believed that colonialism exasperated any that did exist and was certainly the reason that homophobia became state-sponsored (Human Rights Watch 2008; Ireland 2013). Today, many Africans staunchly believe that homosexuality was imported from the West, so determining how accepted or practiced homosexuality was or was not prior to colonization is challenging and further complicated by the fact that many of the words used to describe homosexuality were actually imported from the West (Epprecht 1998). Nevertheless, evidence of same-sex relations in Africa can be traced all the way back to drawings by Bushmen, are well documented by anthropologists, and were often described by colonialists as consensual

(M'Baye 2013; Msibi 2011). So, while there is no indication that these acts were celebrated prior to colonization, neither is there to suggest that homosexuality was any more than ignored in a "don't ask, don't tell" fashion (Epprecht 1998; Msibi 2011).

Prior to institutionalizing homophobia in many African countries, Britain first imported sodomy laws (modeled after their own) into India in 1860 with Section 377 of the Indian Penal Code, which criminalized homosexual sex and imposed sentences of up to life in prison (Human Rights Watch 2008). Section 377 then became the model for anti-sodomy laws in a host of other British colonies. Thus, the twisted reality is that many of the anti-sodomy laws that stain Africa and the rest of the globe were not necessarily about each country's individual desire to criminalize homosexual sex, but rather about Britain using a country's own criminal legal system to import imperialism. Regardless of the origins of the laws, however, they have persisted and serve to breed and promote a contemporary culture of heteronormativity and violent homophobia around the world.

> On our way to the police station, the police officers insulted us and beat us with batons on our heads and bodies. They kept saying they were going to burn us for being dirty pedes [faggots] …. The next morning they began to question us about our homosexuality, and on Tuesday, they took us to Channel Two and to Cameroon Radio and Television. They paraded us on the news saying the police had dismantled a network of homosexuals.
>
> Christian, Cameroon
> *Human Rights Watch 2010a: 2*

Antigay laws are undoubtedly most prominent in Africa, with homosexuality (not necessarily limited to sodomy) being illegal in 32 African countries. Though official data on arrests for homosexuality is largely inaccessible or even non-existent, a plethora of anecdotal evidence suggests that African gays and lesbians are in constant fear and danger of arrest and prosecution, often despite any concrete evidence of their homosexuality. In Cameroon, for example, gays and lesbians are arrested by the dozens in establishments suspected to be gay bars and are even arrested in their own homes based on lists of "presumed" homosexuals published in local newspapers or merely on the suspicions of family and neighbors. In one such case in 2006, four young women were arrested for lesbianism – the only evidence of which being a "tip" from one of the girls' grandmother. They were each sentenced to three years of probation (Human Rights Watch 2010a).

In 2011, well-known Ugandan gay rights activist David Kato was bludgeoned to death in his home after winning an injunction against the Ugandan newspaper *Rolling Stone*, which had published his address and picture on a list of "Top Homosexuals" under a headline that read "Hang Them" (Rice 2011; Walsh 2011). Ugandan officials have been battling back-and-forth since 2014 over the *Anti-Homosexuality Act* that would criminalize the promotion of homosexuality and make consensual same-sex sex punishable by death (Human Rights Watch 2019a). As lawmakers have passed, repealed, and threatened to reintroduce the bill, the country has seen an increase in brutal attacks against LGBT people, including another well-known activist and HIV peer educator, Brian Wasswa, who was bludgeoned to death in his home in 2019 (Human Rights Watch 2019a).

Further examples of selective enforcement and arbitrary punishment across the continent are abundant. For example, in 2018, 170 people were charged with homosexuality in Morocco, two Zambian men were sentenced to 15 years imprisonment for consensual sex, and in Senegal a man was prosecuted for homosexuality when a video of him engaged in consensual sex surfaced (Mendos 2019). The woman who secretly filmed the couple was also convicted on charges of "distribution of content against morality" (Mendos 2019: 13). In 2019, a 23-year-old Tunisian man was convicted of homosexuality when he was the victim of a rape, an Egyptian television host was jailed for one year simply for interviewing a gay man, and the LGBT community was targeted in several raids throughout Uganda, including 125 arrests for "nuisance" in an LGBTQ friendly bar (Human Rights Watch 2019b; Mendos 2019). In several of these instances, arrestees were forced to submit to anal examinations by authorities.

Nevertheless, just because a country has an anti-sodomy law does not necessarily mean that it is enforced with the same tenacity as other laws. Though same-sex relations are illegal in Kenya, for example, there are very few convictions under the law. Still, the sentiment of the law does promote a homophobic culture, and consequently, LGBTI citizens report widespread police harassment, abuse, and corruption (Finerty 2013; Kenya Human Rights Commission 2011). A study conducted by the Kenya Human Rights Commission (2011) revealed that LGBTI citizens, especially gay male sex workers, are frequently arrested on fabricated charges, or are forced to pay bribes or have sex with officers to avoid them. One Kenyan doctor described having to pay a bribe of 100,000 shillings (approximately $1,000 USD) to avoid being paraded naked in front of his neighbors and the local media before being arrested. Another victim of police violence described being raped at an officer's home when he was unable to come up with a bail of 500 shillings. The rape was unprotected and he contracted gonorrhea. Without a doubt, these instances are made possible through the fear and stigma caused by Kenya's anti-homosexuality laws. Officials are keenly aware that victims are unlikely to report or challenge abuse and humiliation.

In addition to the harassment and brutality described above, homosexual acts remain punishable by death in Iran, Yemen, Saudi Arabia, Somalia, Sudan, and parts of Africa's most populated country, Nigeria (Mendos 2019). While reports of citizens being sentenced to death in these countries surface frequently, news of actual executions rarely make it to the mainstream. The exception to this is Iran, where it is estimated that between 4,000 and 6,000 gay and lesbian Iranians have been executed since 1979 for same-sex sexual behavior (Yadegarfard 2019). NGOs (non-governmental organizations) and alternative news sources have reported multiple executions for *lavat* (the Sharia term for sodomy) in the past few decades. To name a few instances, at least two men were hanged in 2005 (Human Rights Watch 2005), at least three more were hanged in 2011 (Dehghan 2011), two were hanged in March 2014 (Kredo 2014), and still at least two more were hanged in August 2014 (Michaelson 2014). It is safe to assume that executions for *lavat* occur much more frequently than we are aware, since trials regarding moral violations are often held in secret and the Iranian government limits what the press reveals in order to avoid global scrutiny for its public and frequent use of the death penalty in general (Human Rights Watch 2010b). Media reports have also uncovered executions for homosexuality in Saudi Arabia in 2018, where five men, who were coerced to admit to homosexual acts, were killed alongside others in a mass execution (Mendos 2019).

The United States is thought to have moved past criminalizing homosexuality via the 2003 landmark Supreme Court case of *Lawrence v. Texas*. The defendant, John Lawrence, was prosecuted in 1998 for violating a Texas law regarding "homosexual conduct" when the police entered his home (for a supposed weapons incident) and discovered him engaging in consensual sex with another man. Lawrence appealed his conviction and the Supreme Court declared the Texas law to be a violation of the constitutional right to privacy. The ruling was considered by and large to be a sweeping victory for the gay rights movement, but the effects of sodomy-related laws continue to haunt the Queer community throughout the United States.

One case in point is in the state of Louisiana, which is one of a dozen states that refuse to strike down their unconstitutional sodomy laws. The police in Louisiana continue to use the law to harass gay men, and in 2015 the Baton Rouge Sheriff's Office arrested men for engaging in consensual sex, claiming that they (the officers) "didn't know" the law was unconstitutional (Ermac 2015). Louisiana also expanded its crimes against nature (CAN) statute to include solicitation for the purpose of prostitution. The expanded law required those prosecuted to register as a sex offender for 15 years. To be clear, there are laws against solicitation for prostitution in Louisiana that are separate from the CAN expansion. Those prosecuted under the solicitation laws (a misdemeanor), however, did not face the consequence of registering, as did those charged with a felony under the CAN law. In her role as Director of the *Sex Workers Project* at the Urban Justice Center, Andrea Ritchie (2013) discovered that, unsurprisingly, those charged under the CAN law were by and large gay men of color and transgender women. She also found that in certain regions, Black women were disproportionately affected by the CAN laws – for example, of all the CAN-related registered sex offenders in Orleans Parish in 2011, 75 percent were women and 80 percent were Black (Ritchie 2013).

The result of the Louisiana law and those similar to it can be devastating, as most of the convicted were impoverished to begin with and now face even greater economic strain in light of fees for registering (hundreds of dollars) and the even greater difficulty of gaining employment while registered as a sex offender. Ritchie (2013: 369) describes how this sort of injustice sets the stage for the experiences and impact of intersectionality when she notes that "[b]eyond such explicit policing of racialized gender, individuals perceived to be transgressing racialized gender norms are consciously or subconsciously framed as both inherently 'disorderly' and profoundly sexualized." Though massive organizing and legal protest resulted in the elimination of the registration requirement of the Louisiana CAN law, Queer people, particularly those of color, continue to face gendered, racialized, and sexualized profiling by law enforcement, a direct result of centuries of dehumanizing and criminalizing queerness.

Despite the pervasiveness of anti-sodomy laws around the world and especially in African countries, there have been calls to repeal them, including from United Nations Secretary-General Ban Ki-Moon, former Secretary of State Hillary Clinton, and, ironically, the former British Prime Minister David Cameron (Kretz 2013). The push to decriminalize homosexuality, however, concerns even some members of the Queer community (especially in African countries) because the threat of backlash is so palpable. In particular, there are concerns that decriminalization will result in discrimination and physical violence against the Queer community beyond what already exists. African citizens overwhelmingly disapprove of homosexuality and many believe that there would not be homosexuality in Africa if it were not for Western influences and colonization (Kretz 2013). This seems a rather counterintuitive attitude given the origin of the sodomy laws, but nevertheless, it creates a homophobic climate conducive to violent backlash in the wake of any decriminalization measure interpreted to be some form of contemporary colonization.

Indeed, the United States did experience a wave of antigay backlash after *Lawrence v. Texas* (2003) decriminalized gay sex. In the year immediately following the decision, 11 states introduced constitutional amendments defining marriage as between cisgender men and women, and then President George W. Bush announced his support for a federal constitutional amendment. In 2006, eight more states introduced constitutional bans on gay marriage. It wasn't until 2008 that public attitudes and state laws began to shift in favor of equality and, as of June

26, 2015, all 50 states have marriage equality. In hindsight, the immediate backlash may have paved the way for this change in momentum.

It is too early for a victory dance, however, as US states continue to boast a variety of anti-LGBTQ legislation, such as religious exemption laws, whereby private business owners, health care professionals, and welfare agencies can deny Queer citizens services and treatment based on religious objections. Imagine that you are eating lunch at the counter of a local restaurant, and between your bites of burger, the owner asks you to leave. You ask why and the owner replies that they don't serve "your kind" – your kind meaning, gay. If this sounds familiar to you, it should, because it happened countless times in US history, culminating in what has come to be known as the "Woolworth lunch counter" incident of 1960 when several young Black men sat down to eat at a Woolworth's in North Carolina and were denied service because they were Black. The young men refused to leave the restaurant and their sit-in sparked a six-month-long protest that ultimately led to the desegregation of the Woolworth lunch counter in July of 1960. Over sixty years later, here we are again, for if you are gay or transgender, this similar bigotry could happen to you. What's worse is that it could happen to you when you need life-saving medical care. A *lack* of laws also impacts the Queer community in the United States, as many states do not prohibit discrimination in housing, public accommodations, and credit services on the basis of sexual orientation and/or gender identity. Except for people convicted of certain crimes, Queer people are the only US citizens that can legally be denied a place to live, denied lines of credit to make purchases and, until a 2020 Supreme Court ruling, fired from their jobs simply for who they are.

Several states also have laws limiting pro-LGBTQ speech in education, particularly as it relates to sex education. In Alabama and Texas, for example, sex education must emphasize that "homosexuality is not an acceptable lifestyle" (Mendos, Botha, Lelis, de le Pena, Savalev, & Tan 2020: 151). Legal scholars argue that these laws, dubbed "no promo homo" laws, are the relics of a larger struggle between the *politics of recognition* (i.e. Queer people fighting for equality) and the *politics of preservation* (i.e. conservatives fighting to preserve "family values") – identity politics playing out through rhetoric and legal battles (Eskridge 2000). Eskridge (2000: 1376) argues that the "state-supported closet" created by these sorts of laws "chills individual self-expression and political participation by GLBT people." No doubt, this is why in some parts of the world special interest groups have successfully lobbied to make it illegal to even express one's support of gay rights.

Perhaps the most well-known example of this is Russia's "gay propaganda law," which makes it a crime to promote homosexuality to minors – in other words, it is illegal to speak to minors about homosexuality in any way that is not disparaging. The law's enforcement has resulted in at least seven guilty convictions, including the arrests and prosecution of two demonstrators, Alexei Kiselyov and Kirill Nepomnyashy, whose crimes were holding signs that read "Gay is Normal" (Human Rights Watch 2014a; Human Rights Watch 2018; *St. Petersburg Times* 2012). Given the cultural climate towards the Queer community in Russia, no doubt confounded by the law, it is no surprise that the last decade has seen a surge of anti-LGBTQ vigilante groups such as *Occupy Pedophilia*, founded by neo-Nazi Maxim Martisinkevich. *Occupy Pedophilia* and similar vigilante groups have kidnapped, detained, sexually abused, and humiliated gay men and teenagers for the purpose of exposing them through videos of the encounters that are subsequently posted on YouTube. One victim of a vigilante group said that "[t]hey [vigilantes] think they have the right to treat us like this. I feel as if I'm not protected by law. All these bandits have been given impunity" (Human Rights Watch 2014a: 34). Despite the fact that Russian law could allow for these crimes to be prosecuted as hate crimes, efforts to do so have been thwarted as a result of both the vagueness of the law and the indifference of the Russian criminal legal system. Meanwhile, Russian citizens publicly supporting Queer rights face termination from their jobs and LGBTQ rights groups and Queer events face constant threat of being protested, bombed, or attacked by mobs organized through social groups on the Internet. Yelena Grigoryeva, a member of the Russian group *Alliance of Heterosexuals and LGBT for Equality*, fell victim to one of these Internet groups in 2019 (Fitzsimons 2019). The website, inspired by the horror film *Saw*, posts the names of LGBT activists and urges its users to "hunt" them. Grigoryeva, whose name and picture were posted on the site, was found stabbed and strangled to death near her home.

Unsurprisingly, these propaganda laws have become a way for some countries to widen the net, so to speak, in terms of criminalizing sexuality. This has been the case in Nigeria, where the arrests and prosecutions for homosexuality have increased since then President Goodluck Jonathan signed a 2014 law banning gay and lesbian public displays of affection, same-sex marriage (14-year sentence), and membership in gay rights groups (10-year sentence). Even though sodomy has been illegal in Nigeria since British rule, the law was rarely enforced. Jonathan's broader antigay law, however, has resulted in hundreds of arrests, including a man allegedly arrested for sending a text message in which he declared his love for another man (Bowcott 2014). Gay men and lesbians around the country live in fear of mass raids by state authorities, such as a same-sex wedding held in 2017 where 53 men were arrested and charged with "belonging to a gang of unlawful society" (Sopelsa 2017). Under the current Nigerian President, Mohammed Buhari, non-governmental agencies in the country have tracked an alarming pattern of violence against LGBTQ people, by both state and non-state actors, "including murder, blackmail and extortion, assault and battery, invasion of privacy, mob attacks, kidnaps, inhumane and degrading treatment, and rape" (The Initiative for Equal Rights 2020).

In 2020, there were 42 United Nations member states that had laws which in some way restricted freedom of expression related to LGBTQ issues (Mendos et al. 2020). Thirty-seven percent of African countries, 3% of Latin American and Caribbean countries, 40% of Asian countries, and 8% of European countries had laws

> criminalising offences against morality and religion, limiting sex education curriculum, prohibiting promotion or propaganda of homosexuality, censorship in media and movies, prosecution for LGBT+ symbols under public manifestation and pornography laws, blocking thematic websites and publications, chasing communications in dating apps, and other ways to limit freedom of expression.
>
> Mendos et al. 2020: 145

Sadly, this was an *increase* from 2019, when 34 UN member states had such laws (Mendos 2019). Thus, the global struggle for Queer rights and recognition has not been a linear journey – rather, it has been marked by a constant series of advances and setbacks.

A looming contemporary dilemma in regards to the persistent criminalization of Queerness is the unwillingness of many nation-states to uphold their own laws and/or a disjuncture between the domestic laws of nation-states and their international legal obligations. A perfect example of this is the previously mentioned violence experienced by Queer individuals and organizations in Russia. The Russian constitution does protect freedom of expression and protects citizens from discrimination, though clearly its application is inequitable. It is when states fail to uphold their own laws that international statutes become applicable, so one would presume that Russia's actions (or inactions, rather) would be addressed by any international legal statutes it has committed itself to. However, even though Russia has signed and ratified the *International Covenant on Civil and Political Rights* (ICCPR), which expressly requires states to allow for freedom of expression and equal treatment under the law, Queer citizens and their allies are seemingly exempt. And even though the UN Human Rights Committee has ruled against Russia in one case of prosecuting someone for violation of the "gay propaganda" law and the UN Committee on Torture has urged Russia to work towards protecting its Queer citizens from discrimination and violence, the state does not appear to be heeding that decision or advice by making any tangible changes.

Similarly, Iran has effectively skirted the reach of international law by keeping much of its legal process shrouded in secrecy. Like Russia, Iran has also signed and ratified the ICCPR, which prohibits countries with the death penalty from using it for anything other than the "most serious crimes" – a term that is never defined, thus being subject to interpretation. Additionally, the ICCPR prohibits the death penalty for juveniles. Consensual gay and lesbian sex is punishable by the death penalty in Iran – on the first offense for men and on the fourth for women (after sentences of 100 lashes for the first three offenses) – a punishment that Human Rights Watch (2010b) insists has been meted out to Iranian citizens, including people who committed offenses as juveniles. Though these and other countries have been criticized and ruled against by international legal bodies, the effects seem to be symbolic, minor, or non-existent.

It is true that, in comparison to other "criminal acts," consensual homosexual sex is rarely prosecuted, and punishment for propaganda is rarer still. Nevertheless, even if laws against same-sex relationships are antiquated and seldom prosecuted, if they exist, then individuals can still be detained and/or arrested and charged, prosecuted, and punished all based on the discretion of the authorities in that particular location (Csete & Cohen 2010). Ultimately, these laws (regardless of how often they are applied) legitimize homophobic attitudes and perpetuate interpersonal and institutional violence against the Queer community and certainly lend credence to the fear that Queer folks have regarding all arms of the criminal legal system, as highlighted by the experiences of transgender and gender nonconforming individuals around the world.

Criminalizing gender nonconformity

Though laws governing queer sexual behavior vary across the globe, laws meant to reinforce cultural gender norms and punish gender nonconformity seem to be far-reaching and are becoming more commonplace. Throughout history and even in recent years, transgender individuals around the world have been harassed by law enforcement, arrested, charged, and prosecuted specifically because of or as a result of their gender presentation, including in the United States, Kuwait, Malaysia, Israel, and the United Kingdom, among others (Dwyer 2011; Gross 2009; Human Rights Watch 2012; Human Rights Watch 2014a).

Often, laws intended to reinforce gender norms come in the form of "impersonation laws," whereby people are punished for "impersonating" someone of the opposite sex. These cases sometimes arise when a cisgender individual (often female) discovers that her or his romantic partner is transgender (often a transgender male) and claims that the sex was only consensual because she or he thought the "offender" was a biological male (or female). One such case was heard in the United Kingdom in 2013, where a 13-year-old transgender boy named Scott McNally pursued a three-year online relationship with a 12-year-old girl. After three years of online interaction the two met and engaged in sexual activity in 2011 – McNally was 17 and the other child was 16 at the time. Upon learning of McNally's biological sex, the "victim" claimed that had she known Scott was "biologically female," she would not have consented to sex. Ultimately the courts agreed that the interactions between the two constituted rape by deception, and McNally pleaded guilty to six charges of assault. He was convicted to three years in a juvenile facility and a *lifetime* on the sex offender registry (Dixon 2013). Not surprisingly, McNally was vilified by the media, deadnamed (referred to by the name he was given at birth) and said to have "fooled the 16-year-old and her family and friends with her disguise" and "lured her into intimate encounters, promising her marriage and children" (Dixon 2013). In their study of the media depiction of transgender murder victims, Schilt and Westbrook (2009) found this "deception" frame to be present 56 percent of the time. So, whether represented as an offender or a victim, it is the trans person's gender presentation that is framed as the problem, not transphobia.

It must be pointed out that what is unique about McNally's case is that the defendant and the plaintiff were close in age, and their relationship was not in violation of the UK's age of consent laws. To the contrary, the majority of "rape by deception" cases do appear to include the violation of age of consent laws, often proving to be a convenient way to punish gender nonconformity. Such was the case for Chris Wilson, a Scottish transgender man who allegedly had sexual relations with two teenage girls – one of whom said she was 16, the age of consent – when he was 20 years old. Wilson told her that he was 17 years old. He was sentenced to 240 hours of community service and placed on the sex offender registry. Interestingly, even though his alleged offense was statutory rape, he was not charged with such. Rather, he was charged with sexual intimacy by fraud, which suggests his conviction was, like McNally, about his gender identity and not about concern for his "victims." As in McNally's case, the media coverage of Wilson's case didn't focus on sexual assault so much as it did his gender identity. The BBC (2013) ran the headline "Sex fraud woman put on probation" for a story about "a woman who posed as a man" – though the article claimed that Chris had lived as a male since childhood, the author consistently used female pronouns.

Alex Sharpe, a Professor of Law at Keele University, makes an excellent point about the implicit double standard that characterizes cases like McNally's and Wilson's – bias that we wouldn't see if the "offender" represented other marginalized groups, such as racial minorities. She points out that no court of law would convict a light-skinned, mixed-race person of rape by deception if the white person that she or he had sex with became outraged and felt "violated" upon learning of the individual's mixed-race background (Sharpe 2013). The cases described here are undoubtedly about the policing and punishment of gender nonconformity and not about the protection of "innocent victims" from deceit or sexual assault.

Some would argue that these cases, while obviously related to the gender presentation of the defendants, would not have been pursued had the individuals not been sexually involved. Though this may be true, there are many examples globally where transgender individuals have faced mistreatment and abuse by law enforcement, arrest, and punishment for no other reason than the clothing they wear or their gendered mannerisms. This occurred historically in the United States and continues to occur around the world, as described below. Though most US anti-Queer laws of the past were largely used to regulate the behavior of gay men, it was butch lesbians who were often the victims of "cross-dressing" laws (Eskridge 1997). Both California and New York had laws against wearing a disguise or "masquerading" in public, and the city of Miami, Florida, outlawed impersonating a female and "dress not customarily worn by his or her sex" (Eskridge 1997: 723). Toledo, Ohio, Chicago, Illinois, and other cities across the country had similar statutes (Mogul, Ritchie, & Whitlock 2011). Neither of the two state laws was exclusively meant to address gender nonconformity, but those arrested were frequently lesbians wearing traditionally male clothing. The purported general guideline that law enforcement officers in New York used was that the individual had to be wearing at least three articles of clothing that matched the "offenders" biological sex. Many of the "cross-dressing" arrests were made as part of larger "anti-homosexual" raids of popular gay hangouts in the 1950s. Twelve female patrons, for example, were arrested for "mannish dress" during a 1957 vice raid of Jimmie White's Tavern in Tampa, Florida (Eskridge 1997). As will be discussed in Chapter 4, however, these raids are not simply relics of the past.

Though these antiquated laws were eventually removed from the books, trans people across the United States are still arrested for their appearance, often under the guise of solicitation offenses. This is exactly what happened to Arizona State University student Monica Jones, a transgender woman of color who was arrested in 2013 and convicted of "manifesting prostitution," which is to say she was interacting with passengers in cars (Kellaway 2015). Though Jones's conviction was overturned in January of 2015, trans women (especially trans women of color) face constant threat of harassment and arrest by police – a phenomenon so common that it has been dubbed "walking while trans." A report released by the National Center for Transgender Equality in 2016 revealed that 40% of the 27,715 transgender or gender nonconforming research participants had interacted with the police in the last year. Of those individuals, 58 percent had experienced harassment by police, with Black respondents reporting the highest rate of harassment (74%) and whites the lowest (55%). Of those who had experienced harassment, 4 percent had been physically assaulted and 3 percent had been sexually assaulted by law enforcement officers (James, Herman, Rankin, Keisling, Mottet, & Anafi 2016). While some who reported harassment were sex workers, many were not, suggesting that "walking while trans" is a very real danger for everyone who challenges traditional gender norms, regardless of the context of their interaction with law enforcement.

While law enforcement in the United States must now find creative ways (i.e. solicitation laws) to arrest people for their gender nonconformity, laws similar to the old masquerade laws of the United States are still found in other countries today, including Kuwait and Malaysia.

> Every time they catch me they expect me to repent. If I wear women's clothes, I get caught. If I wear men's clothes, I get caught. If I wear something in between, I get caught. And in all these situations I get sexually harassed. You begin to understand that getting arrested becomes part of your everyday life.
>
> Ghadeer, Kuwait *Human Rights Watch 2012: 34*

In 2007, Kuwait amended an older public nuisance law to allow the punishment (of up to one year in prison) of anyone "imitating the opposite sex in any way" (Human Rights Watch 2012: 1). Not only does the law not specify what constitutes "imitating" but, since there is no means to legally change one's sex in Kuwait, the law also affects individuals who have undergone gender confirmation surgery. Not surprisingly, the law ushered in police abuse towards transgender women, and led to their being arrested when approaching police to report other crimes. The law has amplified public scrutiny of trans women, and that heightened awareness has led ordinary citizens and healthcare workers to purposely report trans women that they see in public or find themselves treating. Transgender women also describe crimes being committed against them primarily because the perpetrator knows that if she reports the offense, she'll be charged with imitation. A woman named Haneen described to Human Rights Watch (2012) how her rapist literally drove her to a patrol car and dared her to get out of his vehicle and report the brutal attack against her.

> They were rough. One of them squeezed my breasts. I was completely humiliated ....They stripped me completely naked. One of them took a police baton and poked at my genitals. Everyone was looking – the men [Religious Department officials] as well as the women. They took photos of my naked body.
>
> Victoria, Malaysia *Human Rights Watch 2014b: 27*

In Malaysia, transgender citizens, especially trans women, face prosecution and incarceration for "cross-dressing" under Sharia law (Human Rights Watch 2014b). Though the laws vary by state in Malaysia, prison sentences for "posing" as someone of the opposite sex can range from six months to three years and can result in fines as much as a month's worth of salary. According to Human Rights Watch (2014b), the Islamic departments that enforce Sharia law often do so with the assistance of civil officers. The individuals arrested are given no representation in Islamic courts and, unsurprisingly, are usually found guilty.

The COVID-19 pandemic has also made it easier for police in some countries to harass and punish transgender people for failing to conform to gender norms. Panama, for example, instituted a gendered quarantine schedule, whereby men and women were only allowed out in public on opposite days (Human Rights Watch 2020). Transgender Panamanians report being harassed, arrested, fined by police, and prohibited from purchasing needed supplies whether they venture out on assigned days that match their gender identity or they venture out on days corresponding with their identification documentation. One transgender woman was arrested while shopping on a day designated for men. Once at the police station she was inappropriately touched, humiliated, and threatened to be placed in a holding cell with 200 men. It cost her $50 USD to be released. According to the woman, "The [Covid-19] measures have empowered police to discriminate and we, transgender people, need urgent help" (Human Rights Watch 2020: n.p.).

Interestingly, antigay and antitransgender laws and sentiments are not entwined in all countries. In India, where homosexuality is punishable by incarceration, being transgender is now a legally protected status (Sampath 2015). Transgender and intersex individuals, long referred to in India as *hijra*, have recently been given the right to identify as *hijra* on all government documents. Now nearly half a million Indian citizens will be recognized as members of the third sex. In keeping with the country's overall homophobic climate, however, the law was very specific to note that it did not extend to gays, lesbians, or bisexuals. In other countries that recognize *hijra* as a third gender, such as Bangladesh, a lack of clarity in the definition of *hijra* has created a climate conducive to humiliation and abuse (Human Rights Watch 2016). Bangladeshi *hijra*, for example, were thrilled to learn that the government was inviting them to apply for employment, which would mean relief from begging and sex work on the streets for survival. They lined up to be interviewed, only to learn that they would be subject to a medical exam (and sometimes prodded by non-medical personnel, like janitors) to determine that they were "authentic" *hijra* (Human Rights Watch 2016).

One final example of criminalizing gender nonconformity would be the introduction of discriminatory public accommodations laws, colloquially referred to as "bathroom bills," in the United States. A national debate about bathroom use by trans folks was spurred by the passing of the North Carolina Public Facilities & Privacy Act (also known as HB2 or House Bill 2) in 2016, which was introduced in response to the passing of a *non*-discrimination ordinance in Charlotte, NC. While Charlotte's ordinance protected trans people's right to use gender-affirming public spaces, HB2 prohibited trans people from using public bathrooms and other sex-segregated spaces (e.g., locker rooms) that aligned with their gender identity, and instead forced people to use the restroom that aligned with the sex they were assigned on their birth certificate.

HB2, and similar laws subsequently introduced around the country, were promoted by proponents as measures meant to protect cisgender women and girls from sexual assault in public restrooms, though the limited research that does exist on that threat suggests that such incidents are extremely rare and are not impacted by legislation (Hasenbush, Flores, & Herman 2019). There is evidence to suggest, however, that restricting trans and non-binary youth from using the restrooms and locker rooms that match their gender identity *does* correlate to an increased risk of sexual assault for them (Murchison, Agenor, Reisner, & Watson 2019). While HB2 was the only "bathroom bill" to be successfully passed (and later repealed) in the United States, similar legislation continues to surface in state legislative sessions across the country (Kralik 2019). Regardless of whether or not these laws are passed, the ideology of transphobia that they promote has severe consequences for the transgender community, to include physical violence (Lenning, Brightman, & Buist 2021).

It should be recognized that the governments of some nations have made public apologies for their past treatment of Queer people, particularly for laws that criminalized their existence and/or behaviors (Redd & Russell 2020). While the recognition of these injustices is long overdue, apologies alone are not sufficiently reparative. As Redd and Russell (2020) point out in their analysis of an apology from the Australian state of Victoria, the way that these apologies are offered undermines the injustices that they are meant to highlight. For example, in the Victorian apology, state leaders claimed that the past laws criminalizing homosexuality were *inexplicable* – that they could not "possibly explain why we made these laws" and that it is "inconceivable for us today" (Redd & Russell 2020: 594). The problem with this is that when you claim complete ignorance of the origins of these laws, you have failed to recognize what it is about the historical, national, or cultural context that prompted them – thus effectively failing to prevent future injustices from occurring. It is akin to the US government apologizing for Jim Crow laws while failing to recognize their roots in the country's history of colonialism and white supremacy ("We have no idea why segregation happened! It's inconceivable!"). It is that failure to recognize that colonial history, and further to confront and eradicate white supremacy, that explains why racial oppression and disparity persists in the United States well after the segregatory laws of the past have been removed from the books. Symbolic apologies that invite those wronged to "forget the past" and "pat the state on the back" for saying sorry only "promotes a 'proper' orientation towards the past: one tinged with shame and regret, which paradoxically allows the state and other powerful institutions to reclaim moral capital and pride in the present," regardless of whether or not the state's present treatment of Queer people reflects the sentiment of the apology (Redd & Russell 2020: 599).

The examples of criminalized queerness given throughout this chapter provide the context for what is described in the following chapters on victimization and offending, law enforcement, legal systems, and corrections. It is widely accepted in criminology that racial minorities, especially in the United States, experience discrimination and disparity in the criminal legal system in large part due to the historical practice of criminalizing and punishing their very existence (e.g. slavery and Jim Crow laws). Indeed, the scars left by racism have proven to be nearly impossible to erase and are most distinctly revealed in the criminal legal system. Thus, it should be no surprise that Queer people, especially Queer people of color, whose sexual behavior and bodies are still criminalized and punished to extreme degrees, have unique and largely negative experiences with and within the criminal legal system.

Activities and discussion questions

- Given what you have learned in this chapter, why do you think the authors have chosen to use the term "criminal legal system" rather than "criminal justice system"? Which term do you think best describes the current system? What other terms could be used?
- Visit the International Lesbian, Gay, Bisexual, Trans and Intersex Association (www.ilga.org) and explore their State-Sponsored Homophobia Reports (see Resources). Look at the latest report to compare legislation from various countries, or compare yearly reports to identify positive and negative changes in legislation on a global scale.

- Explore the various equality maps created by the Movement Advancement Project (www.lgbtmap.org/). If you live in the United States, compare the state you live in to others. If you reside outside of the United States, discuss how legislation in the United States is similar to or different from the laws of your own country.
- Based on what you learned in the chapter, how would you describe the relationship between civil rights (equal treatment under the law) and violence against LGBTQ people?

Recommended viewing

A Jihad for Love, 2007. [Film] Directed by Parvez Sharma. USA: Halal Films.

Before Stonewall, 1984. [Film] Directed by Greta Schiller and Robert Rosenberg. USA: Before Stonewall, Inc.

Born This Way, 2013. [Film] Directed by Shaun Kadlec and Deb Tullmann. USA: The Film Collaborative.

Call Me Kuchu, 2012. [Film] Directed by Katherine Fairfax Wright and Malika Zouhali-Worrall. USA: Cinedigm.

Dangerous Living: Coming Out in the Developing World, 2003. [Film] Directed by John Scagliotti. USA: After Stonewall Productions.

Equal, 2020. [Series] Directed by Stephen Kijak and Kimberly Reed. USA: HBOMax.

God Loves Uganda, 2013. [Film] Directed by Roger Ross Williams. USA: Full Credit Productions.

Hunted: The War Against Gays In Russia, 2014. [Film] Directed by Ben Steele. USA: HBO.

Paragraph 175, 2000. [Film] Directed by Rob Epstein and Jeffrey Friedman. USA: New Yorker Films.

Screaming Queens: The Riot at Compton's Cafeteria, 2005. [Film] Directed by Victor Silverman and Susan Stryker. USA: Frameline.

Stonewall Uprising, 2010. [Film] Directed by Kate Davis and David Heilbroner. USA: First Run Features.

TransMilitary, 2018. [Film] Directed by Gabriel Silverman and Fiona Dawson. USA: SideXSide Studios.

Note

1 Antiquated and offensive language, like homosexual, are used throughout this chapter to reflect the terminology used in the laws and policies we discuss.

References

BBC. 2013. Sex fraud woman put on probation. BBC News, April 9. Accessed from www.bbc.com/news/uk-scotland-north-east-orkney-shetland-22078298.

Bowcott, O. 2014. Nigeria arrests dozens as anti-gay law comes into force. *The Guardian*, January 14. Accessed from www.theguardian.com/world/2014/jan/14/nigeria-arrests-dozens-anti-gay-law.

Csete, J. & Cohen, J. 2010. Health benefits of legal services for criminalized populations: The case of people who use drugs, sex workers and sexual and gender minorities. *Journal of Law, Medicine & Ethics, 38*, (4): 816–831.

Dehghan, S.K. 2011. Iran executes three men on homosexuality charges. *The Guardian*, September 7. Accessed from www.theguardian.com/world/2011/sep/07/iran-executes-men-homosexuality-charges.

Dixon, H. 2013. 18-year-old woman masqueraded as a boy to get girl in bed. *The Daily Telegraph*, March 21. Accessed from www.telegraph.co.uk/news/uknews/crime/9946687/18-year-old-woman-masqueraded-as-boy-to-get-girl-into-bed.html.

Dwyer, A. 2011. "It's not like we're going to jump them": How transgressing heteronormativity shapes police interactions with LGBT young people. *Youth Justice, 11*, (3): 203–220.

Epprecht, M. 1998. The "unsaying" of indigenous homosexualities in Zimbabwe: Mapping a blindspot in an African masculinity. *Journal of Southern African Studies, 24*, (4): 631–651.

Ermac, R. 2015. Baton Rouge police chief apologizes for 'unconstitutional' sodomy arrests. *The Advocate*. Accessed from www.advocate.com/politics/2015/02/19/baton-rouge-police-chief-apologizes-unconstitutional-sodomy-arrests.

Eskridge, W. 1997. Privacy jurisprudence and the apartheid of the closet: 1946–1961. *Florida State University Law Review, 24*, (4): 703–838.

Eskridge, W. 2000. No promo homo: The sedimentation of antigay discourse and the channeling effect of judicial review. *New York University Law Review, 75*, (5): 1327–1411.

Finerty, C.E. 2013. Being gay in Kenya: The implications of Kenya's new constitution for its anti-sodomy laws. *Cornell International Law Journal, 45*: 431–459.

Fitzsimons, T. 2019. Russian LGBTQ activist is killed after being listed on gay-hunting website. NBC News, July 23. Accessed from www.nbcnews.com/feature/nbc-out/russian-lgbtq-activist-killed-after-being-listed-saw-inspired-site-n1032841.

Gross, A. 2009. Gender outlaws before the law: The courts of the borderland. *Harvard Journal of Law and Gender, 32*, (1): 165–230.

Hasenbush, A., Flores, A.R., & Herman, J.L. 2019. Gender identity nondiscrimination laws in public accommodations: A review of evidence regarding safety and privacy in public restrooms, locker rooms, and changing rooms. *Sexuality, Research, & Public Policy, 16*, (1): 70–83.

Human Rights Watch. 2005. Iran: Two more executions for homosexual conduct. Accessed from www.hrw.org/news/2005/11/21/iran-two-more-exe cutions-homosexual-conduct.

Human Rights Watch. 2008. *This alien legacy: The origins of "sodomy" laws in British colonialism.* Printed in the United States of America.

Human Rights Watch. 2010a. *Criminalizing identities: Rights abuses in Cameroon based on sexual orientation and gender identity.* Printed in the United States of America.

Human Rights Watch. 2010b. *"We are a buried generation": Discrimination and violence against sexual minorities in Iran.* Printed in the United States of America.

Human Rights Watch. 2012. *"They hunt us down for fun": Discrimination and police violence against transgender women in Kuwait.* Printed in the United States of America.

Human Rights Watch. 2014a. *License to harm: Violence and harassment against LGBT people and activists in Russia.* Printed in the United States of America.

Human Rights Watch. 2014b. *"I'm scared to be a woman": Human rights abuses against transgender people in Malaysia.* Printed in the United States of America.

Human Rights Watch. 2016. *"I want to live with my head held high": Abuses in Bangladesh's legal recognition of hijras.* Printed in the United States of America.

Human Rights Watch. 2018. No support: Russia's 'gay propaganda' law imperils LGBT youth. Accessed from www.hrw.org/report/2018/12/11/no-support/russias-gay-propaganda-law-imperils-lgbt-youth#.

Human Rights Watch. 2019a. Uganda: Brutal killing of gay activist: Amid attacks, officials threaten death penalty for LGBT people. Accessed from www.hrw.org/news/2019/10/15/uganda-brutal-killing-gay-activist#.

Human Rights Watch. 2019b. Uganda: Stop police harassment of LGBT people: Drop charges against dozens detained in recent roundups. Accessed from www.hrw.org/news/2019/11/17/uganda-stop-police-harassment-lgbt-people#.

Human Rights Watch. 2020. Panama: Set transgender-sensitive quarantine guidelines: Gender-based quarantine leading to arbitrary arrests, fines. Accessed from www.hrw.org/news/2020/04/23/panama-set-transgender-sensitive-quarantine-guidelines.

Ireland, P.R. 2013. A macro-level analysis of the scope, causes and consequences of homophobia in Africa. *African Studies Review, 56*, (2): 47–66.

Itaborahy, L.P. & Zhu, Z. 2014. *State-sponsored homophobia. A world survey of laws: Criminalization, protection & recognition of same-sex love.* Geneva: International Lesbian Gay Bisexual Trans and Intersex Association.

James, S.E., Herman, J.L., Rankin, S., Keisling, M., Mottet, L., & Anafi, M., 2016. *The report of the 2015 U.S. transgender survey*. Washington, DC: National Center for Transgender Equality.

Kellaway, M. 2015. Arizona appeals court overturns Monica Jones's conviction for "walking while trans." *The Advocate*, January 27. Accessed from www.advocate.com/politics/transgender/2015/01/27/arizona-appeals-court-overturns-monica-joness-conviction-walking-whi.

Kenya Human Rights Commission. 2011. *The outlawed among us: A study of the LGBTI community's search for equality and non-discrimination in Kenya*. Nairobi, Kenya: Kenya Human Rights Commission.

Kralik, J. 2019. *"Bathroom bill" legislative tracking*. Washington, DC: National Council of State Legislators. Accessed from www.ncsl.org/research/educat ion/-bathroom-bill-legislative-tracking635951130.aspx

Kredo, A. 2014. Iran executes two for "perversion." *The Washington Free Beacon*, March 3. Accessed from http://freebeacon.com/national-security/iran-executes-two-for-perversion/.

Kretz, A.J. 2013. From "kill the gays" to "kill the gay rights movement": The future of homosexuality legislation in Africa. *Journal of International Human Rights*, *11*, (2): 207–244.

Lawrence v. Texas. 539 U.S. 558 (2003).

Lenning, E., Brightman, S., & Buist, C.L. 2021. The trifecta of violence: A socio-historical comparison of lynching and violence against transgender women. *Critical Criminology*, *29*, (1): 151–172.

M'Baye, B. 2013. The origins of Senegalese homophobia: Discourses on homo-sexuals and transgender people in colonial and postcolonial Senegal. *African Studies Review*, *56*, (2): 109–128.

Mendos, L.R. 2019. *State-sponsored homophobia 2019: Global legislation overview update*. Geneva: International Lesbian, Gay, Bisexual, Trans and Intersex Association (IGLA World).

Mendos, L.R., Botha, K., Lelis, R.C., de la Pena, E.L., Savalev, I., & Tan, D. 2020. *State-sponsored homophobia 2020: Global legislation overview update*. Geneva: International Lesbian, Gay, Bisexual, Trans and Intersex Association (IGLA World).

Michaelson, J. 2014. Iran's new gay executions. *The Daily Beast*, August 12. Accessed from www.thedailybeast.com/articles/2014/08/12/iran-s-new-gay-executions.html.

Mogul, J.L., Ritchie, A., & Whitlock, K. 2011. *Queer (in)justice: The criminaliza-tion of LGBT people in the United States*. Boston, MA: Beacon Press.

Msibi, T. 2011. The lies we have been told: On (homo) sexuality in Africa. *Africa Today*, *58*, (1): 55–77.

Murchison, G.R., Agenor, M., Reisner, S.L., & Watson, R.J. 2019. School restroom and locker room restrictions and sexual assault risk among transgender youth. *Pediatrics*, *143*, (6): e20182902.

Ottosson, D. 2008. *State-sponsored homophobia: A world survey of laws prohibiting same-sex activity between consenting adults.* International Lesbian and Gay Association.

Redd, C. & Russell, E.K. 2020. 'It all started here, and it ends here too': Homosexual criminalisation and the queer politics of apology. *Criminology & Criminal Justice, 20,* (5): 590–603.

Rice, X. 2011. Ugandan gay rights activist David Kato found murdered. *The Guardian,* January 27. Accessed from www.theguardian.com/world/2011/jan/27/ugandan-gay-rights-activist-murdered.

Ritchie, A. 2013. Crimes against nature: Challenging criminalization of queerness and black women's sexuality. *Loyola Journal of Public Interest Law, 14,* (2): 355–374.

Sampath, R. 2015. India has outlawed homosexuality. But it's better to be transgender there than in the U.S. *Washington Post,* January 29. Accessed from www.washingtonpost.com/posteverything/wp/2015/01/29/india-has-outlawed-homosexuality-but-its-better-to-be-transgender-there-than-in-the-u-s/.

Schilt, K. & Westbrook, L. 2009. Doing gender, doing heteronormativity: "Gender normals," transgender people, and the social maintenance of heterosexuality. *Gender & Society, 23,* (4): 440–464.

Sharpe, A. 2013. We must not uphold gender norms at the expense of human dignity: Sexual intimacy, gender variance and criminal law. *New Statesman,* May 1. Accessed from www.newstatesman.com/politics/2013/05/we-must-not-uphold-gender-norms-expense-human-dignity.

Sopelsa, B. 2017. 53 arrested in Nigeria for celebrating gay wedding, police say. NBC News, April 20. Accessed from www.nbcnews.com/feature/nbc-out/53-arrested-nigeria-celebrating-gay-wedding-police-n748931.

St. Petersburg Times. 2012. "Gay is normal" sign gets demonstrators arrested in St. Petersburg. *St. Petersburg Times,* Issue #1702, April 6. Accessed from www.sptimesrussia.com/index.php?action_id=2&story_id=35439.

The Initiative for Equal Rights. 2020. Human rights violations report based on real or perceived sexual orientation, gender identity/expression and sex characteristics (SOGIESC) in Nigeria. Accessed from https://theinitiativeforequalrights.org/wp-content/uploads/2020/12/2020-Human-Rights-Violations-Report-based-on-SOGIESC.pdf.

Walsh, T. 2011. Ugandan gay rights activist bludgeoned to death. CNN, January 27. Accessed from www.cnn.com/2011/WORLD/africa/01/27/uganda.gay.activist.killed/.

Yadegarfard, M. 2019. How are Iranian gay men coping with systemic suppression under Islamic law? A qualitative study. *Sexuality & Culture,* 23: 1250–1273.

3

QUEER CRIMINOLOGY AT THE INTERSECTIONS

Victimization and offending

Before we turn our attention to the three major components of the criminal legal system, it is necessary to explore how Queer people get tangled up in the system – namely, as victims and offenders. Whether they experience victimization or engage in criminal activity (or both), it is important to point out that the Queer community is not homogeneous. In addition to representing a broad range of gender and sexual identities, Queer people are diverse in all other demographic categories including, but not limited to, age, race, socioeconomic status, ethnicity, geographic location, ability, and religious affiliation. All of these identities impact one's experiences, both in everyday life and in their interactions with the criminal legal system, making each an important variable in our understanding of victimization and offending. Queer people, especially those with multiple stigmatizing identities (e.g., Queer people of color), experience extreme marginalization. According to Epstein (2021: 9):

> Marginalization is the social process by which individuals and groups find themselves on the fringes of society. It blocks

DOI: 10.4324/9781003165163-3

people from rights, opportunities, and resources that others take for granted. Marginalization can be confounded by intersectionality, where co-existing identities make one person's life significantly more difficult than another's.

Thus, research on Queer victims and offenders must be conducted through an intersectional lens.

Victimization

The previous chapter outlined the many ways Queer people are victimized by the state through laws and policies that criminalize their existence. That criminalization creates an environment where Queer people are dehumanized, othered, and therefore at greater risk of experiencing violence. As Lenning, Brightman, and Buist (2021: 153) explain:

> enacting violent policies reaffirms violent ideologies in the eyes of the public which, in turn, emboldens individuals (both citizens and state actors) to take violent actions against the subjugated and marginalized groups in society with little sense of culpability or fear of consequence.

Many of these violent actions occur as a result of and are inextricably linked to violent ideologies such as homophobia and transphobia, as well as a host of other "isms" like racism, sexism, ageism, ableism, and ethnocentrism, and they qualify, either theoretically or legally, as hate crimes. As a significant amount of the literature surrounding Queer victimization focuses on hate crimes, we begin by considering crimes that are explicitly motivated by homophobia and transphobia, and that are often confounded by other violent ideologies.

Though "hate crime" is a seemingly straightforward term that most of us are familiar with, it is not as easy to define as one might assume (Chakraborti & Garland 2015). Which criminal acts deserve the label of hate crime varies by and within academic disciplines, by country, and by states, and hate crimes are inconsistently recognized by law as distinctly unique from other criminal acts, and therefore deserving of special attention or enhanced sentencing. On a basic level, though, a hate crime can be understood as "an offence which is known to the criminal law and is committed in a context that includes identity-based hostility" (Schweppe, Haynes, & Walters 2018: 8–9). Importantly, a hate crime is not a specific type of offense. Though we often think of hate crimes as extremely violent crimes, like murder and physical assault, they also include threats, intimidation, vandalism, property damage, or other offenses. An offense becomes a hate crime when the victim has (or is perceived to have) a specific protected identity *and* the offender is motivated to commit the offense because of that actual or perceived identity. Which identities are considered "protected" vary by geographic location, but often include race, ethnicity, sex, religion, and (dis)ability and, to lesser extents, sexual orientation and gender identity. For example, in the United States there are thirteen states that do not recognize sexual orientation or gender identity to be protected categories within their hate crime laws, and eleven more include sexual orientation but not gender identity (Movement Advancement Project 2021).

While definitions may change slightly throughout location or region, the United States, the United Kingdom, and Canada understand and define hate crimes in much the same way, and tend to see similar trends in their hate crime data. For example, in 2020 Statistics Canada (2021) indicated a decrease in reported crime in general, but a 37 percent increase in reported hate crimes – the highest increase the country had seen in 12 years. The same report indicated that in most of the hate crimes victims were targeted due to race or ethnicity, with Chinese, Korean, and South Asian citizens seeing a pronounced increase in risk. This is strikingly similar to the anti-Asian hate that spread throughout the United States during the global pandemic, which many attribute to the Trump administration's use of the terms "Kung Flu" and "Chinese Virus" to describe COVID-19 (Associated Press 2021). As reported by CBS News, the Center for the Study of Hate and Extremism at California State University found that hate crimes against Asian American and Pacific Islanders rose by 146 percent in 2020 (Associated Press 2021). Just as race is the most significant motivating factor for hate crimes in the United States and Canada, it is as well in the United Kingdom, accounting for nearly three-quarters of the country's hate crime offenses (Home Office 2020).

While hate crime data can help us get a general sense of the motivation behind and scope of bias-motivated offending, sources of hate crime data are fraught with inconsistencies and thus questionable in terms of their accuracy. The United Kingdom government, for example, admits that while their data indicates an 8 percent increase in hate crimes from 2019 to 2020, findings from the Crime Survey for England and Wales shows a decline in hate crimes by 38 percent (Home Office 2020). Likewise, hate crime data in the United States also varies by source. The official source of hate crime data in the U.S. is the Uniform Crime Reports (UCR), compiled by the Federal Bureau of Investigation (FBI). Unfortunately, UCR data only captures information from police departments that voluntarily submit it, and even then only captures offenses reported to police in the first place. Other sources of data, such as the National Crime Victimization Survey (NCVS), paint a very different picture than the UCR. In 2016, when the FBI reported 6,121 hate crimes, the NCVS captured nearly a quarter of a million (Schwencke 2017). Discrepancies between UCR and NCVS data suggests that for every 100 hate crimes that occur in the United States, fewer than four are actually reported to the FBI (Movement Advancement Project 2021).

In order for any incident to be included in the UCR data as a hate crime, the reporting police department or the federal government would have to apply the label of hate crime to the offense as well as identify the motivation for the offense, a process that is wholly subjective. The Pulse nightclub shooting of 2016 perfectly highlights the problematic nature of classification. In the early morning hours of June 12th, 2016, 29-year-old Omar Mateen entered Pulse, a well-known gay nightclub in Orlando, Florida, and opened fire on over 300 patrons, most of whom were Latinx. Mateen murdered forty-nine people and injured fifty-three others, making it the deadliest mass shooting the United States had seen up to that point in history. Because Mateen pledged his "allegiance to Abu Bakr al-Baghdadi of the Islamic State" in a 911 call immediately following the shootings (FBI Tampa 2016), the incident was quickly classified by the FBI as an act of terrorism and not, to the dismay of the LGBTQ community, a hate crime. In his final Facebook message and declaration to the world, Mateen declared that "The real muslims will never accept the *filthy* ways of the west" (Ogles 2018, emphasis added). While the Pulse massacre was no doubt an act of terrorism, it is hard to believe that Mateen's assault on an LGBTQ nightclub, hosting a Latin night, in the middle of LGBTQ Pride Month, was a random fluke and not a strategically chosen target. Were it not for the designation of "Islamic terrorism," one has to wonder if the victims of Pulse would have received the same level of public outpourings of love and grief and support that they did (Dwyer & Panfil 2017).

> I could just see him shooting at everyone and I can hear the [shots getting] closer, and I look over and he shoots the girl next to me. And I'm just there laying down and I'm thinking, "I'm next. I'm dead."
>
> *Angel Colon, Pulse survivor (Zambelich & Hurt 2016)*

Regardless of how the Pulse massacre was officially classified, the effect that it had on the Queer community, both in the United States and abroad, was and is still palpable (Pickles 2020; Ramirez, Gonzalez, & Galupo 2018).

Even when crimes seem to be obviously motivated by hate, prosecutors are often slow to add hate crime charges, and police investigations tend to be fraught with questionable investigative tactics. An attack against Holden White, an 18-year-old teenager from Louisiana, highlights these issues (Avery 2021). White's attacker used Grindr, a gay dating app, to lure him to his father's home under the guise of playing video games. Seneca Chance, who was 19, then brutally assaulted White, choking him, stabbing him, beating him over the head, and nearly severing his hands by cutting his wrists. Seneca, who himself called 911 to report that he had killed a man, was charged with second-degree attempted murder. Though White was rushed to the hospital, police did not bother to request a rape kit, initially chalking the attack up to a "lover's quarrel." Since White, who survived, was rendered unconscious by the vicious attack, he will never know if he was the victim of rape. It wasn't until many months later that the prosecutor added hate crime charges, which could add five years to Seneca's sentence if he is found guilty. According to the Department of Justice (2021: n.p.), White's attack was part of Chance's "overarching scheme to kidnap and murder gay men whom he met online." A federal indictment revealed that Chance admitted that he intended to dismember his victims and save their body parts as "trophies, mementos, and food" (DOJ 2021). Seneca is not the only person to use Grindr as a vehicle for committing vicious crimes – there have been prosecutions for similar crimes in several U.S. states (e.g. Texas, Oklahoma, Michigan), Australia, Belgium, and Britain (Aviles 2019; Clifford 2021; Moran 2020; Sear 2021).

It is important to consider that hate crimes against members of the Queer community do not only affect those who would legally be recognized as victims of hate crimes. Queer people are far too often the victims of bias-motivated violence, regardless of whether or not the state recognizes the offenses against them as hate crimes. Further, hate crimes have a reverberating or rippling effect, meaning that they impact perceptions of safety, levels of fear, and trust in law enforcement, especially by citizens who share common characteristics with the primary victim(s) (e.g., Ramirez et al. 2017; Walters, Paterson, Brown, & McDonnell 2020).

One area of queer criminological research that is growing, despite a relative lack of data, is work exploring violence against transgender people, specifically homicides. While no official data addresses these incidents, non-governmental agencies (NGOs) like the Human Rights Campaign and Transgender Europe have been tracking fatal violence against trans people for years, largely through media reports and anonymous tips. Through its Trans Murder Monitoring (TMM) project, Transgender Europe has been recording the murders of transgender and gender non-conforming people since 2008, and their findings are unsettling. Between January 2008 and September 2019, for example, they identified 3,314 murders in 74 different countries (Fedorko, Kurmanov, & Berredo 2020). Between 2013 and early 2020, the Human Rights Campaign (2020), which only tracks murders in the U.S., identified at least 202 murders of transgender people in thirty states across the country. Sixty-six percent of those victims were Black transgender women. Both organizations admit that these numbers, while shocking, are likely gross underestimates of fatal violence against trans people because "some victims' deaths may go unreported, while others may not be identified as transgender or gender non-conforming" by law enforcement and/or the media (Human Rights Campaign 2020: 2).

While not all of these fatal incidents qualify as hate crimes, many of them are extremely brutal – so much so that it is impossible to deny the offender's animosity towards the victim. A gut-wrenching example of this is the 2017 murder of 17-year-old transgender teen Ally Lee Steinfeld. Just four months after coming out on social media as a transgender woman and as "mostly lesbian but pansexual," Ally was fatally assaulted by four other teenagers (Ballentine & Salter 2017). She was beaten, stabbed, her genitals were mutilated, and her eyes were gouged out before her murderers burned her body and left her remains in a chicken coop in Cabool, Missouri. To the shock of LGBTQ organizations around the country, the local prosecutor Parke Stevens, Jr. declined to charge any of the offenders with a hate crime, saying "I would say murder in the first degree is all that matters. That is a hate crime in itself" (Ballentine & Salter 2017). Andrew Vrba, who stabbed Ally, was found guilty and sentenced to life in prison without parole. His three co-defendants pleaded guilty to charges ranging from abandonment of a corpse to second-degree murder and were sentenced to four years, eight years, and twenty years. The two co-defendants with the shortest sentences have since been paroled (Rehwald 2020).

> The desecration of Steinfield's body is a direct correlation to the way trans bodies are spoken about – in so-called bathroom bills, in public transitions and in death. This is especially true for trans women, and trans feminine individuals, whose vulnerability to violence is amplified by misogyny.
> *Audacia Ray, Anti-Violence Project (Brammer 2018)*

Missouri happens to be one of the 22 U.S. states that includes both sexual orientation and gender identity in its hate crime statutes. However, since Ally's death was never labeled a hate crime, and since police departments don't report victims' names when they submit to the UCR, we'll never know if Ally was the single gender-identity-related hate crime that Missouri reported to the FBI in 2017.

Like most murders of transgender victims, Ally's murder was, as the media described it, "grisly" (e.g., Ballentine & Salter 2017; Rehwald

2020). Also, like 74% of transgender murder victims, Ally was misgendered after her death, being referred to throughout Vrba's trial by both the prosecutor and the defense with male pronouns and the name she was given at birth. She was also a trans woman, and trans women account for the vast majority (84%) of transgender murder victims (Human Rights Campaign 2020). Unlike most trans murder victims, however, Ally Lee was white. Eighty-five percent of transgender and gender non-conforming murder victims in the United States are people of color (Human Rights Campaign 2020).

Despite the efforts of LGBTQ organizations to recognize transgender victims of homicide, it is rare that we hear about these cases in the mainstream media unless, like Ally, they are white. Muhlaysia Booker, a 22-year-old Black trans woman from Dallas, did make national headlines – not necessarily for her murder, but for an incident that occurred a month prior to her death in May of 2019. On April 12th, 2019, Muhlaysia allegedly backed her car into another vehicle, and the driver of that car demanded that she pay for damages on the spot, holding her at gunpoint. The scene quickly drew a crowd, and one onlooker offered a man named Edward Thomas $200 to beat Muhlaysia up. Thomas, along with several others, began repeatedly kicking and punching Muhlaysia while yelling transphobic slurs, injuring her. The assault did not stop until several women stepped in, grabbed Muhlaysia, and dragged her to safety in a nearby vehicle. Most of the incident was captured on cell phone video that quickly went viral, which is why Muhlaysia Booker became a recognizable figure in the news. Despite the media attention, her attacker was convicted only of misdemeanor assault. The defense attorney, who misgendered Muhlaysia and referred to her by the wrong name, "reportedly downplayed Booker's injuries as 'scratches' and referred to the assault as 'mutual combat' between two men" (Donaghue 2019: n.p.). Muhlaysia was murdered on May 18th, 2019 in what the police called an "unrelated incident." Her alleged killer, Kendrell Lavar Lyles, is suspected to have murdered several other people in the Dallas area (Allen 2019).

Sadly, Muhlaysia isn't the only transgender victim to have a brutal assault against them posted on the internet for an international audience to gawk at. A 2016 study conducted by Witness Media Lab found that similar videos are being uploaded, shared, and viewed online far more often than one might expect (Stevenson & Broadus 2016). Using the search terms "tranny fight" and "stud fight" on YouTube, World Star Hip Hop, Live Leak, and Fly Height, researchers found a total of 329 videos of physical assaults against transgender and gender non-conforming individuals, including a woman who was beaten until she had a seizure and another who was stripped naked on a public subway in Atlanta, Georgia. The Atlanta video, which was an assault on two transgender women, was especially graphic, and viewers left over 1,500 comments, including "A man that's all no woman and will never be don't care how many dicks he suck and fuck nasty gay bastard" (Stevenson & Broadus 2016: 36). The 329 videos were viewed over 80 million times, shared over 600,000 times, and "liked" by over half a million viewers.

While it is true that these viral videos are being uploaded, viewed, and liked by people who are presumably transphobic and therefore predisposed to holding negative views about trans people, violence against trans people is gaining some traction in the mainstream media, and those depictions shape the consciousness of the general public. How the media represents and frames acts of violence against trans people matters, as it impacts what the public knows about these often fatal acts, how they think about violence and trans people, and consequently influences the way that the public and the criminal legal system responds to such transgressions. While some news outlets report on these crimes in a thoughtful manner, most of the coverage "tends to be reductive, essentialist, and, in some cases, degrading" and "habitually dehumanizes trans victims and denies their victimhood, which obscures the reality of this social problem" (DeJong, Holt, Helm, & Morgan 2021: 132). Media analyses of the coverage of trans murder victims find that victims are frequently misgendered (referred to using pronouns that match their sex assigned at birth and not their gender) and deadnamed (referred to by the name they were given at birth and not the name they use), and that the victims themselves were often blamed for the violence against them, either for "deceiving" their murderer or for engaging in some behavior deemed "risky" (DeJong et al. 2021; Wood, Carrillo, & Monk-Turner 2019). No matter the tone or accuracy of the media coverage, one thing is for sure, and that is that trans murder victims are slowly beginning to get the attention they deserve. Queer victims of intimate partner violence and sexual assault, crimes that are far more commonly committed among and against Queer people, are rarely subject to public attention, however, and thus they remain in the shadows.

Research on intimate partner violence and sexual assault victimization and offending continues to focus on abuse by cisgender male offenders against cisgender female victims. Although research on intimate partner violence (IPV) in the Queer community has been researched for decades, the amount of existing research is still limited. Interestingly, existing studies have long suggested that same-sex IPV rates are similar if not higher than in cisgender relationships (see Messinger 2020; Renzetti 1992; Tesch, Bekerian, English, & Harrington 2010; Tjaden, Thoennes, & Allison 1999). Further, more recent research specific to transgender victims of IPV has often found a disproportionately high rate of abuse and unique barriers faced in these relationships. The work of Xavier Guadalupe-Diaz (2019) is essential reading for those interested in a more comprehensive account of the lived experiences of transgender victims of IPV through the use of detailed qualitative narrative interviews. Additionally, Adam Messinger (2020: 5) introduced the five myths of LGBTQ IPV which are as follows: "LGBTQ IPV is rare, LGBTQ IPV is less severe, LGBTQ IPV abusers are masculine, LGBTQ IPV is the same as all other IPV, and LGBTQ IPV should not be discussed." As indicated by Messinger and most LGBTQ IPV researchers, Queer folks experience IPV at similar or higher rates than heterosexual, or non-Queer identified individuals. The research does exist and it continues to gather momentum within queer criminology, to borrow from Messinger's introductory chapter, making the invisible visible.

Therefore, if within the world of queer criminology, feminist criminology, and critical criminology we have numerous scholars who have addressed this phenomenon, then why is it that police officers and other service providers in the criminal legal system are either uneducated, untrained, and/or personally and professionally ignorant about this issue? This is but one example as to the importance of using criminological research as an informative tool that can be used in training and policy development within the criminal legal system. For instance, if there is an overall ignorance or prejudice regarding queer IPV, that ignorance and prejudice leads to discrimination in providing service to victims and offenders alike.

Specific barriers that LGBTQ+ people experience when dealing with IPV can be located within policing, victims' rights and advocacy, courts, and corrections, and other social services. One example might be a social worker assigned to a hospital emergency room who may encounter victims of abuse on a regular basis and must assess the safety of individuals who appear to have experienced abuse either at the moment of their interaction or in the past, such as if they are safe with those they are living with. In any situation this is a challenge, as most IPV victims are paralyzed with fear of their abusers and this fear, in addition to countless other factors, may prevent them from being honest with a professional in this role – again often social workers who are expected to be experts in counseling, emotional well-being, addiction, abuse, and overall physical and mental health.

Shelter services are also of great concern – as much of the literature has indicated, shelters are often designed based on sex assigned at birth and therefore, assistance for transgender or gender non-conforming individuals is virtually non-existent; as Slakoff and Seigel (2022: 282) remind us:

> transgender women are more vulnerable to harm and have fewer resources for coping. If transgender women have nowhere to go, they risk additional harms at the hands of police, as well an increased likelihood of homelessness and intimate partner and sexual violence.

One area that has been gaining momentum within criminal legal and criminological research is trauma-informed care (TIC). TIC assumes that every person may have experienced some kind of trauma in their lives and administers treatment and assistance while respecting the likelihood of these experiences and working to avoid re-victimizing the individual needing help. As indicated by the University at Buffalo (2002: n.p.), "Trauma-informed care required a system to make a paradigm shift from asking, 'What is wrong with this person' to 'What has happened to this person.'" More recent research (Antebi-Gruszka & Scheer 2021) highlights the five dimensions of TIC from Goodman,

Sullivan, Serrata, Perilla, Wilson, Fauci, & DiGiovanni's (2016) research; the dimensions are: fostering agency and mutual respect, providing psychoeducation, increasing opportunities to connect with other survivors, building on clients' strengths and finally, practicing cultural sensitivity. When examining the services for LGBTQ+ survivors of IPV within the criminal legal system, services, and programs there is likely little opportunity to provide a trauma-informed care plan as we continue to see wholly inadequate assistance provided to the Queer community of abuse victims and offenders. It is also worth reiterating that this lack of attention is especially felt in the transgender and bisexual communities, as research continues to indicate that these two populations experience the highest percentages of IPV in the Queer community. One study found that "TIC did relate significantly to greater empowerment, greater emotion regulation, and lower social withdrawal; however, TIC did not relate to lower shame" (Scheer & Poteat 2021: 6682). This study also indicated that mental health was not improved using TIC; however, the other findings mentioned are integral in learning more about how this line of treatment can be of great benefit to the LGBTQ+ community.

Other concerns for LGBTQ+ victims, are often universal fears of being outed if they leave, report the abuse, leave their abuser, or seek services (if available). All of these issues and the overall fear and distrust that Queer folks have of police and the criminal legal system in general contribute to the reasons why reporting abuse to the police is often not a viable option to them. There are multiple concerns over barriers to services, including police services (and possible subsequent interactions with courts and corrections) that should be considered. First, as we have discussed, there are unique concerns that LGBTQ+ people have that are not of concern to heterosexual or gender-conforming individuals such as shelters, physical and emotional support, financial assistance, and more. These all contribute to why Queer folks are often unlikely to report their abuse to police. There continues to be training and policy sparsity in policing, especially regarding interaction with Queer populations, which we attribute to the structure and culture of policing that has long championed anti-LGBTQ+ policy and overall sentiment, and operates broadly within a heteronormative capacity and hegemonic masculinity. The lack of trust in police is detailed later in Chapter 4 until then, however, it is important to remember the history of victim-blaming that survivors of IPV experience within the system that re-victimizes them and further exacerbates trauma. This is an especially salient point regarding Queer individuals.

As indicated throughout this chapter and the text as a whole, official data on the experiences of Queer people in the criminal legal system are still painfully lacking, but perhaps this is especially true of individuals who identify as bisexual. This collective, the "B" in LGBTQ+, is frequently ignored in the research as well as by NGOs and popular news sources, even though existing research indicates that bisexual individuals are the most likely to experience IPV (Addington 2019; see Black, Basile, Breiding, Smith, Walters, Merrick, Chen & Stevens 2011).

Taken together we recognize the systems' failure to address these serious implications from the lack of education, understanding, and compassion towards Queer victims and survivors of IPV. We also recognize that in the time of COVID-19, these failures are compounded and intensified, with perhaps even more barriers to safety as families quarantine in their shared spaces. As indicated by the Human Rights Campaign (2020: n.p.) "our isolated environment, as well as the numerous financial and additional stressors brought by COVID-19, creates an increased risk of IPV – a risk which is that much higher for LGBTQ people."

Finally, a comprehensive discussion of queer victimization would be incomplete without recognizing and unpacking some form(s) of state violence. While the previous chapter discussed state violence extensively, and the next several chapters will home in on how Queer people are victimized within the branches of the criminal legal system specifically, the most pervasive form of state violence against Queer people is negligence. Particularly when they are victims of crime, Queer people are often ignored, not taken seriously, or blamed for the crimes committed against them. Not only does this mean that the Queer community, rightfully so, has a general distrust of the police (see Chapter 4), it also means that crimes against them can go unsolved due to a general lack of concern for the victims, even when those crimes span many years and claim many victims.

Though we could offer many examples, the case of Canadian serial killer Bruce McArthur serves as a haunting example of state negligence.

Over the course of seven years (2010–2017) McArthur killed and dismembered eight different people, all of whom had ties to Toronto's "Gay Village" (Epstein 2021). Though each victim was unique, all were gay or bisexual, six were people of color (mostly Middle Eastern and South Asian), and most "were at the intersection of multiple identities, making them particularly vulnerable to a serial predator" (Epstein 2021: 8). Despite warnings from Toronto's Queer community that a serial killer was on the loose, Toronto police consistently denied that a serial killer was responsible, even just a few weeks before McArthur's arrest and subsequent confession (Coletta 2021).

In a report submitted on behalf of an independent civilian review of missing persons cases in Toronto, Judge Gloria J. Epstein (2021: 1) summed the McArthur case up as politely as possible: "The police could have done better." Though it was not within the review board or Judge Epstein's power to find the Toronto Police Department, or any member of it, guilty of misconduct or civil or criminal liability, the failures outlined by the report are appalling. While they are too numerous to list here, most of the failures related to lack of communication between officers and units, failure to enter data into databases, failing to make connections between McArthur's previous conviction (for beating a man over the head with a pipe in the Gay Village) and the killings, and failing to link the victims through common characteristics and behaviors (like having interactions with McArthur on the Internet). Throughout the flawed investigation officers interviewed McArthur on two different occasions, letting him go both times, despite the fact that one of the interviews occurred because he choked a man in a van. Police let him go when McArthur claimed he was having consensual sex with his accuser (Coletta 2021). The investigation into the missing men ebbed and flowed over the years, and didn't seem to gain any serious traction until Andrew Kinsman, the only white victim and a well-respected activist in the Gay Village, went missing (Epstein 2021). While some accuse the police of systemic bias because of the victims' multiple marginalized identities, and others claim no bias at all, we agree with Judge Epstein (2021: 56) that "both the perception and the reality of discrimination-free policing are essential."

Though serial killing is an anomaly in the "grand scheme of crime," McArthur's case is telling precisely *because* he is a serial killer. If eight different people can be victims of the same person (who is known by police to be a threat), all of whom have ties to one geographic location within a specific city, and all of whom identify with a common community, and still not receive a swift response from police, just imagine all of the Queer victims of isolated, interpersonal crimes who are never given the attention they deserve or receive the justice owed to them.

State negligence is often a form of secondary victimization, which is a type of harm experienced by crime victims as they attempt to navigate the systems designed to aid and protect them. These harms can manifest in a variety of ways, and include victim-blaming by service providers, the denial of a person's victim status, failure to intervene or act on behalf of a victim, and neglecting to prevent future harm(s). While many victims face secondary victimization, perhaps none experience it to the degree that asylum seekers do, especially those seeking refuge in the United States.

As we discussed in the previous chapter, Queer people are criminalized all over the world and experience extreme forms of violence, often at the hands of state agents. When this state-sanctioned violence becomes so pervasive that it is unbearable, some choose to flee to countries seen as sanctuaries, including the United States. Due to politicized and constantly shifting immigration policies, asylum seekers are not guaranteed respite just because they leave their home countries, and oftentimes face similar or even greater threats once they cross international borders. The violence and obstacles facing Queer asylum seekers have become more apparent in recent years, in large part due to LGBT people "joining a series of migrant 'caravans' that traveled in groups to the US-Mexico border beginning in 2017" (Human Rights Watch 2020: 2).

One of those migrants was 29-year-old trans woman Camila Díaz Córdova, who was escaping her life in El Salvador, where trans people face widespread abuse and discrimination (Human Rights Watch 2020) and where trans women have a life expectancy that is 41 years lower than the country's overall average (Amnesty International 2020). Camila was one of the 1,228 people who sought asylum in the U.S. from El Salvador between 2007 and 2017 on the basis of "persecution related to gender identity or sexual orientation" (Human Rights Watch 2020: 23). At a young age Camila was rejected by her family, which forced her to engage in sex work for survival. As a sex worker Camila experienced harassment and abuse from police officers (Human Rights Watch 2020) and death threats and extortion by the Barrio 18 gang (Renteria 2019). When she could no longer endure the violence she faced on the street, Camila made her way to the U.S. and turned herself in to immigration authorities in August of 2017, only to be deported back to El Salvador four months later.

Back in El Salvador, Camila returned to sex work once again to support herself, and in 2019 she died from the injuries she sustained when three police officers beat her and threw her out of a moving vehicle. Her murder marks the first time that anyone in El Salvador has ever been convicted of killing a transgender person (Human Rights Watch 2020). Had the U.S. not deported her with so much haste, Camila might still be alive today. On the other hand, had she spent much more time in a U.S. Immigration and Customs Enforcement (ICE) facility than she did, she would have endured being held indefinitely in a facility designated for men, been subject to sexual assault and abuse, spent time in solitary isolation, and possibly been denied medical care (Human Rights Watch 2016). In either case, transgender refugees face state negligence no matter which country they find themselves in.

Whether they are victims of hate crimes, murder, IPV, state negligence, or other forms of crime, Queer victims face unique challenges that can only be understood in the context of the broader social harms they face on a daily basis and in relation to all of the identities they represent. To ignore their victimization is to deny Queer people of their humanity, which only further perpetuates violence against them and contributes to an endless cycle of systemic abuse and neglect. While the criminal legal system appears to be largely uninterested in attending to the crimes committed against Queer people, there seems to be no hesitance to arrest, charge, and punish Queer offenders.

Offending

Relative to victimization, very little is empirically known about queer offending. As best delineated by Panfil (2014), this may be due to several factors, mostly relating to the pervasiveness of stereotypes about

Queer people and also a fear (by queer criminologists) of perpetuating negative stereotypes. This omission, however, can actually perpetuate myths about Queer people, such as the presumption that they are inherently victims, or that they lack agency, power, or control (Panfil 2014). Further, it obfuscates our understanding of the relationship between victimization and one's likelihood or need to offend. In this sense, queer criminology (as opposed to orthodox criminology) is actually well-suited to investigate and confront the issue of queer offending, inasmuch as it seeks to do so in a way that highlights the structural and social conditions that influence Queer people to commit crime.

Further, in using an intersectional lens, queer criminologists can delineate differences between Queer people in regards to the myriad identities that they hold, illuminating the effects of race, class, age, etc., on queer offending and offenders. However, as there is no official crime data that captures all of these demographic categories, this task is far easier said than done. Thus, queer criminologists are left with two choices: draw upon the data collected by non-official sources (like NGOs, largely situated in the West) or create their own data from scratch. The former forces criminologists to analyze data that may not be complete or fully attentive to their research questions, and the latter means conducting original research without the institutional support of grant funding that is more readily available to criminologists studying populations that government agencies are most concerned with.

As was discussed in Chapter 1, Queer people, especially gay men, have historically been considered by criminologists through a lens of sexual deviancy; thus inquiries into their "criminal nature" were by and large in relation to their sexuality (and no other aspect of their identity) and sexual behaviors. Social norms regarding sexual behavior, especially notions of masculinity and heterosexuality, contributed to the idea that gay men were inherently effeminate, mostly white, and predominantly middle class (thus less prone to violent crime), and therefore less worthy of the attention of criminologists studying violent crimes (Panfil 2014).

While criminologists may not have paid much attention to queer criminality in the past, the general public certainly did, and still does, thanks to the media. In fact, much of what we *think* we know about queer offending is entrenched in socially constructed stereotypes that are perpetuated by the media. These stereotypes have been used to create queer criminal archetypes that the public has come to recognize and accept as accurate depictions of queer criminality, though they are little more than gross caricatures. Mogul, Ritchie & Whitlock (2011) identify several queer criminal archetypes that have developed and persisted in the media for a century or more: the queer killer, the sexually deranged predator, the disease spreader, the queer security threat, and young, queer criminal intruders. Each of these archetypes is reified by true cases, but only those cases that are the most sensational – crimes that are rare, lurid, gruesome, and that quench the public's insatiable thirst for commodified true crime narratives.

Perhaps the most pervasive of the archetypes presented by Mogul et al. (2011: 27) is the queer killer, also known as the gleeful gay killer, portrayed by the media as:

> people who torture, kill, and consume lives, not only for the sheer erotic thrill of it, but also to annihilate heterosexual enemies, lovers who disappoint, and anyone else who thwarts the fulfillment of their unnatural, immature desires or seems like a useful stand-in for self-hating, symbolic suicide.

Drawing on the most shocking details of cases like Jeffrey Dahmer, John Wayne Gacy, Dennis Nilsen, and Aileen Wournos, the media has tapped in to our collective psyche, recycling the same stories over and over in mountains of television shows, documentaries, fictionalized film accounts, books, podcasts, and more, so much so that we readily accept without question the idea that Queer people who kill do so, at least in part, to fulfill, suppress, or assert their sexually deviant perversions. In other words, queer killers commit murder "*because* they are queer," while other offenders who commit crimes that are equally as brutal (e.g. Ted Bundy, Richard Ramirez) are never assumed to have killed *because* they are heterosexual (Mogul et al. 2011: 30, emphasis in original).

Sensationalized depictions of the queer killer archetype are a cornerstone of the true crime genre and the more disturbing the case, the more the public is drawn to it. Take, for example, the case of Canadian killer Luka Magnotta, who was convicted of murdering international college student Jun Lin in 2012. The Magnotta case was a media jackpot, containing all of the elements of a bizarre Hollywood film – a former porn star uploads videos of himself torturing kittens (piquing the interest of internet sleuths), and then records himself murdering a man with an ice pick and dismembering and cannibalizing him before uploading that video to the internet and mailing his body parts to Canadian politicians, all of which culminates in an international "catch me if you can" type manhunt. Within two weeks of its release, *Don't F**k with Cats: Hunting an Internet Killer*, the documentary series chronicling the case, became one of the top five most watched documentaries on Netflix in 2019 (Oldham 2020). No doubt some of the people reading this book will head to Google to find out more about Magnotta, or immediately log in to Netflix to binge watch the documentary series – and that is the point. These sensationalized (extremely rare) cases become sources of entertainment and spectacle, not in any way contributing to our actual understanding of queer criminality. As Mogul et al. (2011: 26) point out:

> [these] archetypes and their accompanying scripts are remarkably powerful in directing not only the initial gaze, but also subsequent interpretations and actions, of police, prosecutors, judges, juries, and prison authorities. It is almost impossible to overestimate the societal clout of these symbolic representations.

These exaggerated archetypes bleed out from television screens, social media posts, and salacious headlines, and seep into the collective conscious of society, perpetuating the myths upon which Queer people are criminalized. This symbiotic relationship between socially constructed myths and real-life policies has contributed to the overpolicing and increased surveillance of Queer communities and spaces, which results in the disproportionate involvement of Queer people in the criminal legal system (Asquith, Dwyer, & Simpson 2017). Oftentimes the attention that is put on understanding queer offending is concentrated on sexually based crimes and thus Queer offenders are "festishised in and by the criminal processing system" (Asquith et al. 2017: 172). This fetishization perpetuates stereotypes about Queer sex offenders, especially male offenders who have male victims, and has quantifiable consequences, to include a greater likelihood of being involuntarily civilly committed to a facility for being a "sexually violent person" (SVP). For example, in Texas only 9.4% of registered male sex offenders have a male victim, but 33.5% of civilly committed male perpetrators have same-sex victims, meaning that the rate of civil commitment is three times the rate of offending (Hoppe, Meyer, De Orio, Vogler, & Armstrong 2020). According to Hoppe et al. (2020: 16), "These patterns suggest that gay/bisexual and other MSM[1] are seen as more violent, more dangerous or mentally ill and more deserving commitment under SVP statutes as compared with heterosexuals."

We should note that even though this data highlights a correlation between perceptions of Queer offenders and punishment, it does little to tell us about the offending itself. Further, the methodological limitations of the study reveal how difficult it can be to actually understand queer offending. Since no state or federal correctional agencies record sexual orientation as part of their data collection, the researchers had to use the sex of the victim (all perpetrators in the states considered – Texas and New York – were male) to ascertain the offenders' sexual orientation. In short, if the male perpetrator had a male victim, they were classified as sexual minorities for the purpose of the study (Hoppe et al. 2020). Though the researchers had noble intentions, measuring sexual orientation in this way, especially among sex offenders, is problematic. As Walker (2020) points out, the research indicates that most people who sexually offend against children do so not because of an attraction to children but because children are particularly vulnerable and sex offenders tend to be situational offenders. Simply put, children are easier to sexually assault than adults are. Using that same logic we can surmise that not all sex offenders who have a same-sex victim are gay, but rather they are preying on whomever they perceive to be the easiest target, hoping that the stigma and shame surrounding gay identity labels will deter their victims from coming forward.

Like the Hoppe, et al. (2020) study, most research on "queer offending" is not actually about offending. Basic library and Google searches on "queer offenders" do not generally yield results that tell us anything about *why* queer people offend or *how* those offenses differ in frequency, severity, or commission from crimes committed by cisgender or heterosexual offenders. The exception to this is what we know about survival crimes, which we will turn to shortly, but most studies about "queer offending" are actually studies about queer punishment – that is research that describes the experiences Queer people have once they become entangled in the correctional system. Moreover, much of that work is on punishment related to the most serious of crimes or forms of punishment (like the aforementioned study on civil commitment, a very rare occurrence).

One unique area of research that has been done in the area of queer offending, however, is Panfil's (2017) work on gay gang members, which calls into question the existing knowledge we have about gang membership, gang life, and desistance. Panfil (2017: 232) writes that the men she interviewed were "not running away from their marginalization. Undoubtedly they are resisting racist, classist and heterosexist forces that exclude and devalue them." We would add that queer criminologists must not run away from that marginalization either. Rather than fear that our work on Queer offenders may further marginalize them, we need to embrace the idea that studying Queer offenders can be a form of resistance against the racist, classist, and heterosexist forces that dictate how we think about and understand criminal behavior. Indeed, it is these very forces that place many Queer people at the intersection of offending and victimization.

Intersection of offending and victimization

An individual's identity and overall life experiences often highlight the overlap in offending and victimization. We argue this is true for everyone but Queer people face unique structural conditions that can impact their ability to fully access and participate in institutions necessary for basic survival, such as education, healthcare, and employment, which may force some to engage in crimes commonly referred to as survival crimes. Survival crimes are criminal acts committed for the purpose of achieving some necessary goal when one's ability to achieve that goal through legitimate means is reduced. Survival crimes are not unique to Queer people; however, research suggests that marginalized populations such as Queer folks experience discrimination in multiple areas of their life, often based solely on one's sexuality and/or gender identity, which can influence criminal behavior and consequently contribute to disproportionate rates of involvement in all branches of the criminal legal system.

Perhaps the strongest indicator of survival offending can be located in one's housing status. For example, research has indicated that LGBT youth have a 120 percent higher risk of homelessness than their non-Queer peers (Morton Dworsky, & Samuels 2017). With more Queer youth without shelter, and living on the streets as a result, there is greater likelihood that Queer youth may commit crimes such as regulatory offenses and survival offenses, that can range from petty theft to more dangerous crime such as sex work. As mentioned, there are multiple factors that can contribute to homelessness, poverty being one obvious factor, but when we have an individual who is Queer, poor, and Black, these intersections converge, resulting not only in homelessness but living in constant fear of being victimized, which for Queer youth may have also been the case in their homes. Research continues to support the idea that homelessness creates a unique vulnerability for persons not only to be the victims of crime but to commit crimes as well. As this all relates to the above conversation regarding Queer youth especially, Woods (2018) indicates three major concerns brought forth from varying research, which include homelessness, foster care, and higher rates of poverty among LGBT people. Indeed, the aforementioned concerns are echoed throughout the literature and as we look at these through an intersectional lens the victim and offender overlap continues to be magnified.

One of the most unsettling offenses is survival sex. In a three-year study, interviewing over 280 LGBTQ young people between the ages of 13 and 21, The Urban Institute's participants were mostly cisgender males, bisexual, and of a racial minority, with 37 percent identifying as African-American or Black (Dank, Yu, Yahner, Pelletier, Mora, & Conner (2015). The average age of participants was just under 20 years of age, most were not enrolled in school, and nearly half reported neither graduating nor completing their general equivalency diploma (GED). Finally, 48 percent of participants lived in shelters and another 10 percent reported living on the street. The majority of their participants reported having become involved in trading sex through friends or peers, but the next most common answer was an individual becoming involved when someone approached them. Some participants indicated that they began trading sex through an "exploiter," someone who lured them into commercial sex work through force, fraud, and coercion. Finally, the researchers found that most participants used survival sex, or were exploited through commercial sex, in order to obtain necessities like food and shelter, further noting that "over a quarter of youth found themselves presented with the opportunity to trade sex, typically through a client who approached them and offered money, shelter, or other resources in exchange for sexual acts" (Dank, Yahner, Madden, Bañuelos, Yu, Ritchie, Mora & Conner 2015: 21).

In another study Swaner, Labriola, Rempel, Walker, and Spadafore (2016) interviewed nearly 950 13–24-year old's' in six different states who identified as being involved in sex trade. One notable, overall finding echoes the negative impact that homelessness, trauma and more have on their ability to experience legitimate work, find housing, and obtain an education. The authors go on to note that not unlike the "exploiters" in the Dank et al. (2015) study that

> even youth who are not subjected to emotional, sexual, or physical violence by a pimp are still disadvantaged by social structures (including poverty and discrimination) that restrict available life choices and leave some youth particularly vulnerable to entry into the underground economy...
>
> Swaner et al. 2016: xv

Research capturing the experiences of Queer adult sex workers, such as the National Transgender Discrimination Survey, echo the findings on youth engaged in survival sex (Fitzgerald, Elspeth, Hickey, Biko, & Tobin 2015). Over 12 percent of trans people surveyed, mostly Black and Latinx people, reported engaging in sex work or trading sex for shelter. The majority of those folks reported experiencing past violence in school and adverse job outcomes in the traditional workforce, and almost half had experienced homelessness at some point in their lives. Nearly 80 percent of trans sex workers reported interactions with police, most of which were uncomfortable, to include mistreatment and physical and sexual assault by officers. When those police interactions resulted in arrest or formal charges, respondents experienced bias in the court system and harassment by correctional officers (Fitzgerald et al. 2015).

It seems that much of the existing (and Western-centric) research on Queer offending centers on survival crimes, often focused on juveniles committing those crimes or, like the Magnotta case, the sensationalized archetype Queer criminals who are impatiently waiting to pick you up at a bar, drug your drink, kill you in any number of gruesome ways, cut you up, and cook you and eat you for dinner (see Jeffrey Dahmer). This, as mentioned in Chapter 1, also supports Woods's (2015) contention that criminologists in general are guilty of failing to conduct diverse research on Queer people or focusing solely on sexually deviant offenders when they do.

However, common-sense tells us this cannot be the case – surely there are offenders who identify as a member of the LGBTQ+ community who commit any number of crimes that a heterosexual or cisgender person might. In fact, regarding offending youth, Keuroghlian (as cited in Lee 2018: n.p.) draws our attention to the minority stress model when it comes to LGBT+ youth offending, and notes that "There's nothing inherently more criminal about this population. It's due to life circumstances due to stigma and discrimination."

It is also worth considering that because of a history of stigma, Queer people's offending has been highly subjective and defined by anti-LGBTQ+ legislation existing in anti-LGBTQ+ locations throughout the world. Again, as evidenced in the archetypes mentioned above, any discussion of Queer offenders would be incomplete without foundational knowledge on the criminalization of queerness discussed in the last chapter. For instance as detailed by Nadal (2020), in the not-so-distant past military personnel in the United States would face not only being dishonorably discharged if they were found to be gay, but they could also be court martialed and face imprisonment for sodomy. Further highlighted by Nadal (2020: 16) are universities expelling students for "engaging in homosexual activity," and the executive order that "forbade [LGBTQ] people from working in the federal government" because according to one United States subcommittee "homosexuals and other sex perverts are not proper persons to be employed in Government" because they were unsuitable and security risks. These stereotypes may seem laughable to some folks reading this today but keep in mind that these biases are the bases for the discrimination against Queer people and the criminalization of their personhood that persists today, going as far as labeling them deviants, criminals, and overall risks to avoid or banish. Teachers were fired (and continue to be) because of their sexuality and its perceived influence on their students. Anti-HIV legislation is also prevalent today with "26 states maintain[ing] specifically HIV-related laws criminalizing exposure" (Nadal 2020: 17).

We know that Queer folks are overrepresented in jails and prisons and, while that research continues to increase, we still know very little about what got them there. All the above mentioned contributes to the increased likelihood that Queer people may enter into the criminal legal system – with lives characterized by little support and lots of victimization the trajectory is often towards crime. Queer folks, regardless of their other multiple identities, may be victims of crime, engaged in criminal offending, or finding themselves at the intersection of both. What we do know about these phenomena, however, is that other identities do matter and they can impact one's level of safety, amplify the disadvantages that lead one to crime, and disproportionately entangle people in a vicious cycle of victimization and offending.

Activities & discussion questions

- Watch *Southwest of Salem: The Story of the San Antonio Four* and answer the following questions: How do stereotypes about women of color and lesbians contribute to the "criminalization" of women? How does intersectionality play a role in this case? Would the case have played out differently (if so, how) if the women were not Latinx lesbians? What if the alleged perpetrators were gay men and the alleged victims were male?
- Explore the hate crime related maps created by the Movement Advancement Project (www.lgbtmap.org/). If you live in the United States, see if your state includes sexual orientation or gender identity in its hate crime legislation and compare the state you live in to others. If you reside outside of the U.S. discuss how hate

crime legislation in the United States is similar to or different from the laws of your own country.

Recommended viewing

Call Her Ganda, 2018. [Film] Directed by PJ Ravel. USA: Unraval Pictures.
Catching a Serial Killer: Bruce McArthur. 2021. [Film] Directed by James Buddy Day. USA: Peacock Alley Entertainment.
Check It, 2016. [Film] Directed by Dana Flor and Toby Oppenheimer. USA Olive Productions.
Don't F**k with Cats: Hunting an Internet Killer. 2019. [Film] Directed by Mark Lewis. USA: Raw Television.
Southwest of Salem: The Story of the San Antonio Four. 2016. [Film] Directed by Deborah Esquenazi. USA: Deborah S. Esquenazi Productions, LLC.
The Death and Life of Marsha P. Johnson. 2017. [Film] Directed by David France. USA: Public Square Films.

Note

1 MSM stands for men who have sex with men.

References

Addington, L.A. 2019. Bisexual Women and Intimate Partner Violence. *The Gender and Policy Report*. Accessed from https://genderpolicyreport.umn.edu/bisexual-women-and-intimate-partner-violence/
Allen, K. 2019. Man charged in murder of Dallas transgender woman Muhlaysia Booker. ABC News, June 12. Accessed from https://abcnews.go.com/US/man-charged-murder-dallas-transgender-women-muhlaysia-booker/story?id=63674104.
Amnesty International. 2020. For many trans women, living in El Salvador is a death sentence. Coronavirus is making it even worse. Amnesty International, August 12. Accessed from www.amnesty.org/en/latest/news/2020/08/trans-women-el-salvador-death-sentence-coronavirus/.
Antebi-Gruszka, N. & Scheer J.R. 2021. Associations Between Trauma-Informed Care Components and Multiple Health and Psychosocial Risks Among LGBTQ Survivors of Intimate Partner Violence. *Journal of Mental Health Counseling*, 43 (2):139–156..
Asquith, N.L., Dwyer, A., & Simpson, P. 2017. A queer criminal career. *Current Issues in Criminal Justice*, 29, (2): 167–180.

Associated Press. 2021. The painful history of anti-Asian hate crimes in America. CBS News, August 1. Accessed from www.cbsnews.com/news/the-painful-history-of-anti-asian-hate-crimes-in-america/.

Avery, D. 2021. Hate crime charges added in gruesome Grindr attack on gay teen. NBC News, January 29. Accessed from www.nbcnews.com/feature/nbc-out/hate-crime-charges-added-gruesome-grindr-attack-gay-teen-n1256155?cid=sm_npd_nn_fb_ot&fbclid=IwAR3jRBEbutf0BjGXrA7rDCz86IJhu9-W3VQT0qy4bPxwye5Vi6ScmMHBGTE.

Aviles, G. 2019. Gay man killed, another critically injured in Grindr meetup. NBC News, July 16. Accessed from www.nbcnews.com/feature/nbc-out/gay-man-killed-another-critically-injured-in-grindr-meetup-n1029881.

Ballentine, S. & Salter, J. 2017. Officials: Transgender teen's grisly death not a hate crime. Associated Press, September 27. Accessed from https://apnews.com/article/sports-crime-mens-college-basketball-college-basketball-hate-crimes-a1031b5a3198453dba9c1a94546c7a77.

Black, M.C., Basile, K.C., Breiding, M.J., Smith, S.G., Walters, M.L., Merrick, M.T., Chen, J., & Stevens, M.R. 2011. *The National Intimate Partner and Sexual Violence Survey (NISVS): 2010 Summary Report.* Atlanta, GA: National Center for Injury Prevention and Control, Centers for Disease Control and Prevention.

Brammer, J.P. 2018. Prosecutors seek death penalty in transgender teen's grisly killing. NBC News, April 14. Accessed from www.nbcnews.com/feature/nbc-out/prosecutors-seek-death-penalty-transgender-teen-s-grisly-murder-n862391.

Chakraborti, N. & Garland, J. 2015. *Hate crime: Impact, causes & responses*, 2nd edition. Los Angeles: Sage.

Clifford, J. 2021. Court orders third teenager to stand trial over alleged Grindr murder, kidnapping charges dropped. ABC Illawarra, June 10. Accessed from www.abc.net.au/news/2021-06-10/third-teenager-committed-in-grindr-murder-peter-keeley/100205282.

Coletta, A. 2021. Review finds 'serious' flaws in investigation of serial killer who preyed on Toronto's LGBTQ community. NBC News, April 13. Accessed from www.washingtonpost.com/world/2021/04/13/canada-bruce-mcarthur-lgbt-serial-killer/.

Dank, M., Yahner, J., Madden, K., Banuelos, I., Yu, L., Ritchie, A., Mora, M., & Conner B. 2015. *Surviving the streets of New York: experiences of LGBTQ youth, YMSM and YWSW engaged in survival sex.* Washington DC: Urban Institute.

Dank, M., Yu, L., Yahner, J., Pelletier, E., Mora, M., & Conner, B. 2015. *Locked In: Interactions with the Criminal Justice and Child Welfare Systems for LGBTQ Youth, YMSM, and YWSW Who Engage in Survival Sex.* Urban Institute.

DeJong, C., Holt, K., Helm, B., & Morgan, S.J. 2021. "A human being like other victims": The media framing of trans homicide in the United States. *Critical Criminology, 29*, (1): 131–149.

Department of Justice. 2021. Louisiana man indicted for attempted murder of a gay man and plot to kidnap and murder other gay man. Office of Public Affairs, March 18. Accessed from www.justice.gov/opa/pr/louisi ana-man-indicted-attempted-murder-gay-man-and-plot-kidnap-and-mur der-other-gay-men.

Donaghue, E. 2019. Man convicted in videotaped assault of transgender woman who was later found dead. CBS News, October 22. Accessed from www.cbsnews.com/news/muhlaysia-booker-case-man-convicted-in-vid eotaped-assault-of-transgender-woman-who-was-later-found-slain/.

Dwyer, A. & Panfil, V. 2017. "We need to lead the charge" – "Talking only to each other is not enough": The Pulse Orlando mass shooting and the futures of queer criminologies*. *The Criminologist, 42*, (3): 1–7.

Epstein, G.J. 2021. Missing and missed: Report of the independent civilian review into missing persons investigations. Toronto Police Services Board. Accessed from https://8e5a70b5-92aa-40ae-a0bd-e885453ee64c.filesusr. com/ugd/a94b60_eb1b274e75764885b9bf5a2347b5fad1.pdf?index=true.

FBI Tampa. 2016. Investigative update regarding Pulse nightclub shooting. June 20th. Accessed from www.fbi.gov/contact-us/field-offices/tampa/news/ press-releases/investigative-update-regarding-pulse-nightclub-shooting.

Fedorko, B., Kurmanov, S. Berredo, L. 2020. A brief guide to monitoring anti-trans violence. Transgender Europe. Accessed from https://transrespect. org/en/brief-guide-to-monitoring-anti-trans-violence/.

Fitzgerald, E., Elspeth, S., Hickey, D., Biko, C., & Tobin, H.J. 2015. Meaningful work: Transgender experiences in the sex trade. Accessed from https:// transequality.org/sites/default/files/Meaningful%20Work-Full%20Rep ort_FINAL_3.pdf.

Goodman, L.A., Sullivan, C.M., Serrata, J., Perilla, J., Wilson, J.M., Fauci, J.E., & DiGiovanni, C.D. 2016. Development and validation of the Trauma-Informed Practice Scales. *Journal of Community Psychology, 44* (6), 747–764.

Home Office. 2020. *Hate crime, England and Wales, 2019/20.* Accessed from https://assets.publishing.service.gov.uk/government/uploads/system/uplo ads/attachment_data/file/925968/hate-crime-1920-hosb2920.pdf.

Hoppe, T., Meyer, I.H., De Orio, S., Vogler, S., & Armstrong, M. 2017. *Civil commitment of people convicted of sex offenses in the United States.* The Williams Institute: UCLA School of Law.

Human Rights Campaign. 2020. HRC Launches Interpersonal Violence Report During COVID-19. Accessed from www.hrc.org/resources/hrc-launches-interpersonal-violence-report-during-covid-19

Human Rights Campaign. 2020. An epidemic of violence: Fatal violence against transgender and gender non-conforming people in the United States in 2020. Accessed from www.hrc.org/resources/an-epidemic-of-violence-fatal-violence-against-transgender-and-gender-non-conforming-people-in-the-u-s-in-2020.

Human Rights Watch 2016. "Do you see how much I'm suffering here?": Abuse against transgender women in US immigration detention. Accessed from www.hrw.org/sites/default/files/report_pdf/us0316_web.pdf.

Human Rights Watch. 2020. "Every day I live in fear": Violence and discrimination against LGBT people in El Salvador, Guatemala, and Honduras, and obstacles to asylum in the United States. Accessed from www.hrw.org/sites/default/files/media_2020/10/centralamerica_lgbt1020_web_0.pdf.

Lee, S.S. 2018 August 1. LGBT+ youth face tougher time as first offenders, study finds. A new study is shedding light on first offenders and mental health struggles. Accessed from https://abcnews.go.com/Health/study-finds-lgbt-youth-face-tougher-time-offenders/story?id=56954256

Lenning, E., Brightman, S., & Buist, C.L. 2021. The trifecta of violence: A socio-historical comparison of lynching and violence against transgender women. *Critical Criminology, 29*, (1): 151–172.

Messinger, A.M. 2020. *LGBTQ intimate partner violence: Lessons for policy, practice, and research.*

Mogul, J.L., Ritchie, A., & Whitlock, K. 2011. *Queer (in)justice: The criminalization of LGBT people in the United States.* Boston, MA: Beacon Press.

Moran, D. 2020. Dad of 4 who worked as chemist accused of cannibalizing his Grindr date. *USA Today*, January 13. Accessed from.

Morton, M.H., Dworsky, A., & Samuels, G.M. 2017. *Missed opportunities: Youth homelessness in America: National estimates.* Chicago, IL: Chapin Hall at the University of Chicago

Movement Advancement Project. 2021. Policy Spotlight: Hate Crime Laws. Accessed from www.lgbtmap.org/file/2021-report-hate-crime-laws.pdf.

Nadal, K.L. 2020. *Queering law and order: LGBTQ communities and the criminal justice system.* Lanham, MD: Lexington Books.

Ogles, J. 2018. Why does the FBI refuse to call the Pulse massacre a hate crime? *The Advocate*, June 11. Accessed from www.advocate.com/crime/2018/6/11/why-does-fbi-refuse-call-pulse-massacre-hate-crime.

Oldham, S. 2020. Don't fuck with cats: Deanna Thompson and director Mark Lewis reflect on their creepy Netflix series. Variety, January 27. Accessed from https://variety.com/2020/tv/news/dont-fuck-with-cats-netflix-luka-magnotta-deanna-thompson-1203479502/.

Panfil, V. 2014. Better left unsaid? The role of agency in queer criminological research. *Critical Criminology, 22*, (1): 99–111.

Panfil, V.R. 2017. *The gang's all queer: The lives of gay gang members*. New York: New York University Press.

Pickles, J. 2020. Sociality of hate: The transmission of victimization of LGBT+ people through social media. *International Review of Victimology*, 27, (3): 311–327.

Ramirez, J.L., Gonzalez, K.A., & Galupo, M.P. 2018. "Invisibility during my own crisis": Responses of LGBT people of color to the Orlando shooting. *Journal of Homosexuality*, 65, (5): 579–599.

Rehwald, J. 2020. Texas county man sentenced to life for 2017 murder of transgender teen. *Springfield News-Leader*, November 20. Accessed from www.news-leader.com/story/news/local/ozarks/2020/11/20/texas-cou nty-man-sentenced-life-2017-murder-transgender-teen/6355776002/.

Renteria, N. 2019. Trans asylum-seeker killed after U.S. deportation back to El Salvador. Accessed from www.reuters.com/article/us-usa-immigrat ion-violence/trans-asylum-seeker-killed-after-u-s-deportation-back-to-el-salvador-idUSKCN1QC03L.

Renzetti, C.M. 1992. *Violent betrayal: Partner abuse in lesbian relationships.* Newbury Park: Sage.

Scheer, J.R. & Poteat, V.P. 2021. Trauma-Informed Care and Health Among LGBTQ Intimate Partner Violence Survivors. *Journal of Interpersonal Violence,* 36, (13–14):6670–6692.

Schwencke, K. 2017. Why America fails at gathering hate crime statistics. ProPublica, December 4th. Accessed from www.propublica.org/article/ why-america-fails-at-gathering-hate-crime-statistics.

Schweppe, J., Haynes, A., & Walters, M.A. 2018. *Lifecycle of a hate crime: Comparative report.* Dublin: ICCL.

Sear, L. 2021. Gay man viciously beaten to death in Belgium's first homophobic murder in nine years. Pink News, March 9. Accessed from www.pinkn ews.co.uk/2021/03/09/belgium-homophobic-murder-grindr-david-p-antwerp-petra-de-sutter-lgbt/.

Slakoff, D.C., & Siegel, J.A. 2022. Barriers to Reporting, Barriers to Services: Challenges for Transgender Survivors of Intimate Partner Violence and Sexual Victimization. In C.L Buist & L.K. Semprevivo (eds.), *Queering Criminology in Theory and Praxis: Re-imagining Justice in the Criminal Legal System and Beyond.* Bristol: Bristol University Press.

Statistics Canada. 2021. After five years of increases, police-reported crimes in Canada was down in 2020, but incidents of hate crime increased sharply. *The Daily*, July 27. Accessed from www150.statcan.gc.ca/n1/en/daily-quotidien/210727/dq210727a-eng.pdf?st=gdLo_Uwc.

Stevenson, K. & Broadus, K. 2016. *Capturing hate: Eyewitness videos provide new source of data on prevalence of transphobic violence.* New York: Witness Media Lab.

Swaner, R. Labriola, M., Rempel, M., Walker, A., & Spadafore, J. 2016. *Youth involvement in the sex trade; A national study.* New York: Center for Court Innovation.

Tesch, B.P., Bekerian, D.A., English, P., & Harrington, E. 2010. Same-Sex Domestic Violence: Why Victims are More at Risk. *International Journal of Police Science & Management, 12*: 526–535.

Tjaden P, Thoennes N, & Allison C.J. 1999. Comparing violence over the life span in samples of same-sex and opposite-sex cohabitants. *Violence and Victims, 14* (4): 413–425.

University at Buffalo. 2022. What is trauma-informed care? Buffalo Center for Social Research. Accessed from https://socialwork.buffalo.edu/social-resea rch/institutes-centers/institute-on-trauma-and-trauma-informed-care/ what-is-trauma-informed-care.html.

Walker, A. 2020. "I'm not like that, so am I gay?": The use of queer-spectrum identity labels among minor-attracted people. *Journal of Homosexuality, 67,* (12): 1736–1759.

Walters, M.A., Paterson, J., Brown, R., & McDonnell, L. 2020. Hate crimes against trans people: Assessing emotions, behaviors, and attitudes towards criminal justice agencies. *Journal of Interpersonal Violence, 35,* (21–22): 4583–4613.

Wood, F., Carillo, A., & Monk-Turner, E. 2019. Visibly unknown: Media depictions of murdered transgender women of color. *Race and Justice, online first.*

Woods, J.B. 2015. The birth of modern criminology and gendered constructions of the homosexual criminal identity. *Journal of Homosexuality, 62*: 131–166.

Woods, J.B. 2018. LGBT Identity and Crime. *Dukeminier Awards: Best Sexual Orientation and Gender Identity Law Review, 17*: 123–194.

Zambelich, A. & Hurt, A. 2016. 3 hours in Orlando: Piecing together an attack and its aftermath. NPR, June 26. Accessed from www.npr.org/2016/06/16/482322488/orlando-shooting-what-happened-update.

4

QUEER CRIMINOLOGY AND LAW ENFORCEMENT

Open the introduction to any criminal justice textbook and, in the chapter on law enforcement, you will find a section that highlights the duties of the job. You will most likely find within those same pages discussion on the characteristics of law enforcement officers themselves, and most certainly one, if not the first, characteristic you will learn of is distrust. Officers of the law, namely police officers, distrust the citizens whom they are tasked to protect and serve. This is due in large part to the potential dangers of the job and the fear of working in a profession where many of the individuals you encounter are presumed criminals. Certainly, this is understandable – as any police officer will tell you, a successful day on the job means they return home safely at the end of the shift. However, while these suspicions may be justified as a means of self-preservation, these tactics are often used to discriminate against citizens based on, among other characteristics, race, age, gender, or sexual orientation. What is interesting is that these populations who are often the targets of selective enforcement share one salient commonality with the officers who police them – distrust.

DOI: 10.4324/9781003165163-4

When we published the first edition, we highlighted in this chapter a distinct mistrust of the police amongst minority populations. We discussed how police action or inaction resulting in the untimely deaths of Black men across the country had spawned the protest movement #blacklivesmatter (beginning after the murder of Trayvon Martin and gaining momentum after the shooting death of Michael Brown and the choking death of Eric Garner). While rioters, along with peaceful protestors, assembled where these events took place and across the country, reliable reporting of just how many Black men and boys are killed by police is not readily available. This can be attributed to unreliable data collection, or the lack of willing participants – for instance, much of the reporting is done voluntarily, and additionally, reports of citizens killed by police are often said to have been done justifiably, which can also be problematic.

> I can't breathe.
>
> Eric Garner, July 17, 2014
> George Floyd, May 25, 2020

When we first wrote the book, we highlighted Eric Garner's last words before dying at the hands of a police officer. Today, we include George Floyd's name, who pleaded with officers using the same words as Garner had six years earlier. Reports have indicated that Floyd stated he couldn't breathe over twenty times before being murdered by Derek Chauvin. What these incidents and data continue to suggest is that minorities (especially Black men) have reason to continue to be suspicious of law enforcement and that officers continue policing the symbolic assailant that historically has been the minority male. The unrest and disdain for police in general may be better documented, and certainly documented more often, with the influence and pervasiveness of the Internet, cell phones, and social media in general, but that doesn't mean these incidents are new or unique experiences for Black men, as they have long been the targets of police brutality and misconduct. A study by Edwards, Lee, and Esposito (2019) found that police violence is the leading cause of death among young men. The research goes on to indicate that Black men are estimated to be 2.5 times more likely and Black women are 1.4 times more likely than their white counterparts to be killed by police. The study also concluded that American Indian/Alaska native men and women are more likely to be killed by police than white men and women (Edwards et al. 2019: n.p.). This serves as a constant reminder that the lives of people of color are not valued – and are in fact devalued – by law enforcement and the criminal legal system in general. In turn, this behavior also suggests that *white lives do matter* – as victims, as offenders, and as practitioners. The fear that the Black community feels in relation to the police impedes the ability of Black men, women, boys, and girls to obtain human agency; in essence, this fear stifles and blocks the ability of an entire group of people to make their own choices without fear of retribution up to and including death.

We have chosen to highlight the fear that minority populations have of law enforcement and include examples to remind you of the unrest that has been felt. Most of you will recall these events without trouble; you will remember watching protests across the country and abroad – the location may change, but the message remains – Black Lives Matter and there must be accountability for behavior that goes far beyond the scope of policing, or even the use of force continuum, because this is homicidal behavior that has resulted in just that. Earlier we discussed George Floyd and his murder at the hands of Derek Chauvin, who has been convicted of all three counts he was charged with (second-degree unintentional murder, third-degree murder, and second-degree manslaughter). You will remember Breonna Taylor's story – shot to death, taking five bullets from police, with one officer firing multiple times into Taylor's apartment. This occurred after Taylor's boyfriend shot an officer in the thigh after being awakened by police as they entered the apartment with a no-knock warrant. Kenneth Walker (Taylor's boyfriend) believed the police to be Taylor's ex-boyfriend (one of the people the officers were looking for that night) and shot thinking that he was breaking in. After Taylor was shot and lay gasping for air, police tended to the injured officer but offered no assistance to Breonna Taylor (see Oppel, Taylor, & Bogel-Burroughs 2021). The community and some news outlets noted the important role that Taylor played working as an emergency room technician and that she had previously been employed as an emergency medical technician, with her family stating that she wanted to become a nurse (Stanglin, Duvall, and

Wolfson 2020). We mention this because it's important to recognize the life behind the murder – however, simply because Taylor worked in health care and has been lauded as a life-saving first responder does not mean that George Floyd's life was any less important because he was murdered after being detained by police for using a counterfeit twenty-dollar bill. Sadly, we could go on and on with these examples because the tragedies of these incidents are nothing new. The BBC (2021) recently compiled a list of some of the better-known police murders of people of color (mostly Black men) in the United States

- July 2014: Eric Garner
- August 2014: Michael Brown
- November 2014: Tamir Rice
- April 2015: Walter Scott
- July 2016: Alton Sterling
- July 2016: Philando Castile
- March 2018: Stephon Clark
- March 2020: Breonna Taylor
- May 2020: George Floyd
- April 2021: Daunte Wright

It would be not only remiss, but a tragic mistake, to assume that the list of people murdered by police in the United States is limited to these victims, who have received additional attention in the media. In fact, CBS news compiled a list of 164 Black men and women killed by police in the United States from January to August of 2020 (see Cohen 2020). That the media coverage of these murders is disproportionate to the rate at which they occur speaks again to the idea that Black lives are of less importance than others in our collective conscience.

You will remember asking why events like this happened in 2014 and then asking the same question in 2021, and it wouldn't take a psychic to tell you that many of us will continue to be asking the same questions in 2025, 2035, 20tilltheendoftime. Why does this brutality continue to persist? As we have indicated thus far, structure and institutions are of great concern. Individual issues matter, of course, but individuals continue to be influenced, socialized, and ultimately constructed/built to embody the institutions they are involved in, and the policing occupation has a long-standing, troubled past and present of a subculture that demands compliance, silence, and allegiance.

Let us return to BLM. You probably saw the hashtag blacklivesmatter come across your Twitter feed or have heard about it on the news. You have likely read the signs being held by people from all walks of life, marching in the streets, demanding justice. Perhaps you have argued with friends, family, and strangers about just what BLM means, and hopefully by now you have come to learn that life isn't lived through a mutually exclusive lens where if you support BLM that automatically means you don't support the police. However, how does this matter to the Queer community? First, it was three Queer-identified women, Alicia Garza, Patrisse Cullors, and Opal Tometi, who created BLM (Garza 2014). These women of color, and their histories of community organizing, have gone on to be championed as "the new civil rights movement." In an early article on the movement, Elizabeth Day (2015: n.p.) wrote, "… the new civil rights movement combines localised power structures with an inclusive ethos that consciously incorporates women, lesbian, gay, bisexual, transgender and queer activists." The movement then and now, is an example of intersectionality in action and activism.

Activism, especially in response to police brutality, is nothing new for the LGBTQ+ community, as there is a distinct fear that Queer folks, especially trans folks, and even more so trans people of color, have of police officers. Indeed, according to The Human Rights Campaign (HRC) (2020), there have been over 200 transgender and gender nonconforming people killed in the Unites States. While police officers were not directly responsible for all of their deaths, investigations have been demanded into the deaths of Tony McDade in Florida and Layleen Polanco while in solitary at Rikers Island (see Selby 2021). It is worth noting that in 2016, National Coalition of Anti-Violence Programs (NCAVP 2017b) found that of those transgender individuals who were murdered, 9 percent were in relation to police violence. We also know that reports spanning the globe conducted by Transgender Europe indicated 350 transgender and gender-diverse murders in a single year (2020) with the most murders occurring in Brazil; additionally, since 2008 the total number of transgender and gender-diverse murders is nearing 3,700 (Transgender Europe 2020). All of the above speaks to the impact of the "matrix of domination" (Collins 2000) and takes into account the many characteristics that impact the intersectionality of oppression. As noted by Crenshaw (1989: 140), "... the intersectional experience is greater than the sum of racism and sexism, any analysis that does not take intersectionality into account cannot sufficiently address the particular manner in which Black women are subordinated." Trans women of color are Black women who have been murdered because of their intersecting identities. In 2016, NCAVP (2017b) reported that, of the total number of anti-LGBTQ homicides, 75 percent were people of color, with the majority of victims identified as Black (56 percent).

> What people need to understand is that when you're talking about Black and brown communities, immigrant communities, communities experiencing poverty, and then you layer that with folks who are LGBTQ, specifically trans and gender nonconforming, [systemic policing] issues aren't necessarily very different, they're just amplified.
>
> *Mateo de la Torre, director of policy and advocacy*
> *at Black and Pink, as cited in Burns (2020)*

The negative relationship between the police and the Queer community has always existed – the policing of gender variance and the policing of same-sex consensual sex have been used to control the behavior of countless many that have performed gender and sexuality outside of the binary heteronormative lens. While this fractured relationship may have always existed, certainly the Stonewall Riots, perhaps more aptly called The Stonewall Rebellion, brought media attention to the malcontent. We see an iconic historical event that occurred over five decades ago in the middle of 1969 repeated with the continued police harassment of the Queer community. As Mogul, Ritchie, and Whitlock (2011: 46) have noted, in 2003 a primarily Black gay club in Highland Park near Detroit, Michigan, was raided by the local sheriff's department. Hundreds of gays, lesbians, and transgender people were violently detained. Officers made them sit in human waste and they were physically and verbally abused, being called "fags" by officers.

Violence that Queer people have experienced at the hands of law enforcement is an example of power as a means to oppress and repress the freedoms of others (Foucault 1980). Mogul et al. (2011) also identify the power that police officers have and how that power can influence not only how a particular area is policed, but how being labeled as different can also impact groups of people. There is little evidence to show that the policing occupation has made any real effort to improve the relationship with the Queer community. Yes, many departments in the United States and abroad have created LGBTQ liaison officers or the equivalent but they have for the most part had little impact. Research continues to show us that the LGBTQ+ community harbors resentment, fear (rightfully so), and overall negative experiences with law enforcement (see Hodge & Sexton 2018). In criminology, labeling theory posits that a behavior in and of itself is not deviant or criminal until others begin to define, label, or essentially construct that behavior as such (Becker 1963). Mogul et al. (2011: 49) note:

> Social constructions of deviance and criminality pervade the myriad routine practices and procedures through which law enforcement agents decide whom to stop on the streets or highways, whom to question, search, and arrest, and whom to subject to brutal force.

In the forthcoming section, we will discuss in greater detail the experiences of brutality, misconduct, and distrust of police officers within the Queer community. We will discuss bias and selective enforcement, and highlight experiences of Queer people in the United States and abroad.

Police brutality and misconduct

The events that took place at The Stonewall Inn in 1969 were a response to the continued police harassment and brutality that LGBTQ+ people consistently faced. Although there is more attention and discussion regarding these issues today, the Queer community has often been overlooked, or considered as a second thought, regarding the focus of the media or within criminology and other disciplines. Regardless of the attention it receives, however, police violence has a deep and lasting impact on the Queer community, just as it has affected other marginalized and oppressed groups. *Fusion* magazine, Kent State University's publication, explored the impact of police brutality on the LGBTQ population and noted the similarities between the civil rights movement and the gay rights movement (see Eckhouse & Saxen 2017). The authors highlight how these movements, and currently the BLM movement, have been the catalyst for drawing attention to police brutality, and go on to state:

> Although it may seem like police brutality has nothing to do with LGBTQ people, especially if they are white, the truth is not so simple … The LGBTQ community is … heterogenous. Some gay people are cis, some trans people are straight, some bisexual people don't have genders and people of all races can be LGBTQ.
>
> Eckhouse & Saxen 2017: 33

This is an accurate depiction of how these movements are connected and why it matters so much to continue couching our research through intersectionality, as Eckhouse and Saxen (2017: 33) go on to state, "Given the community's inherent diversity, different populations within it face different experiences of oppression. In terms of violence and discrimination, including involvement with law enforcement, trans women of color have it harder than most."

Perhaps somewhat surprisingly, there is the lack of a clear and universal definition of what constitutes police brutality. Yes, it may prove difficult to objectively define police brutality and/or excessive use of force but that does not mean it is impossible. We tell our students in research classes across the country that there is a vital importance in the ability to conceptualize terms and being able to clearly define them – law enforcement, regardless of location, should be required to do this as well. Failure to properly define an action can be detrimental to the justice process, the impact of which is most often felt by civilians and not state agents. For example, in the infamous case of The New Jersey 4, three Black, lesbian, gender non-conforming women were identified as a gang because of New York's faulty definition of what constitutes gang behavior. Indeed, the definitions vary at both federal and state levels and typically include language similar to the National Institute of Justice (2011, original from California legislature), which states that a criminal street gang:

> ... means any ongoing organization, association or group of three or more persons ... having as one of its primary activities the commission of one or more ... criminal acts ... a common name or common identifying sign or symbol ... whose members individually or collectively engage in or have engaged in a pattern of criminal gang activity.
>
> National Institute of Justice 2011

The National Institute of Justice has commented that the above is a common definition at the state level, although New York, at the time of the NJ4 incident, implemented a differing definition that lowered the number of people in a group to two. All of this is to say that while many of us might believe we can easily define something or that we "just know" what an action is, that does not matter regarding the criminal legal system regarding arrest, charging, prosecution, and on and on. In this example, a problematic definition led to the overcharging of four women, none of whom were gang-affiliated, who were guilty only of protecting themselves against violence.

Often in police-involved violence any given incident will be *subjectively* evaluated and scrutinized. All too often, police see one thing, victims another, and the public and media have their own perspectives and interpretations. With that being said, one broad definition comes from Cao (2003: 1; emphasis in the original) who defines police brutality as "citizens' *judgment* that they have not been treated with full rights and dignity by police as expected in a democratic society." In July 2020, the United States Department of Justice offered several definitions for a variety of unacceptable police behaviors that could potentially be investigated by the DOJ including a more general definition of "law enforcement misconduct" and more specific definitions of "physical assault," "sexual misconduct," "deliberate indifference to a serious medical condition or a substantial risk of harm," and "failure to intervene." These federal level distinctions are in place to "enforce Constitutional limits on conduct by law enforcement officers …" and includes this excerpt: "Whoever, under color of any law … willfully subjects any person … to the deprivation of any rights, privileges, or immunities secured or protected by the Constitution or laws of the United States [shall be guilty of a crime]." Amnesty International (n.d.) defines police brutality as … "various human rights violations by police. This might include beatings, racial abuse, unlawful killings, torture, or indiscriminate use of riot control agents at protests."

Quite frankly, we could fill an entire chapter or more on these varying definitions and actions alone, and we know that others in positions of power in the U.S. have indicated their dislike of the lack of specificity in the DOJ's descriptions above. In fact, in April of 2021, the Brennan Center for Justice released a policy report (see Merkl 2021, emphasis on the original) that included a foreword from the former Attorney General, Eric H. Holder Jr., on statute 18 U.S.C. § 242 (also known as Deprivation of Rights under Code of Law). Holder wrote:

> Unlike nearly all other criminal laws, the statute does not clearly define what conduct is a criminal act. It describes the *circumstances* under which a person, acting with the authority of government, can be held criminally responsible for violating someone's constitutional rights, but it does not make clear to officials what particular *actions* they cannot take.
>
> Merkl 2021

Police accountability is lacking, to say the least. The FBI has begun data collection on police use of force, but reporting is not mandatory and has been low. The Bureau of Justice Statistics (BJS) reports contact between police and the public and indicate in their 2018 findings that approximately 2 percent of the 61.5 million people in the United States who have had contact with the police report experiencing police threats or use of force. This amounts to about 1.3 million people with an increased likelihood that males, Blacks, Hispanics, and younger people will experience threats of use of force from police. Please, don't let it be lost on you that Queer folks are not included in the research, not only from the BJS but from nearly every major reporting agency. We'll return to this momentarily.

The CATO Institute's National Police Misconduct Reporting Project (2010) found that there were over 4,800 reports of police misconduct that involved over 6,600 sworn law enforcement officers, including over 350 cases that involved administrative or high-ranking officers. These incidents of misconduct resulted in over 6,800 victims and 247 deaths, and cost over 345 million dollars in civil judgments or settlements. Of the reported incidents, excessive force led the complaints with nearly 24 percent of the cases, followed by sexual misconduct complaints at 9.3 percent. The next highest complaints were fraud or theft, accounting for just over 7 percent of cases, and false arrest at nearly 7 percent.

As noted above, Queer victims are rarely represented in major reports on use of force or excessive force, but make no mistake, Queer victims of police brutality exist in great numbers and are often grossly underreported. The U.S. Transgender Survey (James, Herman, Rankin, Keisling, Mottet, & Anafi 2016: 12) which includes responses from nearly 28,000 transgender and gender variant participants in the United States and surrounding territories, highlights that "more than half (58%) of respondents experienced some form of mistreatment" from police. Fifty-seven percent stated they felt uncomfortable asking for police assistance, and survey participants who were under correctional supervision in jails, prisons, or detention facilities stated they experienced "high rates for physical and sexual assault by facility staff and other inmates" (James, et al. 2016: 13). Over 20 percent reported assault from staff and other inmates, while 20 percent were sexually assaulted. In all, survey findings concluded that among the respondents, transgender individuals were five times more likely to be sexually assaulted by staff and over nine times more likely to be sexually assaulted by inmates than their cisgender peers.

Additionally, in terms of LGBTQ IPV survivors' interactions with police, 35 percent reported indifference from law enforcement while 31 percent stated the police were hostile towards them (NCAVP 2017a). The report also indicates that "Black survivors were 2.8 times more likely to experience excessive force from police than survivors who did not identify as Black" (NCAVP 2017b: 15). The Queer community has a history of being overpoliced and in turn overrepresented in the criminal legal system at a disproportionate level. As stated above, this has resulted in lasting distrust and fear of law enforcement. One real life example of victim blaming and revictimization at the hands of the police is the harrowing case of rape survivor Brandon Teena.

In Nebraska in the winter (December 24th or 25th) of 1993, Brandon Teena was beaten and raped by John Lotter and Tim Nissen after they had discovered that Brandon was assigned female at birth. Brandon filed a report with law enforcement, but the subsequent interview conducted, primarily by Sheriff Charles Laux, revealed the ways in which trans victims are often further victimized by law enforcement. During the interview, which for all intents and purposes was an interrogation, Laux asked Brandon what he had in his underpants when Lotter and Nissen removed them, insinuating that Brandon used deception to appear male. Specifically, Laux asked Brandon if he used a sock to appear as if he had a penis, to which Brandon admitted. Later, when Brandon told Laux that the assailants did not touch him sexually immediately after finding out that he was assigned female at birth, Laux responds that he doesn't believe that the men would not have touched Brandon in some way, going so far as to say that he did not believe that after pulling Brandon's pants down that Lotter and Nissen would not "stick his hand in you or his finger in you." Laux stated several times that he did not believe Brandon's story even though Brandon told Laux in great detail that he was beaten by Lotter and Nissen before being taken to their car and raped. Laux then asked Brandon how he was sitting in the car when Lotter and Nissen began to "poke" him.

Laux's entire tone and demeanor was nothing short of accusatory, again, repeating his disbelief that the event even took place while stating that because Brandon was drunk he could not believe that his rapists would not have "played with" Brandon "a little bit." Further, Laux repeatedly asked Brandon how his legs were positioned in the car and if Lotter and/or Nissen penetrated him vaginally or anally. Laux accused Brandon of changing his statement about his position in the car and essentially accused him of lying, stating that he could play the tape back in order to prove it to Brandon, to which Brandon told him to do so. Court findings concluded that Brandon had not changed his account of the brutal attack. Laux then asked Brandon why he wanted to appear male and asked, "why do you run around with girls instead of guys beings [sic] you're a girl yourself? Why do you make girls think you're a guy?" Brandon responded that he was unsure as to why he did it and asked Laux what the relevance of those questions was, with Laux replying that he was attempting to ascertain all of the information pertaining to the night that Brandon was raped. Brandon later commented that he did not think that was important to the case and indicated that he had a "sexual identity crisis" but that he could not explain it.

As noted, this interaction is quite clearly an example of victim blaming and secondary victimization, but we can also see the Sheriff attempting to establish reasons why Lotter and Nissen would have beaten and raped Brandon – which relates to gay and trans panic defenses so often used in cases such as this, as Chapter 5 will highlight. Despite the fact that police obtained evidence that would support Brandon's attack and rape, that other officers believed Brandon, that Lotter and Nissen both admitted to assaulting Brandon, that numerous statements from Brandon and others corroborated the initial statement, and that Brandon was afraid that Lotter and Nissen would retaliate against him for going to the police, no immediate action was taken and Lotter and Nissen remained free. Approximately one week later, Lotter and Nissen murdered Brandon and two others (see *Brandon Estate of Brandon v. County of Richardson* 2001; Buist & Stone 2014; O'Hanlon 2001).

It is our cultural norms surrounding sexuality and gender presentation that make members of the Queer community vulnerable to abuse at the hands of law enforcement. As we have shown, members of the Queer community, especially those who identify as transgender or non-binary, not only distrust the police and law enforcement in general, but fear the police as well. In countries around the world, Queer people are abused and victimized by officers who are sworn to uphold the law. In Uzbekistan, for example, gay men especially fear being "outed" or bullied by police and are harassed and detained and interrogated for no legal reason, and therefore avoid police interaction even to their detriment because they do not feel protected or served by law enforcement agents. (Human Rights Watch 2021). Human Rights Campaign (2020) also reported on abuse of power in Cameroon where "security forces" continue to arrest men for same-sex consensual sex.

Further, HRW (2021: n.p.) quoted a 22-year-old transgender woman revealing that "police told us we are devils, not humans, not normal. They beat a trans woman in the face, slapped her twice in front of me." Despite the legality of consensual gay sex in Kyrgyzstan, the social stigma of homosexuality creates a space for extreme abuses against the Queer community and impunity for the offending officers. A Human Rights Watch report (2014) detailing the police brutality against gay men in Kyrgyzstan describes one victim's rape at the hands of police officers. The victim described being forced to the ground and that another officer

> ... took his penis out and started forcing it in my mouth. One officer was holding me from behind and really hurting my arms .... Then he let my hands go, and took his pants off. They also said that they would also fuck me in the ass.
>
> Human Rights Watch 2014: 39–40

This is a reminder that laws on the books and laws in action can be and are often contrasting applications. The EU (European Union) LGBT equality survey, with over 90,000 respondents from EU member states and Croatia, found that in 43 percent of the most serious incidents of hate-motivated violence against Queer persons, half admitted that they did not think police would do anything about their victimization. Further, the report noted that one third of the participants indicated that they did not report hate crime victimization to the police because they feared a "transphobic or homophobic reaction from the police" (European Union Agency for Fundamental Rights 2014: 68).

In 2021 the European Union Agency for Fundamental Rights (FRA) drew attention to the importance of "supportive effective policymaking," but evidence shows that this policymaking, while necessary, is not sufficient in preventing violence, discrimination, and fear against and amongst Queer people in the 30 countries included in their report, which surveyed nearly 140,000 people aged 15 and older who identify as LGBT or I (intersex). The authors note that there has been little positive change in the 7 years between surveys which indicates the impact of discrimination on the lives of LGBTI persons and their overall quality of life (European Union Agency for Fundamental Rights 2020).

In Uganda where, as indicated in Chapter 2, all homosexual acts are considered illegal, gays and lesbians have reported being abused by police officers including "intrusive physical examinations" or being ignored or threatened by police. Gays and lesbians indicated that officers would refuse to investigate cases filed involving gay and lesbian victims or would charge them with a variety of behaviors that violate Ugandan criminal codes against homosexuality. They also noted that they experienced physical abuse from law enforcement and prison officials, as well as being coerced into making statements about themselves that were incriminating (BBC 2015). More recently, Uganda's president has made homophobic comments, there has been documented increases in LGBT harassment towards Queer individuals and allies (Bhalla 2021), and a new Sexual Offenses Bill "contains a clause to criminalize same-sex relationships. The bill prescribes a five-year-jail term for anyone guilty of same-sex acts ..." (Deutsche Welle 2021).

Selective enforcement

Abuses of power in policing are manifested in more ways than just the physical, although they often go hand in hand. When addressing the selective enforcement (who to question, arrest, and so on) that police officers implement through the use of discretionary tactics, we must note that these tactics often represent the personal beliefs and ideologies of the officer and/or department, larger political agendas, or antiquated discriminatory policy. Because of this and because of the overall fear that Queer people have of law enforcement officers and officials, the victimization of Queer people often goes unreported or is ignored, or they are revictimized by those who are supposed to be protecting them and their rights.

Gruenwald and Kelly (2014) reported that violence towards the LGBT community is oftentimes exceptionally brutal – in 30 percent of LGBT homicides, multiple weapons are used, and in 42 percent of homicides, there are multiple offenders. As with all hate-motivated crimes, the numbers are vastly underreported and therefore there is little to no way of knowing just how many homicides result from anti-Queer violence. What research has indicated is that because there is a constant disconnect between the Queer community and law enforcement and because members of the Queer community feel as though they are targeted by police, there is little reason to believe that all violence against the community is reported, or when reported, that those incidences are properly investigated. The National Coalition of Anti-Violence Programs' (2017b) report on hate violence in 2016 noted that anti-LGBTQ homicides had doubled in 5 years from 25 in 2012 to 52 in 2017. Reuters (2020) reports that 63 LGBTQI community members in Columbia had been killed in the first 8 months of 2020.

One example of LGBTQ distrust of police relates to domestic violence. As Greenberg (2011) indicates, trans women are less likely to seek help from police officers in cases of domestic violence and trans people of color are even less likely to report. The decision not to report is often for the same reasons that cisgender Black women are reluctant to report their victimization to police – because they already distrust the police and see no viable options in reporting an incident that will only further victimize themselves or their communities. Greenberg (2011: 232) goes on to note that transgender victims often express that they themselves are seen/treated as offenders simply because of their identity; "reading a trans woman as trans may cause the officer to doubt her story of abuse, especially if her abuser is perceived as a cisgender woman." The example provided by Greenberg (2011) also highlights the detriments of selective enforcement in policing, as officers may not take seriously Queer domestic assaults or trauma from emotional violence, or rightly identify the aggressor in each instance. As an example, law enforcement might be more apt to use gender role stereotypes in deciding who to detain or ultimately arrest.

Additionally, transgender men and women often feel as though police officers use stop and frisk techniques not as a means of preventing crime but rather as a means to assess one's sex, or as Greenberg (2011) calls them, "gender checks." Other problems associated with police responses to domestic violence and intimate partner abuse cases involving transgender individuals is the refusal of officers to assist because they assume that the victims are prostitutes (this speaks both to selective enforcement based on gender identity as well as selective enforcement based on personal ideology). Conversely, trans women have reported being disproportionately targeted based on what the community has referred to as "walking while trans." This concept mirrors the racial disparities found with regards to selective enforcement focused on Black men when driving, or what Harris (1999) first coined, Driving While Black. This concept refers to pretextual traffic stops (deemed legal by the Supreme Court) of Black men, using the traffic stop as a means to produce reasonable suspicion and probable cause in order to search the men and their vehicles, hoping to ascertain and obtain illegal drugs. Returning to the concept of walking while trans, a study conducted by the Department of Justice on the New Orleans Police Department found that "members of the LGBT community complained that NOPD officers subject them to unjustified arrests for prostitution, targeting bars frequented by the community and sometimes fabricating evidence of solicitation for compensation" (Greenberg 2011: 231).

Walking while trans is, as mentioned, akin to driving while Black, whereas both unofficial policies of police lead to selective enforcement and disproportionate arrest of people of color. Published reports and research continues to highlight the fear that transgender women, especially transgender women of color, have of police officers and their overall safety because they are being targeted based on their race and gender identity. One well-known case, briefly mentioned in Chapter 2, is that of Monica Jones, who in 2014 was arrested in Phoenix, Arizona under what is referred to there as a manifestation ordinance – Jones has stated that she believes she was being profiled by police as a sex worker as she walked the public streets in her area (see Stangio 2014). The Arizona ordinance essentially states that anyone who talks to or even waves at a car can be considered to be soliciting sex (see Harjai 2016). A student at Arizona State University at the time of her arrest, Monica noted that she often walks, and one might go on to assume that many a college student has walked, and talked, and waved at cars without arrest for solicitation. In 2015, a Superior Court Judge vacated her conviction and stated that Jones did not receive a fair trial because her past prostitution charges were used against her (see Harjai 2016). The case study of Monica Jones is just one of many examples of how policies and practices such as walking while trans are wholly detrimental to transgender women of color, so much so that large and influential cities and states like New York have repealed anti-loitering laws (known as the walking while trans ban) with New York Governor Andrew Cuomo stating, "repealing the archaic 'walking while trans' ban is a critical step toward reforming our policing system and reducing the harassment and criminalization transgender people face simply for being themselves" (as quoted by Diaz 2021: n.p.).

Regardless of the repeals, although positive, LGBTQ people continue to report police abuse and mistreatment, and being profiled as sex workers (see Make the Road 2012). The overall displeasure, distrust, and acrimonious relationship with and in the police persist, although there have been arguments made for changes in attitudes with younger generations (Dario, Fradella, Verhagen, & Parry 2020). While the findings of Dario and colleagues (2020) are moving towards hopeful, the bulk of the research continues to suggest the opposite. For example, one project found that LGBT participants' perceptions of police were significantly more negative than other participants. Perceptions from the transgender identified persons that were surveyed included being more likely to be treated unfairly by police (see Owen, Burke, Few-Demo, & Natwick 2018).

In Australia, Dwyer's (2011) research indicated that police interaction with LGBT youth impacted the way police treated them and how the police chose to use discretion. Much like in the United States, Australian youth felt harassed and victimized and in turn were reluctant to report their victimizations to law enforcement. Indeed, if there is an increase in the negative interactions between young LGBT people, this will in turn impact their belief in police legitimacy (Dwyer 2011). Dwyer (2011) also indicated that police tried to assess sexual orientation based on gender constructions of masculinities and femininities and gender performance, i.e., feminine boys were harassed based on their outward appearance, or "how the body can be performed in ways that visibly enact queerness and in turn is constituted as a body to be watched and regulated by police" (Dwyer 2011: 216).

In the United States, a 2014 report from the Office of Juvenile Justice and Delinquency investigated "LGBTQ Youth in the Juvenile Justice System" (in this case the "Q" stood for "questioning" rather than "Queer"). Much of this report will be detailed in Chapter 6 but until then, it should be noted that similar to the Australian-based study on young people, in the United States, LGBTQ juveniles are more likely to be stopped by police, which leads to a disproportionate representation of LGBT youth in the juvenile system. What is important to keep in mind is that with an increased number of LGBTQ-identified young people on the streets, it is not unlikely that they will have contact with the police. But what is of major importance here is to remember that once in the criminal legal system there is an increased likelihood that one will remain trapped in the criminal legal system. For instance, research has found that disproportionate minority contact with police leads to an overrepresentation of young minorities in courtrooms and correctional facilities.

Historically, this research has focused on the disproportionate contact that people, primarily young people of color, have with police, but research has also indicated that the media often influences the public perception of crime and criminals and the perception of people of color as offenders. Images of offenders as young, minority, poor, and from urban settings (Reiman & Leighton 2012; see Russell 1998) can certainly affect the ways in which police officers choose to selectively enforce law-breaking behavior even if those behaviors are nonviolent, such as hanging out in a local park or on a street corner. This influence should be considered when we examine the ways in which young people who identify or are labeled as Queer are treated by law enforcement and understand that these youth are also being contacted by police officers in disproportionate numbers. This contact serves no greater good, but instead serves to further marginalize minority populations in the United States and abroad. Research has shown that while Queer youth make up no more than 7 percent of the U.S. population, they currently represent up to 15 percent of the population within our juvenile justice system (Hunt & Moodie-Mills 2012; Office of Juvenile Justice and Delinquency Prevention OJJDP 2014). Further, as indicated earlier, many of these young people are forced out of their homes and into the streets because of their sexual orientation and/or gender identity, and tend to commit survival crimes rather than predatory violence. Finally, the impact of intersectionality is quite real for these young people, as over 60 percent of these Queer youth are Black or Latino (Hunt & Moodie-Mills 2012).

In the following section, we turn our attention to the differential treatment that Queer law enforcement officers experience on the job. Several studies will be highlighted that do show some improvement in the working conditions for Queer officers in police departments around the world. However, officers still report feeling marginalized and harassed at work and many of them fear being out or outed on the job. First, we must discuss the policing structure and culture that is in place and may influence the negative ways in which Queer officers are treated.

Queer and blue

In order to address the experiences of officers who identify as lesbian, gay, bisexual, transgender, or queer, we must first discuss the policing subculture. Historically, policing has been a male-dominated field that values masculine traits while devaluing traits that are commonly attributed to women. Therefore, physical aggression is viewed as an essential component of police work instead of or above verbal communication; or an officer will value communication skills but will argue that at some point the talking has to end and the fight has to begin – therefore physical strength is required. Mind you, there is rarely any discussion of the value of the tools that all officers have at their disposal regardless of their sex (Corsianos 2009; Wells & Alt 2005). In 2021, women still made up less than 20 percent of law enforcement officials. Regardless of a new generation of police officers that may not identify gender stereotypes on the job as much as before, women are still seen as the outsiders within a male profession. Women officers who present in a more masculine way on the job often comment that this works as more of a benefit than detriment to them (Corsianos 2009; Miller, Forest, & Jurik 2003). In fact, Miller et al. (2003) noted that lesbians who are out on the job feel as though because this is almost expected, they are not as marginalized as gay men are. However, overwhelmingly, research has indicated that gay and lesbian officers experience a heightened sense of marginalization and harassment compared to other minority groups on the job (Colvin 2009; Moran 2007; see also Bernstein & Kostelac 2002; Buhrke 1996; Burke 1994; Miller et al. 2003).

Focusing on the value placed on masculinity and the vast numbers of men working in policing is important because they both serve to explain the heteronormative culture that is pervasive in male-dominated jobs, or more specifically, the influence of compulsory heterosexuality within the policing occupation (Miller et al. 2003). Therefore, identifying as anything other than straight can prove detrimental, perhaps especially to gay male officers. Some of the findings in Miller et al. (2003) reveal that gay and lesbian officers felt as though they were constantly scrutinized, were excluded by their heterosexual colleagues, and were victims of a variety of antigay behaviors. Other concerns voiced were fear that if officers were out on the job, their fellow officers would fail to back them up on duty calls, and that they feared being viewed as distrustful if others found out they were gay, as well as experiencing a lack of camaraderie on the job (Miller et al. 2003). Since officers distrust the public and put an immense amount of trust in their fellow officers, being shunned by your colleagues can have potentially dangerous, even life-threatening results. While some have found support for being out on the job (see Colvin 2009; Jones 2015), there must be consideration for officers who are not out to their families or friends, let alone at work. Just as some officers interviewed by Colvin (2009) and Miller et al. (2003) have indicated that being out can benefit them (allow them to be open about their relationship status, gain respect of other officers, speak freely about their personal lives, etc.) this can also have a backlash effect with regards to overt or covert harassment and lack of support on the job, including going on calls and requiring back-up that may never arrive.

Other qualitative studies have brought attention to the victimization, harassment, and marginalization of gay and lesbian officers. For instance, in her book, *A Matter of Trust*, Buhrke (1996) presents narrative interviews with over 40 men and women, representing over 30 different departments in law enforcement, detailing their personal experiences on the job. Buhrke begins the introduction of her research by revealing her personal experiences as a police officer and being viewed as a "traitor" amongst the Queer community. This sentiment continues in 2021 with calls to ban police from participating in Pride events in the U.S. and abroad. Documented reports have indicated a move to ban officers from events in New York, California, Washington,

DC, and Canada, most citing solidarity with Black activists in demonstration against police brutality. One such ban comes from NYC PRIDE who announced in May of 2021 that they would not allow police officers at Pride events for at least five years based on their efforts to keep Pride a safe space. Their statement in part noted, "The sense of safety that law enforcement is meant to provide can instead be threatening, and at times dangerous, to those in our community who are most often targeted with excessive force and/or without reason" (NYC Pride 2021). The statement also highlighted the experiences of BIPOC (Black, Indigenous, and People of Color) LGBTQ+ individuals and challenged police to "acknowledge their harm and to correct course moving forward, in hopes of making an impactful change" (NYC Pride 2021).

> Officers all too often are not accepted by their police community because they are gay and lesbian, and because they are cops, they are rejected by the lesbian and gay community.
>
> *Buhrke 1996: 2*

Research indicates that gay and lesbian officers remain committed to policing as a profession and often times are just as embedded in the organizational environment of the job as any other officer (e.g. Burke 1994; Corsianos 2009; Miller et al. 2003). This level of commitment to the profession and dedication to the work is exemplified by the Queer officers who stay on the job despite facing harassment and stereotypes that are shrouded in the patriarchal masculinist organization of policing itself. An extreme example of this is highlighted in a study by Buist (2011), in which a lesbian officer commented that while on the job, she had experienced varying levels of harassment including being stalked by a coworker, another coworker identifying her as lesbian although she wasn't out, and having investigations opened against her and her partner, all of which ultimately led to her leaving law enforcement. Despite the torment, she later returned to the academy and policing because of her dedication and love of the job, regardless of the hate she had experienced. Indeed, many of the lesbian officers who discussed their personal histories on the job noted that although they experienced more incidents of harassment because of their sexual orientation, they remained in law enforcement because they loved the work. Still, they admitted that as women and as lesbians they felt as though they had to work much harder than anyone else to prove that they belonged (Buist 2011). As indicated in previous studies (see Miller et al. 2003) Corsianos (2009: 105) notes that lesbians "like other officers … wanted to be recognized for their traditional policing goals."

One of the major issues that will no doubt continue to impact Queer officers' decisions to be on the job, let alone out on the job, may be attributed to the ideology of fellow officers as well as their superiors, up to and including the head of their respective agencies. Not to mention the political climate and influence both at the federal and state levels. While there has been a federal ban on discrimination that is based on sexual orientation, this does not mean that every state follows the same policy. In the United States today, not all states consider sexual orientation or gender orientation to be protected classes and this certainly may be a contributing factor as to why some officers choose to stay in the closet rather than disclosing their sexual and/or gender orientation. Many departments across the country and abroad have begun to implement new training strategies with the intention of recruiting officers with more diverse backgrounds as well as updating their codes of conduct to reflect a more diverse workforce and implementing and requiring new training techniques for officers who come into contact with Queer communities and individuals. The question, however, remains: Do these approaches work? Also, how can the policing style used by a department influence the way in which training is implemented and instituted?

Policing style and training

In a study conducted in England and Wales, Jones (2015) surveyed 836 police officers to assess if a move to diversify policing was successful. Jones highlighted many of the findings from Burke's (1994) work that addressed the negative experiences faced by LGB people, which included feeling hostility and aggression from police, that their concerns and protection were ignored by police officers, and that LGB officers themselves felt as though they were viewed as deviant because of their sexual orientation. Jones's (2015) latest report concentrates on the attempt to bring law enforcement more up-to-date regarding not only the public's image of the police departments but the ways in which the officers do their jobs and relate to and/or accept each other. Specifically, the departments in England and Wales were focused on improving their department in order to

> ... fracture the dominance of white, heterosexual men in polic-
> ing and resultant informal working practices, through active
> recruitment of officers from a broad spectrum of cultural and
> demographic backgrounds.
>
> Jones 2015: 3

The findings of Jones's (2015) survey were promising, noting that there was positive change in the departments in England and Wales. Indeed, Jones (2015: 5) reported that over 70 percent of survey respondents indicated that their departments "do enough for LGB cops" and that they are "satisfied or very satisfied" as police officers in their departments, and over 80 percent of respondents noted that they had not encountered prejudice on the job because they identified as LGBTQ. Much of these positive results may be attributed to the change in legislation in England and Wales, as well as the decision of the police there to implement their own changes to their police code of conduct to include "respect and courtesy, honesty, and integrity, personal autonomy, lawfulness and professional equity" (Jones 2015: 6). Although these findings are positive to say the least, officers still reported feelings of distress and discrimination, but at a lower percentage than before the changes were implemented.

Additionally, Jones (2015) highlights a salient point regarding sexuality and sexual orientation. He notes that we must appreciate that sexual orientation or identity is dynamic and that to attempt to understand sexuality is also to recognize the intricacies that accompany sexual as well as gender identities. As indicated in Chapter 1, we must be cognizant and aware that sexuality for some may be considered a construction that is influenced by a litany of factors and tied into the influence of the patriarchal society in which we live. Further, these ideas that we develop based on gender role expectations are often manifested through imitation and reproduction of those expectations of masculinity and femininity (Butler 1990; West & Zimmerman 1987). Instead of essentialist and absolutist thinking regarding sexual orientation and/or gender identity, we should be able to recognize the continuum of sexuality that exists or may exist for some. Conversely, the criminal legal system, when functioning properly, identifies behavior based on codified laws that are often interpreted literally as opposed to focusing on the myriad interpretations that may exist. Here, we have police officers who are tasked with being the frontline guardians of law enforcement and therefore they may be even less apt to adopt an understanding of the possibility of fluidity as applied to identity. Officers often rely heavily upon their use of discretion, at times to the detriment of citizens and officers alike (see selective enforcement). Therefore, officers continue to classify individuals based on what they *know*, because the unknown is what they most fear.

The style of policing that is promoted and implemented within the policing occupation will have a significant impact on the effectiveness of diversity training among officers. The move from the professional era of policing into a more problem-oriented era and now into community-oriented policing may indeed not only serve to foster tolerance, understanding, and acceptance of Queer officers and citizens, but it may also begin to attract different kinds of people to the law enforcement profession in general. Keep in mind that more traditional forms of policing – such as the problem-oriented and broken-windows styles, along with and perhaps especially zero-tolerance or quality-of-life policing – have proven to promote distrust of citizens towards officers. For example, when William Bratton instituted zero-tolerance policing in the NYPD, he argued that the method of policing would help to clean up the streets and subway stations of the homeless population. Essentially, this style of policing enforces a variety of laws against loitering and vagrancy. When describing subway stations throughout the city he commented:

> Every platform seemed to have a cardboard city where the homeless had taken up residence. This was a city that had stopped caring about itself. There was a sense of permissive society allowing certain things that would not have been permitted years ago.
> Bratton 1998: 34

While Bratton had argued that quality-of-life policing is similar to problem-oriented and community-oriented policing, this argument is problematic especially since upon instituting zero-tolerance policing, citizen complaint reports of police brutality increased by 75 percent and Amnesty International found a 60 percent increase in citizen complaints in the early to mid-1990s (Green 1999). More recently, the NYPD has been in the center of debate regarding stop and frisk laws that unduly impact people of color. Any style of policing, such as zero-tolerance law enforcement, has a tendency to clean the streets at the detriment of minority populations, often poor, homeless people of color. But at the same time, we must keep in mind that our youth population is also targeted and affected by the enforcement of these laws, and certainly our Queer youth as they experience higher rates of homelessness.

Instead of using styles of policing that are reactionary, community policing involves the concerns of the residents and business owners promoting what Alpert, Durham, and Stroshine (2006: 97) identify as the open-systems theory: A design that is "flexible, adaptive, and organic." While Alpert et al. (2006) argue that this particular approach to community policing would fall within the professional model, there is certainly room for debate here as professional styles of policing are more reactionary than proactive, which is one of the central tenets of community-oriented policing strategies. Greene (2004) suggests that law enforcement officers should view the public as "clients," which in essence brings attention to the importance of knowing the community that the officers patrol; therefore, interaction with the community members will better allow them to assess the needs of that community. Several different scholars have indicated that the structure of policing in and of itself, the paramilitaristic hierarchical model that values masculinity and aggression, prevents the successful implementation of community policing styles. However, Greenberg (1999) asserts that it is not the structure that should be blamed, but instead the people working within the structure that should be held accountable, namely those in supervisory roles, for the failure to successfully implement community policing and establish positive relationships with the members of the community. This is certainly an interesting observation; however, if the organization itself was restructured in a way that did not support individuals' prejudiced beliefs or encourage those beliefs, a message would be sent that intolerance is unacceptable – this was evidenced in the aforementioned study by Jones (2015) that found a dramatic change in the experiences of Queer officers once new and more inclusive training had been implemented.

The Ontario Association of Chiefs of Police issued a report, "Best Practices in Policing and LGBTQ Communities in Ontario," in 2013, which was the first of its kind to be published in Canada (Kirkup 2013). The report addressed past practices that promoted tensions between the police and the LGBTQ community throughout Toronto and detailed the importance of implementing policing strategies that were inclusive of all members of the communities they policed, noting that "police services should reflect the communities they serve" (Kirkup 2013: 9). The report also highlighted the Canadian Association of Chiefs of Police adoption of Resolution 2 in 2004 that noted the importance of policing free of bias, and that rather focused on "fairness, dignity, and ethics" (Kirkup 2013: 6). This mirrors the code of conduct that police in England and Wales adopted (Jones 2015) that connotes the importance of respect and honesty among others. Another important aspect in how training should reflect the changing face of communities and policing itself is in recognizing the importance of respecting "safe spaces" of Queer members. Moran (2007: 418) points out "safe spaces are often created in response to homophobic violence exploring personal, community, commercial and institutional responses to threatened and actual violence." Police, therefore, must understand that these locations are seen not only as safe spaces for Queer folks, but sacred places as well; places where individuals who feel marginalized in many if not all of the social settings they reside in can feel accepted and protected. Police officers who have no knowledge of the prejudices that Queer people have experienced are less likely to understand just how important these places are and how valued they are by the community of people that they serve.

In relation to the importance of safe spaces, it is also important to understand that the population in a particular area will influence the knowledge of the community itself. If there is not a known presence of Queer folks in a particular area, these areas may in fact be the locations where police need the most training and awareness regarding issues that impact people who are unlike themselves. As for police officers who are Queer, one could surmise that the smaller the department, the less likely an officer will feel safe being out or coming out on the job. Either way, we continue to see prejudiced attitudes towards Queer officers regardless of the size of the police department. We also must understand that hate and prejudice are not always known on the job, but rather suspected. This again speaks to personal politics and ideology that departments can do little about until those prejudices manifest themselves. For example, Lyons, DeValve, and Garner (2008: 110) found that of the 747 police chiefs in Texas they surveyed, nearly 50 percent of them reported that they had "trouble working with a gay man," while over 60 percent reported that "homosexuality constitutes a 'moral turpitude,'" and 56 percent indicated that being gay was a "perversion." Additionally, 58 percent of their participants "believed that lesbians and gay men have a choice in their desires."

Law enforcement is facing a backlash of their own – especially with the use of social media, every misstep and poor decision is broadcast on the nightly news and across Twitter feeds throughout the world. But, unlike most professions, when police officers make poor decisions, people can die. When those decisions are couched within prejudice and hatred, there is little that policing style, training, or even legislation can do to protect those who are the victims of police violence or victims of the discrimination that prevents officers from protecting and serving the public regardless of sexual orientation, gender identity, or the color of one's skin, among so many other intersecting oppressions.

Returning to the discussion of community policing, this conversation is relevant, especially in the face of what appears to be increased (or perhaps the increased knowledge of) brutality and selective enforcement of minority citizens. As noted, theoretically speaking, community-oriented policing focuses on proactive interpersonal connections and interactions between officers and the public. There are problems associated with this as most police departments would espouse that they utilize community-oriented practices; however, this is rarely the case. Again, if the structure of policing or law enforcement in general is couched within paramilitaristic, patriarchal, hypermasculine ideals, these strategies will never result in the relational approach that is community-oriented policing. Instead, the institution will continue to operate by utilizing aggressive tactics that in turn, as shown, result in increased civilian complaints and distrust between civilians and officers, between officers and civilians, and in the case of Queer officers, between officers and officers.

If community-oriented policing is to be effective, then it needs to be implemented correctly and completely – no more half measures that are implemented perhaps because federal funding is granted to departments who claim some degree of community policing. The Bureau of Justice Statistics reports that 83 percent of officers in the United States work in departments that claim to use community police officers (Hickman & Reaves 2006). Therefore, the odds are that departments that report having community policing officers and promote community policing tactics are likely to be implementing selective enforcement and disproportionate profiling strategies that impact Queer communities, communities of color, and poor communities. Instead of simply stating that community policing is being utilized, there needs to be an effort to incorporate the tenets of community-oriented policing beyond the surface-level work of checking in with community leaders and/or giving officers some modicum of responsibility in decision making on patrol.

So how does law enforcement properly and successfully implement community-oriented policing? First, we would suggest that departments use successful models to guide them in changing their own policy and approaches to policing. Next, we would suggest supervisory positions within the department that monitor the successful implementation of community-oriented policing strategies and working groups of officers who are assigned community roles, much like a community liaison within the police department. In general, we would also recommend a move away from the traditional, aggressive style of policing that has done little to serve communities, states, and nations. This would require a complete change in the structure of the institution of policing and would not come without substantial backlash. We understand that this is not likely to occur, but if recruitment strategies were changed, and codes of conduct updated and enforced and violation of such codes were punished, we may see a more inclusive law enforcement component of the criminal legal system. Research, although scant, has indicated that some positive changes can develop.

Still, Queer officers remain marginalized within their departments. Their best defense is most likely changing legislation that protects against discrimination based on sexual and/or gender orientation, but that legislation has yet to be implemented in all 50 states in the United States. Further, while legislation will allow for protections in the eyes of the law, this does not mean that it will guarantee equal treatment for Queer officers.

Activities and discussion questions

- Research your local police departments. Do they have a good or bad record with the Queer community in your area? Do they have support for Queer officers? Do your findings reflect the research?
- Are there any Queer support groups for teens, parents, and so on? Any local resources that provide services?
- Is there evidence that the policing occupation has changed for the better in the last 20 years? If so, how so? If not, explain your answer.

Recommended viewing

Badge of Pride, 2010 [Film] Directed by Min Sook Lee. Canada: Hungry Eyes Film and Television.

Boys Don't Cry, 1999 [Film] Directed by Kimberly Peirce. USA: Fox Searchlight.

The Brandon Teena Story, 1998 [Film] Directed by Susan Muska and Gréta Olafsdóttir. USA: Zeitgeist Films.

References

Alpert, G.P., Durham, R.G., & Stroshine, M.S. 2006. *Policing: Continuity and change*. Long Grove, IL: Waveland Press.

Amnesty International. n.d. Police Violence. Accessed from www.amnesty.org/en/what-we-do/police-brutality/.

BBC. 2015. Ugandan gay people "abused by police." *BBC News*, February 27. Accessed from www.bbc.com/news/world-africa-31658311.

BBC. 2021. George Floyd: Timeline of black deaths and protests 2021. *BBC News*, April 22. Accessed from www.bbc.com/news/world-us-canada-52905408.

Becker, H. 1963. *Outsiders*. New York, NY: The Free Press.

Bernstein, M. & Kostelac, C. 2002. Lavender and blue: Attitudes about homosexuality and behavior toward lesbian and gay men among police officers. *Journal of Contemporary Criminal Justice, 18*, (3): 302–328.

Bhalla, N. 2021. Anti-gay rhetoric ramps up fear among LGBT+ Ugandans ahead of polls. *Reuters*, January 6. Accessed from www.reuters.com/article/us-uganda-lgbt-election/anti-gay-rhetoric-ramps-up-fear-among-lgbt-ugandans-ahead-of-polls-idUSKBN29B22W.

Brandon Estate of Brandon v. County of Richardson. 2001. Accessed from http://caselaw.findlaw.com/ne-supreme-court/1275811.html.

Bratton, W.J. 1998. *Crime is down in New York City: Blame the police*. In Norman Dennis (ed.), *Zero tolerance: Policing a free society*. (pp. 29–42). London: IEA.

Buhrke, R. 1996. *A matter of justice: Lesbians and gay men in law enforcement*. New York, NY: Routledge.

Buist, C. 2011. "Don't let the job change you; you change the job": The lived experiences of women in policing. *Dissertations*. Paper 335. Accessed from http://scholarworks.wmich.edu/dissertations/355.

Buist, C.L. & Stone, C. 2014. Transgender victims and offenders: Failures of the United States criminal justice system and the necessity of queer criminology. *Critical Criminology, 22*, (1): 35–47.

Burke, M. 1994. Homosexuality as deviance: The case of the gay police officer. *British Journal of Criminology, 34* (2): 192–203.

Burns, K. 2020. Why police often single out trans people for violence: The deaths of Layleen Polanco and Tony McDade highlight how Black trans Americans are treated and criminalized. *Vox*, June 23. Accessed from www.vox.com/identities/2020/6/23/21295432/police-black-trans-people-violence.

Butler, J. 1990. *Gender Trouble*. New York, NY: Routledge.

Cao, L. 2003. *Curbing police brutality: What works? A reanalysis of citizen complaints at the organizational level*. Washington, DC: United States Department of Justice: National Criminal Justice Reference Service.

Cato Institute. 2010. *National Police Misconduct Reporting Project*. Accessed from www.policemisconduct.net/statistics/2010-annual-report/#_Sexual_Misconduct.

Cohen, L. 2020. Police in the U.S. killed 164 Black people in the first 8 months of 2020. These are their names (Part I: January–April). *CBS News*, September 10. Accessed from www.cbsnews.com/pictures/black-people-killed-by-police-in-the-u-s-in-2020/.

Collins, P. 2000. *Black feminist thought: Knowledge, consciousness, and the politics of empowerment*. New York, NY: Routledge.

Colvin, R. 2009. Shared perceptions among lesbian and gay police officers: Barriers and opportunities in the law enforcement work environment. *Police Quarterly, 12*, (1): 86–101.

Corsianos, M. 2009. *Policing and gendered justice: Examining the possibilities.* Toronto, Canada: University of Toronto Press.

Crenshaw, K. 1989. Demarginalizing the intersection of race and sex: A Black feminist critique of antidiscrimination doctrine, feminist theory and anti-racist politics. *University of Chicago Legal Forum, 1989*: (1): 140. Accessed from https://chicagounbound.uchicago.edu/cgi/viewcontent.cgi?article=1052&context=uclf.

Day, E. 2015. #BlackLivesMatter: the birth of a new civil rights movement. *The Guardian*, July 19. Accessed from www.theguardian.com/world/2015/jul/19/blacklivesmatter-birth-civil-rights-movement.

Diaz, J. 2021. New York Repeals "Walking While Trans" Law. *NPR*, February 3. Accessed from www.npr.org/2021/02/03/963513022/new-york-repeals-walking-while-trans-law.

Dario, L.M., Fradella, H.F., Verhagen, M., & Parry, M.M. 2020. Assessing LGBT people's perceptions of police legitimacy. *Journal of Homosexuality, 67*, (7): 885–915. Accessed from https://doi.org/10.1080/00918369.2018.1560127.

Deutsche Welle. 2021. Uncertain future for LGBT+ rights in Uganda as controversial bill is passed. *DW*, May 5. Accessed from www.dw.com/en/uncertain-future-for-lgbt-rights-in-uganda-as-controversial-bill-is-passed/a-57437925.

Dwyer, A. 2011. "It's not like we're going to jump them": How transgressing heteronormativity shapes police interactions with LGBT young people. *Youth Justice, 11*, (3): 203–220.

Eckhouse, M.J. & Saxen, M.M. 2017. *Police brutality and why it is an LGBTQ issue.* Fusion and Spring. Accessed from www.kent.edu/sites/defaultfiles/file/Police_Brutality.pdf

Edwards, F., Lee, H., & Esposito, M. 2019. Risk of being killed by police use of force in the United States by age, race-ethnicity, and sex. *Proceedings of the National Academy of Sciences of the United States of America, 116*, (34): 16793–16798.

European Union Agency for Fundamental Rights. 2014. *EU LGBT survey: European Union lesbian, gay, bisexual and transgender survey.* Luxembourg: Publications Office of the European Union.

European Union Agency for Fundamental Rights. 2020. A long way to go for LGBTI equality. EU-LGBTI II. Accessed from https://op.europa.eu/en/publication-detail/-/publication/f6ab7c98-d2d2-11ea-adf7-01aa75ed71a1.

Foucault, M. 1980. *Power/knowledge: Selected interviews and other writings.* New York, NY: Pantheon Press.

Garza, A. 2014. A herstory of the #blacklivesmatter movement by Alicia Garza. *The Feminist Wire*, October 7. Accessed from http://thefeministwire.com/2014/10/blacklivesmatter-2/.

Green, J. 1999. Zero tolerance: A case study of police policies and practices in New York City. *Crime and Delinquency, 45*, (2): 171–187.

Greenberg, K. 2011. Still hidden in the closet: Trans women and domestic violence. *Berkeley Journal of Gender, Law & Justice, 27,* (2): 198–251.

Greenberg, S. 1999. *Is it time to change law enforcement's paramilitary structure?* In J.D. Sewell & S.A. Egger (eds.), *Controversial issues in policing* (pp. 139–153). Brockleigh, NJ: Allyn and Bacon.

Greene, J.R. 2004. *Community policing and police organization*. In W.G. Skogan (ed.), *Community policing: Can it work?* (pp. 30–54). Belmont, CA: Thomson Wadsworth.

Gruenwald, J. & Kelly, K. 2014. Exploring anti-LGBT homicide by mode of victim selection. *Criminal Justice and Behavior, 41,* (9): 1130–1152.

Harjai, K. 2016 June 6. Monica Jones and the Problem of "Walking While Trans" Innocence Project. Accessed from https://innocenceproject.org/monica-jones-walking-while-trans/.

Harris, D. 1999. The stories, the statistic, and the law: Why "driving while black" matters. *Minnesota Law Review, 84*: 265–326.

Hickman, M.J. & Reaves, B.A. 2006. *Local police departments, 2003.* Washington, DC: Bureau of Justice Statistics.

Hodge, J.P. & Sexton, L. 2018. Examining the Blue Line in the Rainbow: The Interactions and Perceptions of Law Enforcement Among Lesbian, Gay, Bisexual, Transgender and Queer Communities. *Police Practice and Research: An International Journal.*

Human Rights Campaign. 2020. *An Epidemic of Violence: Fatal Violence Against Transgender and Gender Non-Conforming People in the Unites States in 2020.* Accessed from https://hrc-prod-requests.s3-us-west-2.amazonaws.com/FatalViolence-2020Report-Final.pdf?mtime=20201119101455&focal=none.

Human Rights Watch. 2014. *"They said we deserved this": Police violence against gay and bisexual men in Kyrgyzstan.* United States of America: Human Rights Watch.

Human Rights Watch. 2021. World report 2021. Accessed from www.hrw.org/sites/default/files/media_2021/01/2021_hrw_world_report.pdf.

Hunt, J. & Moodie-Mills, A. 2012. *The unfair criminalization of gay and transgender youth: An overview of the experiences of LGBT youth in juvenile justice system.* Washington, DC: Center for American Progress.

James, S.E., Herman, J.L., Rankin, S., Keisling, M., Mottet, L., & Anafi, M. 2016. *The Report of the 2015 U.S. Transgender Survey.* Washington, DC: National Center for Transgender Equality.

Jones, M. 2015. Who forgot lesbian, gay, and bisexual police officers? Findings from a national survey. *Policing, 9,* (1): 1–12.

Kirkup, K. 2013. *Best practices in policing and LGBTQ communities in Ontario.* Ontario, Canada: Ontario Association of Chiefs of Police.

Lyons Jr., P.M., DeValve, M.J., & Garner, R.L. 2008. Texas police chiefs' attitudes toward gay and lesbian police officers. *Police Quarterly*, *11*, (1): 102–117.

Make the Road. 2012. *Transgressive Policing: Police Abuse of LGBTQ Communities of Color in Jackson Heights*. New York.

Merkl, T.A. 2021. *Protecting Against Police Brutality and Official Misconduct. A New Federal Criminal Civil Rights Framework*. Brennan Center for Justice New York University School of Law, April 29. Accessed from www.brenna ncenter.org/our-work/research-reports/protecting-against-police-brutal ity-and-official-misconduct.

Miller, S.L., Forest, K.B., & Jurik, N.C. 2003. Diversity in blue: Lesbian and gay police officers in a masculine occupation. *Men and Masculinities, 5*, (4): 355–385.

Mogul, J.L., Ritchie, A., & Whitlock, K. 2011. *Queer (in)justice: The criminaliza-tion of LGBT people in the United States*. Boston, MA: Beacon Press.

Moran, L.J. 2007. "Invisible minorities": Challenging community and neigh-bourhood models of policing. *Criminology & Criminal Justice*, 7, (4): 417–441.

National Coalition of Anti-Violence Programs (NCAVP). 2017a. *Lesbian, Gay, Bisexual, Transgender, Queer, and HIV-Affected Hate Violence in 2016*. New York, NY: Emily Waters.

National Coalition of Anti-Violence Programs (NCAVP. 2017b. *A Crisis of Hate: A Mid Year Report on Homicides Against Lesbian, Gay, Bisexual and Transgender People*: Emily Waters, Sue Yacka-Bible

National Institute of Justice. 2011 October 27. What is a Gang? Definitions. Accessed from https://nij.ojp.gov/topics/articles/what-gang-definitions.

NYC Pride. 2021 May 15. NYC Pride announces new policies to address police presence. Accessed from www.nycpride.org/news-press-media/nyc-pride-announces-new-policies-to-address-police-presence.

Office of Juvenile Justice and Delinquency Prevention (OJJDP). 2014. *LGBTQ Youth in the Juvenile Justice System*. Washington, DC: N/A.

O'Hanlon, K. 2001. Brandon Teena's mother sues sheriff. *ABC News*, January 13. Accessed from http://abcnews.go.com/US/story?id=94389.

Oppel, R.A, Taylor, D.B., & Bogel-Burroughs, N. 2021. What to Know about Breonna Taylor's Death. *New York Times*, April 26. Accessed from www.nyti mes.com/article/breonna-taylor-police.html.

Owen, S.S., Burke, T.W., Few-Demo, A.L., & Natwick, J. 2018. Perceptions of the police by LGBT communities. *American Journal of Criminal Justice, 43*, (3), 668–693. Accessed from https://doi.org/10.1007/s12103-017-9420-8.

Reiman, J. & Leighton, P. 2012. *The rich get richer and the poor get prison: Ideology, class, and criminal justice*. Boston, MA: Pearson.

Reuters 2020. September 15. More than 60 LGBT, intersex people killed in Colombia in the first eight months of 2020. Accessed from www.reuters. com/article/us-colombia-lgbt/more-than-60-lgbt-intersex-people-killed-in-colombia-in-first-eight-months-of-2020-idUSKBN26634G.

Russell, K. 1998. *The color of crime: Racial hoaxes, white fear, black protectionism, police harassments, and other microaggressions.* New York, NY: New York University Press.

Selby, D. 2021. 'We were made out to be these horrible monsters': How homophobia led to the wrongful conviction of four Texas women. *Innocence Project*, June 1. Accessed from https://innocenceproject.org/lbgtq-pride-month-san-antonio-four-police-violence/.

Stangio, C. 2014. Arrested for walking while trans: An interview with Monica Jones. *ACLU*, April 2. Accessed from www.aclu.org/blog/criminal-law-ref orm/arrested-walking-while-trans-interview-monica-jones.

Stanglin, D., Duvall, T., & Wolfson A. 2020. Breonna Taylor 'truths' includes misinformation. *USA Today*, September 26. Accessed from www.usatoday. com/story/news/factcheck/2020/09/26/fact-check-posts-breonna-tay lor-truths-include-misinformation/3531905001/.

Transgender Europe. 2020 TMM Update Trans Day of Remembrance 2020. *Transrespect versus Transphobia Worldwide*, November 11. Accessed from https://transrespect.org/en/tmm-update-tdor-2020/.

Wells, S.K. & Alt, B.L. 2005. *Police women: Life with the badge.* Westport, CT: Praeger.

West, C. & Zimmerman, D.H. 1987. Doing gender. *Gender & Society 1*, (2): 125–151.

5

QUEER CRIMINOLOGY AND LEGAL SYSTEMS

While Chapter 4 focused on Queer experiences with or as law enforcement officers, here we turn our attention to what happens in courtrooms and legislative bodies around the globe. Not only will we explore the ways that Queer rights have been battled out in the courts and how laws and criminal trials affect Queer offenders and victims, but we will also identify how non-Queer offenders have come to use systems of homophobia and heteronormativity to their advantage. Additionally, we will explore how laws can (or cannot) be used to address crimes committed against the Queer community.

The battle for queer rights

As delineated in Chapter 2, queerness in and of itself continues to be criminalized throughout the world, so it is not surprising that Queer people are denied access to and equal treatment in nearly every social institution including employment, marriage, and education, among others. The denial of these rights affects all Queer citizens, including those entrenched in the criminal legal system,

DOI: 10.4324/9781003165163-5

and the attainment or denial of those rights are oft determined by judges in a court of law or by a country's legislative body.

One's ability to gain access to the social institutions that define everyday life is ultimately dependent upon legal identity – that is, the documented proof that a person exists and that determines the demographic categories that he, she, or they are defined by. For transgender people, obtaining legal documentation that reflects one's true identity is becoming increasingly difficult and complicated (e.g., Holroyd 2020; Human Rights Watch 2019; Knight 2019; Yurcaba 2021). In Japan, for example, a trans person who wishes to obtain legal recognition of their gender identity must be at least 20 years old, unmarried, and childless, and must jump a series of cost-prohibitive and unnecessary hurdles, including being diagnosed with gender identity disorder (GID), undergoing sterilization, and undergoing gender reaffirming genital surgery (Human Rights Watch 2019). Other countries, like Hungary, don't provide any process, let alone a complicated one, to change legal documentation, effectively banning transgender people from ever being legally recognized as their true selves (Holroyd 2020). Arizona state representative John Fillmore, who proposed a bill banning the legal recognition of non-binary people (even though the state did not recognize them anyway) said, "What's going to happen when someday someone wakes up and they want to go to a far extreme and identify as a chicken or something, for crying out loud" (Yurcaba 2021). Without appropriate legal documentation that aligns with their gender identity, trans people are essentially forced to not participate in the social institutions that define our lives (e.g., employment, marriage, school), or to do so inauthentically and without protection from discrimination and violence.

According to a report submitted to the International Lesbian Gay Bisexual Trans and Intersex Association (Mendos, Botha, Lelis, De la Pena, Savalev, & Tan 2020), employment discrimination based on sexual orientation is prohibited in only 81 UN member states – that's less than half of them. This means that Queer people working within the criminal legal system in those countries must constantly fear the loss of their livelihood, regardless of how well they perform their job duties. Until a 2020 Supreme Court ruling fewer than half the states in the United States had banned such discrimination. Queer criminal justice practitioners living in 28 different states could have been fired for their identity alone, which is exactly what happened to Crystal Moore, the openly lesbian police chief of Latta, South Carolina. Moore was fired from her position by Mayor Earl Bullard, a man who made no secret of his antigay beliefs (Collins 2014). Despite the fact that South Carolina allowed for discrimination based on sexual orientation, the citizens of Latta rallied behind Moore – not only did Moore get reinstated, but Bullard was stripped of most of his power by a majority vote in an ad-hoc election. While Moore's case resulted in a victory of sorts, it left her with $20,000 in legal bills and does not change the fact that Bullard was completely within his rights to fire her based on her sexuality. Despite the newly amended federal law, Queer employees in the United States still face discrimination in the hiring process, and while on the job, harassment and abuse in the workplace (James, Herman, Rankin, Keisling, Mottet, & Anafi 2016; Sears & Mallory 2011).

Same-sex couples can legally marry in 28 countries and can join in some sort of civil union in 34 others – altogether that is 33 percent of UN member countries and more than double what we reported in the first edition of this book (Mendos et al. 2020). The Netherlands became the first country to legislate marriage equality as recently as 2000, followed three years later by Belgium (Pew Research Center 2013). Though the wave of legal marriage equality around the world has been seen as a victory for gay rights, the increasing recognition of same-sex marriage is not without negative consequence, as there has been notable backlash. Immediately before France legalized same-sex marriage in 2013, more than 45,000 citizens rallied against the proposed legislation – just one of dozens of demonstrations that required the presence of police suited in riot gear (Erlanger & Sayare 2013). The legislation was followed by a startling uptick in anti-LGBTQ violence, with the group *SOS Homophobie* reporting a 78 percent increase in homophobic incidents (3,500 in total) from the year prior (Potts 2014).

In the United States, where all states now have marriage equality, there has also been considerable backlash. Some nonviolent examples of this backlash were shared in Chapter 2, but lesbian, gay and bisexual citizens who have married legally have also faced some blatantly violent physical repercussions. For example, only nine days after marrying her female partner and being featured on local television stations as a result, a 28-year-old, Michigan woman was beaten unconscious by a group of men who yelled "Hey bitch, aren't you that faggot from the news?" (Ferrigno 2014). The victim's marriage was one of around 300 that occurred the day after a district court judge ruled the state's ban on same-sex marriage unconstitutional – just 24 hours later, a stay prevented any more marriages from occurring and the state's ban was upheld until the Supreme Court ruled same-sex marriage legal in June 2015. Despite the crime clearly being related to the victim's sexual orientation, Michigan's hate crime law would not apply even if her assailants were caught, as it does not include sexual orientation as a protected status.

Before even reaching the age of employability or being able to (possibly) marry, Queer youth face rampant discrimination and violence in school (Kosciw, Clark, Truong, & Zongrone 2020). According to the 2019 school climate survey, conducted by the Gay Lesbian and Straight Education Network (GLSEN), over half of LGBTQ students do not feel safe at school because of their sexual orientation and 42.5 percent do not feel safe as a result of their gender expression (Kosciw et al. 2020). This feeling of unease is perpetuated by negative comments and language regarding sexual and gender identity, over half of which students report hearing from school faculty and staff, and is validated by experiences of physical and violent attacks. Consequently, Queer students who experience victimization miss more school, have lower GPAs, experience greater rates of depression, report low levels of self-esteem, and are less likely to pursue college than their peers who do not experience victimization. All of these experiences contribute to the unique pathways that impact Queer youth, and in turn result in disproportionate interactions with police, courts, and eventually corrections within the criminal legal system.

In addition to being at greater risk of victimization, Queer youth may also be labeled as "offenders" more often than non-Queer youth and, consequently, may be disproportionately funneled into the school-to-prison pipeline (Himmelstein & Bruckner 2011; Kosciw et al. 2020; Snapp, Hoenig, Fields, & Russell 2014). Himmelstein and Bruckner (2011) found that Queer youth, especially non-heterosexual females, were more likely than their heterosexual peers to face a variety of sanctions including expulsion, arrest, detainment, and conviction. Another study by Snapp et al. (2014) contextualized these findings with examples of Queer youth being disproportionately punished for an array of behaviors including public displays of affection (both actual and rumored), violating school dress code, defending themselves from bullies, and truancy (which may of course be related to the aforementioned victimization). A brief released by the Gay-Straight Alliance Network (Burdge, Licona, & Hyemingway 2014) reveals that LGBT youth of color perceive themselves to be under greater surveillance by school police officers, faculty, and other school officials than their non-Queer peers, a finding not inconsistent with what is already known about racial disparity in the school-to-prison pipeline. Once again, the significance of intersectionality is revealed.

While on the surface, one's rights to authentic legal recognition, non-discriminatory employment, marriage, and safe schools seem to be civil issues, they are deeply entwined with the criminal legal system. As long as trans people are denied the right to be legally and authentically recognized, there is an increased chance that they will avoid or be denied access to social institutions, which may lead to an increased likelihood of criminal behavior – for example, engaging in survival crimes in lieu of legitimate employment. As long as there are no employment protections for sexual or gender minorities, Queer criminal legal practitioners will not have job security. As long as marriage equality (and other civil rights denied to Queer people) continues to divide people around the world, law enforcement will be left with the responsibility of policing protest and attending to the victims of backlash. As long as Queer youth are disproportionately funneled into the school-to-prison pipeline, the criminal legal system has no hope of fixing the vicious cycle of mass incarceration. Thus, the advancement of Queer rights in the civil arena should be of central concern to criminal legal practitioners and criminologists, but it cannot be left in their hands alone to protect the Queer community or to forge the fight for sexual and gender equality.

The advancement of Queer rights is largely due to and dependent upon LGBTI advocacy groups around the globe, and these organizations receive a majority of their financial support from philanthropic foundations and governments located in the global North, particularly from the United States and Western Europe (Wallace, Nepon, &

Postic 2020). A study by Funders for LGBTQ Issues (Wallace et al. 2020) found that of the roughly $560 million supporting LGBTI organizations in 2017 and 2018, 58 percent stayed in the global North (which constitutes only 7 percent of the global population), 31 percent went to countries in the East and the global South, and 11 percent was given to organizations whose work spans multiple countries or regions. Though $560 million may seem like a substantial amount of money no matter how it is divvied up, it is really just a drop in the bucket. It constitutes only 31 cents of every $100 spent by global foundations and only 4 cents for every $100 donated by governments. This funding is crucial, as many LGBTI-serving organizations operate with few or no paid employees and most, especially outside of the global North, are newly established (Espinoza 2007) and are unregistered out of fear of repercussions or because the governments under which they operate have placed barriers upon them (Daly 2018). Domestic and international communities are truly at a crossroads in terms of LGBTQ+ rights. More than ever before, identity politics are playing out around the world and the results of that battle remain to be seen. Legal scholars continue to debate the role that legal decisions regarding civil rights will have for the overall advancement of Queer equality (Keck 2009). As illuminated here and in Chapter 2, there is no doubt that backlash does occur in the immediate wake of pro-LGBTQ+ legal decisions, but there is not a consensus about whether this backlash is simply an inevitable hiccup that will eventually dissipate, or if it can have a long-term and devastating effect on the overall path to equality. Some have argued that the magnitude of this backlash has been overstated. In his analysis of same-sex marriage decisions (and the resulting backlash) in the United States, Keck (2009: 182) concludes that "the backlash narrative captures several important features of the recent history of LGBT rights litigation, but it does not support the sweeping and one-sided conclusions that have often been drawn from it." Whichever is truly the case, there is no denying that Queer people continue to take two steps forward and then find themselves forced to take one step back in regards to their equal rights. Moreover, the backlash that clearly exists, no matter how temporary, does affect social attitudes and therefore has an immediate effect on the treatment of Queer people in social institutions, including as employees, jurors, defendants, and victims in a court of law.

Queer experiences in the courtroom

While research on Queer experiences in the courtroom is scant, it is safe to say that "challenges linked to sexuality and gender identity in criminal courts can compromise legitimacy and fairness in the criminal justice system" (Woods 2019: 77). Whether as lawyers, judges, jurors, defendants, civil litigants, or victims, Queer people that find themselves in a court of law face widespread homophobia and discrimination (Brower 2011; Cramer 2002; Farr 2000; Lee 2013; Meidinger 2012; Mogul 2005; Mogul, Ritchie, & Whitlock 2011; Shay 2014; Shortnacy 2001: Woods 2019). The first large-scale exploration into courtroom bias regarding sexual orientation was conducted by the *Sexual Orientation Fairness Subcommittee* (SOFS 2001) of the *Access and Fairness Advisory Committee* of the Judicial Council in California in 1998 and 1999. The subcommittee used information garnered from five focus groups to develop a survey instrument that they distributed to gay and lesbian court users (n=1,225) and employees of all sexual orientations (n=1,525). Though most of the court users felt that they were treated the same as their heterosexual counterparts, over half (56 percent) reported experiencing or seeing negative comments or actions against gays and lesbians. Most of those negative experiences were reportedly felt when sexual orientation became an issue in relation to the case and most of the negative comments or actions were made by lawyers or court employees, not other court users. Of the court employees, 20 percent reported hearing derogatory comments or jokes about gays or lesbians, most often made by lawyers and judges – almost half did not report the behavior that they witnessed to anyone.

It is perhaps, though, not the people who responded to the survey that reveal the most about the courtroom atmosphere, but rather those that chose not to complete the survey, such as one court employee who replied: "I have received your survey on sexual orientation and found it to be degrading and offensive .... I am sure the Judicial Council could find better use of the talent, time and money that is being wasted on a minority of court personnel" (SOFS 2001: 13).

That there were any individuals unwilling to complete the survey because the mere thought of doing so was repulsive and/or a waste of their time suggests that anti-Queer sentiment in the courtroom is even more pervasive than the study revealed.

In 1997, a similar but smaller study conducted by the Arizona State Bar of the Board of Governors created a *Task Force on Gay and Lesbian Issues* to assess the experiences of gays and lesbians in Arizona courtrooms (Cramer 2002). The Task Force sent surveys to 291 judges (29 percent response rate), 450 attorneys (29 percent response rate), 465 law students at one University (22 percent response rate), 476 law students at another University (12 percent response rate), and 800 Queer community members (48 percent response rate). The results were bleaker than the California study. Seventy seven percent of judges and lawyers reported hearing disparaging remarks about gays and lesbians, often in public areas of the courthouse. Even more law students (90 percent) reported hearing negative comments. Based on these findings and further evidence of discriminatory treatment (e.g. 13 percent of judges reported negative treatment of gays and lesbians in open court), the Task Force concluded that these incidents of negative treatment were significant and in need of being addressed via mandated education on sexual diversity for court employees. Subsequently, the State Bar added this component to an existing required course on professionalism and the Arizona Supreme Court included sexual orientation to their Ethical Rule against manifesting prejudice.

In a more general sense and much like many members of the public, gay men and lesbians are most likely to find themselves in a court of law as a result of jury duty (Brower 2011). As only some jurisdictions disallow peremptory strikes based on sexual orientation, potential gay, lesbian, and bisexual jurors (and realistically trans jurors) have reason to fear unwanted "outing" or expect discrimination in the voir dire process (Shay 2014). Conversely, Queer defendants could benefit from a voir dire process that questions a potential juror's biases regarding sexuality and gender identity. Thus, the voir dire process is of great significance to the outcomes of the cases that actually result in a jury trial. As Brower (2011: 672) points out, these "experiences shape how gay people perceive the quality of justice and access to the judicial system" including, presumably, how they will be treated as defendants or victims.

The biases and discrimination that Queer people face in larger society follow them into the courtroom, especially if they are facing charges for sexual offenses. Queer sex offenders are often overcharged and, consequently, accept unfair plea deals (Mogul et al. 2011). Prosecutorial discretion is especially problematic for Queer youth who find themselves charged with statutory rape because they are not extended the "Romeo and Juliet" exception afforded to heterosexual youth by most states (Meidinger 2012).

The "Romeo and Juliet" exception is when the defendant and the victim are close in age, engaged in clearly consensual sex, and are perceived to be committed to one another – some states actually define a range of age differences that would be deemed acceptable in this sort of situation. The problem is that prosecutors are less likely to perceive Queer youth to be in "appropriate" committed relationships, and the legally defined age ranges often exclude same-sex encounters. For example, Texas, Alabama, and California all have age range exceptions for statutory rape, but all of them explicitly apply to heterosexual youth only, meaning that Queer youth face harsher punishment for engaging in the same behaviors as their heterosexual peers (Meidinger 2012). Considering the survey findings from California and Arizona, it is safe to assume that the decisions that prosecutors make are couched in negative attitudes towards Queer citizens and are more than likely based on personal beliefs regarding what is or is not "appropriate."

A striking example of this is the Kansas case involving Matthew Limon, a developmentally disabled 18-year-old (ACLU 2005; Meidinger 2012). While attending a residential school for the developmentally disabled, Limon had consensual oral sex with a young man who was 15 – just over three years younger than him. In Kansas, the Romeo and Juliet law can reduce the severity of punishment in cases of consensual sex where the victim is between 14 and 16 years old, the offender is under the age of 19, the victim and offender have no more than a four-year age gap, and the victim and offender "are members of the opposite sex." Because the Romeo and Juliet law didn't apply to Limon's case solely because of the "opposite sex" distinction, he was convicted of sodomy and sentenced to 17 years and two months in prison and ordered to register as a sex offender. Had he engaged in heterosexual sex and thus been able to use the Romeo and Juliet law, Limon would have served approximately 15 months for his crime and would have avoided the stigma of registering as a sex offender altogether. Limon's experience is a disheartening example of where discrimination has been literally codified in the law.

Another example of selective prosecution is in cases of rape by "deception" or "gender fraud," several of which were described in Chapter 2. Transgender men have been prosecuted for rape by deception in Israel, the United States, and more recently in the United Kingdom, where there have been five such prosecutions since 2012 (Ellin 2019; Sharpe 2015; Sharpe 2017). In each of these cases cisgender women had consensual sex with transgender men, sometimes multiple times and in the context of a committed relationship, later claiming that they were unaware of their partner's sex assigned at birth and, had they been, they would not have consented to sex. These prosecutions are problematic for several reasons.

One problem lies with the basic premise of the "deception" claim, which relies on the assumption that a transgender man is not a man (Sharpe 2015). The plaintiffs in these cases claim that they would not have had sex with the defendant if they had known they "weren't men." As Sharpe (2015: 385) points out, such a claim "constitutes nothing less than the ontological degradation of transgender people." From the defendant's perspective, there is no deception. That is, they identify as male and therefore presented themselves as male to the plaintiff (and others), thus the only thing they withheld is their gender history, not their *actual gender identity*.

Another significant problem with the prosecution of cases of rape by "gender fraud," and one that impacts the criminal legal system more broadly, is the notion of "harm" (Sharpe 2015). Central to the fact that these are *criminal* trials is a presumption that a *harm* has occurred. The question then becomes, what is the harm? No physical or diagnosed psychological harm was reported in any of these cases, and the plaintiffs admit that they did in fact have consensual sex with the man (who happens to be transgender) that they intended to. Thus, the only "harm" presented was "feelings of distress, disgust, or revulsion" or, as one plaintiff put it, feeling "literally sickened" (Sharpe 2015: 389). To prosecute someone for the "harm" of offending another person is a very slippery slope. Furthermore, the facts of these cases suggest that the defendants may very well have been in harm's way themselves, had they revealed that they were transgender. Like the Limon case described above, these prosecutions are not so much about protecting a victim from actual harm or even about what the offender did – simply, it is about *who* the offender is.

Even when laws do not discriminate between offenders, court-rooms around the globe are still shrouded in homophobia. These attitudes have a real effect on sentencing outcomes for Queer offenders, sometimes even resulting in the most severe form of punishment – the death penalty (Farr 2000; Mogul 2005; Shortnacy 2001). According to Mogul (2005), for example, 40 percent of women on death row in the United States were implied to be lesbians during their trials, no doubt because prosecutors know that some jurors are likely to hold negative attitudes towards Queer defendants, as evidenced in the findings above. In fact, jurors are three times more likely to be biased towards gay litigants than they are towards Blacks, Asians, Hispanics, and whites (Brower 2011).

It may well have been this bias that sent Bernina Mata to death row in 1999 for stabbing a man to death. Her prosecutor mentioned her sexuality during her bond hearing, before the grand jury, and during a motion to suppress evidence hearing. Additionally, the prosecution insisted that her lesbianism was the motive for the murder. Ten different witnesses were called to testify to her sexual orientation, lesbian-themed books from her home were entered as evidence, and the prosecution mentioned her sexuality 17 different times during their closing arguments (Mogul 2005). During her trial, in open court, Prosecutor Troy Owens made his intention quite clear:

> We are trying to show that [Bernina Mata] has a motive to com-
> mit this crime in that she is a hard core lesbian, and that is why
> she reacted to Mr. Draheim's behavior in this way. A normal

heterosexual woman would not be offended by such conduct as to murder.

Mogul 2005: 473

Unfortunately, Mata's treatment in court is not unique. Characterizing female offenders as man-hating lesbians or as defying traditional gender roles (i.e. being "manly"), at least in capital cases, is well documented (Farr 2000; Mogul 2005; Shortnacy 2001). The media and courtroom descriptions of some female offenders (murderers in particular) are reminiscent of Hollywood movie trailers, such as in the case of Australian Tracey Wigginton, who was also convicted of stabbing a man to death. Upon her release from prison, one *Herald Sun* headline proclaimed: "Satanic lesbian vampire killer Tracey Wigginton terrified Australians in gruesome 1990s trial" (Hunt 2013). A basic Internet search for Wigginton reveals that nearly every article and book written about Wigginton refers to her as a "lesbian vampire killer."

In 2007, similar language was used by the media to describe a group of young, Black lesbians who defended themselves against the unwanted sexual advances of Dwayne Buckle, a case introduced earlier in the book. When the young women, who are now known as the New Jersey 4, told him they were not interested, he reportedly called them "fucking dykes" and told them that he would "fuck them straight." The women went on to say that Buckle spit and threw a cigarette at them and grabbed one of them by the throat before they defended themselves (Italiano 2007). Even Italiano's (2007) description of this case, which outlined the gory details surrounding the incident, used disparaging language about the women involved.

HEADLINE: ATTACK OF THE KILLER LESBIANS

Next thing he knew, he was encircled, beaten and knifed in the gut right there on a Greenwich Village sidewalk – by seven bloodthirsty young lesbians.

Laura Italiano, New York Post, 2007

These descriptions are not without consequence, and lead to capital convictions in cases that would not typically be tried as such (i.e.

murders of individuals, usually known intimately by the offender, by offenders with little to no prior record). In her study of media depictions of death row inmates, Farr (2000: 63) concludes that "the cases are linked through portrayals of the perpetrators as embodiments of defeminized and dehumanized female evil for whom chivalry must be forfeited and the most severe punishment delivered."

In the United States, the most famous use of a woman's lesbianism as fodder for the prosecution was the case of Aileen Wuornos, a sex worker who, between 1989 and 1990, shot and killed seven men believed to be her customers. Wuornos has become one of the most widely recognized criminals in history not just because she is one of the world's few female serial killers, but because her story became the center of a media-fueled frenzy and the topic of dozens of books, a musical opera, television programs, songs, poems, documentaries, and films, including the award-winning Hollywood movie *Monster* starring Charlize Theron. Chesney-Lind and Eliason (2006) point out that the film's depiction of Wuornos is entrenched in stereotypes about female masculinity and lesbianism, in large part to convince the audience that she is evil and unworthy of sympathy, despite the fact that the actual evidence in the case suggests that her crimes were acts of self-defense or related to violence-induced post-traumatic stress disorder. "After all," they note, "a lesbian prostitute that murders men seeking sex from her confirms many popular, heterosexist notions about the relationship between lesbianism, masculinity, and female violence" (Chesney-Lind & Eliason 2006: 39–40). Wuornos was sentenced to death and was executed by lethal injection on October 9, 2002.

Women are not alone in having their sexuality (or presumed sexuality) and gender nonconformity used as evidence against them or as speculation by the prosecution (Shortnacy 2001). Calvin Burdine's sexuality, for example, may have been the proverbial nail in his coffin. In 1983, Burdine was convicted of capital murder after a trial that lasted less than 13 hours. During the sentencing phase of the trial, the prosecutor addressed the jury, telling them that "sending a homosexual to the penitentiary certainly isn't a very bad punishment for a homosexual, and that's what he's asking you to do" (Shortnacy 2001: 347). This statement was preceded by the prosecutor failing to remove jurors that expressed homophobic attitudes and by Burdine's prior consensual sodomy conviction being entered into evidence. Burdine was sentenced to death, but did eventually have a successful appeal – not on the grounds of prosecutorial prejudice or misconduct, but because his lawyer slept through much of his short trial. Consequently, he then pleaded guilty in exchange for three life sentences (Weinstein 2003). The prosecutor's comments during trial regarding Burdine's sexual orientation and the assumption that prison is a sexual playground for Queer identified offenders speaks to the stereotypes that plague the criminal legal system, especially in the punishment phase. These assumptions and problematics will be addressed in greater detail in Chapter 6.

> I was sure that the police were coming to help me. And when they arrived, they were ready to attack me. They were so quick to … make me the aggressor ….And they were like, "Somebody got stabbed" And I was like, "Yeah, I got stabbed in the face." They didn't care.
>
> CeCe McDonald *Signorile 2014*

Despite the negative experiences of Queer offenders, it is logical to conclude that as cultural attitudes regarding sexuality and gender become more progressive, the Queer community will become more apt to engage the criminal legal system when they find themselves victims to crime (Shay 2014). In general, Queer victims are now receiving more public empathy than they have in the past (Smith 2002), but this doesn't necessarily mean that they will receive equitable or appropriate treatment by the courts, especially if they choose to defend themselves from violence. The case of CeCe McDonald is a harrowing example of a person whose victimization was altogether ignored because she made the choice to fight back against her attacker. In 2011, McDonald, a Black trans woman, was assaulted by a white woman outside of a bar as several people yelled racist and transphobic remarks at her and several companions, including "You niggers need to go back to Africa" and "Look at that boy dressed as a girl, tucking his dick in" (Erderly 2014: n.p.). Her attacker dragged her to the ground and slashed her face with a broken glass. As she tried to leave the scene, her assailant's ex-boyfriend ran after her, and McDonald fatally stabbed him with a pair of scissors. Despite the fact that McDonald's action could be seen as self-defense, she was arrested and charged with murder and, in order to avoid up to 80 years in prison, she pleaded guilty to second-degree murder and served 19 months of a 41-month sentence in a men's prison. Since her arrest, conviction, and subsequent release, McDonald has become an iconic figure in the Queer rights movement and a symbol for exposing and challenging transphobia.

Gay/trans panic

Though much of this book highlights the ways in which Queer experiences with the criminal legal system are shaped by homophobia and heteronormativity, we also must recognize that non-Queer people have attempted to use these systems of denigration to their benefit. One example of this is the "gay panic" or "trans panic" defense, which has been used by some defendants to justify violent crimes against members of the Queer community. The defense is a simple one – the defendant claims that the victim made unwanted sexual advances against them and, in self-defense, the defendant commits an act of violence against the victim (thus warranting a lesser charge). Though there is no data on how many times the gay or trans panic defenses have been used, some suggest that the gay panic defense has been employed approximately 45 times in the United States (Perkiss 2013) and Wodda & Panfil (2015) identified at least 13 uses of the trans panic defense. Formerly called the "homosexual panic" defense, it is thought to have been used first in the case of *People v. Rodriguez* (1967), in which the defendant hit a man in the head (killing him) after the victim supposedly grabbed his genitals while he was urinating in an alley. The defense worked for Rodriguez, inasmuch as he was convicted of second rather than first-degree murder (Perkiss 2013). Two of the most widely publicized cases where a gay or trans panic defense was introduced are those involving victims Lawrence King and Gwen Araujo, both from California.

In 2008, openly gay 15-year-old Larry King of Oxnard, California, was shot twice in the back of his head by 14-year-old classmate Brandon McInerney for supposedly flirting with him and publicly asking him to be his Valentine. The shooting occurred in the school computer lab in front of witnesses, so there was no question that McInerney was guilty of killing Larry. What was under question was whether or not he should be tried as an adult (which he was) and if he was guilty of first-degree murder and a hate crime (as the prosecution contended), or if his "panic" and rage over King's advances made his offense voluntary manslaughter (as the defense contended). It was a question the jurors were apparently not equipped to answer, as it was a hung jury that resulted in a mistrial, perhaps because some of the jurors were sympathetic to McInerney and felt as though he was a victim of Larry's advances.

> Where are the civil rights of the one being taunted by another person that is cross-dressing?
> Diane Michaels, Juror for the Brandon McInerney trial
> *Valentine Road* 2013 [Film]

Rather than face another trial, McInerney plead guilty to second-degree murder and was sentenced to 21 years in prison. Some of the jurors from the trial appeared at his sentencing wearing gray bracelets that read, "Save Brandon" (Barlow 2011). The King/McInerney case was tragic, and not just because a young boy lost his life. The case highlighted the intersections of race, as King was of mixed race and McInerney was supposedly dabbling in neo-Nazi propaganda; class, as both boys lived in extreme poverty (indeed, Larry was living in an emergency shelter at the time); and age, as the jurors struggled with the notion of sentencing a 14-year-old as an adult. In many ways, both boys were victims – they had both experienced lives of violence and a failed system, and they both serve as reminders of the complexity of victimization, offending, and punishment.

Gwen Araujo is perhaps the most famous transgender murder victim that the United States has seen since the murder of Brandon Teena (see Chapter 3), in part due to the award-winning Lifetime channel made-for-television movie *A Girl Like Me: The Gwen Araujo Story*. In 2002, Gwen was just 17 years old when four men beat and strangled her to death and buried her in a shallow grave after discovering that she had male genitalia. Gwen had allegedly had sexual relations with two of the men – Jose Merel and Michael Magidson – whose attorneys were able to convince a second jury (the first trial ended in a hung jury) that they had been "reasonably provoked" by Gwen's "deception" (Lee 2013: 828). It is not surprising that panic defenses work in cases like Merel and Magidson, since murders of Queer people (particularly of trans folks) are often framed by the media as being the direct result of the victim's "deception." For example, in an article about Gwen's murder, Merel's mother said, "If you find out the beautiful woman you're with is really a man, I think it would make any man go crazy" (Wodda & Panfil 2015: 952). In their review of news articles concerning the murders of trans people between 1990 and 2005, Schilt and Westbrook (2009) found that journalists framed 56 percent of the violence to be connected to sexual encounters whereby the offender felt "tricked" or "duped" by the victim.

Both men were convicted of second-degree murder and were acquitted of the hate crime charges that had been brought against them. They were sentenced to 15 years to life in prison. The other two men involved – Jason Cazares and Jaron Nabors – pleaded no contest and guilty, respectively, to manslaughter, and received sentences of six and eleven years. It was anger over these sentences that led to the 2006 passing of the Gwen Araujo Justice for Victims Act, which bans the use of "panic strategies" as courtroom defenses. The Act effectively made California the first state to ban the use of gay and trans panic defenses in criminal trials. Since then, at least eight more states and the District of Columbia have banned the use of gay/trans panic defenses (Associated Press 2020).

While the gay panic defense may be used as an attempt to skirt harsh punishment, federal and state hate crime laws are intended to mete out harsher punishments to those whose crimes are motivated by hate. According to the FBI's hate crime statistics, United States law enforcement agencies reported 1,303 hate crime offenses based on sexual orientation bias and 131 based on gender identity bias in 2017, constituting approximately 17.6 percent of all hate crimes reported in that year. While shocking, these statistics are grossly underestimated and are at odds with other sources. While the FBI only reports that two of the hate-motivated murders in 2017 were related to sexual orientation (and zero related to gender identity), the National Coalition of Anti-Violence Programs (Tillery, Ray, Cruz, & Waters 2018) reported

52 antigay or antitransgender hate-related homicides in the same year. According to the NCAVP, this was an 86 percent increase from the previous year, and 40 percent of the victims were transgender women of color.

Though hate crimes are being increasingly recognized around the globe, "the United States has been at the international forefront of developing hate crime legislation and policy," beginning with the Civil Rights Act of 1968 (Chakraborti & Garland 2015: 142). The Matthew Shepard and James Byrd, Jr. Hate Crimes Prevention Act (hereafter referred to as the HCPA) was passed in 2009, giving the federal government more leverage in the prosecution of crimes involving bodily harm due to someone's race, color, religion, national origin, disability, sexual orientation, and gender identity, especially where state-level hate crime laws fall short. Both of the men that the HCPA memorialized were violently murdered in 1998 – Matthew died from injuries he sustained when two men beat him and tied him to a fence post because he was a gay man, and James (who was Black) died from being tied to the back of pick-up truck by three white supremacists and dragged several miles.

Currently, there are 46 states that have their own hate crime statutes, but 15 of those states do not include sexual orientation or gender identity as protected characteristics, and most of the remaining states only recognize one or the other (Human Rights Campaign 2020). There are 42 other countries (most of them in Europe) that consider hate crimes related to sexual orientation to be an aggravating circumstance (Mendos 2019). Spain became the first to do so in 1998 (Itaborahy & Zhu 2014), and scholars continue to urge other countries to follow suit (Prunas, Clerici, Gentile, Muccino, Veneroni, & Zoja 2014). There are 39 countries that have banned "incitement of hatred" based on sexual orientation, effectively prohibiting hate speech (Mendos 2019). It is fear of this sort of legislation that has led to challenges of the constitutionality of the HCPA in the United States, including in the 2012 Michigan case of *Glenn v. Holder* (2012).

Gary Glenn (then President of the American Family Association of Michigan) and his co-plaintiffs (all pastors at Christian churches) alleged that the HCPA violated their rights to freedom of speech in regard to their "opposition to homosexuality, homosexual activism, and the homosexual agenda" (see *Glenn v. Holder* 2012). Though the plaintiffs did not act or intend to act violently against gays or lesbians, they argued that the HCPA would cause them to be placed under unwarranted surveillance as a result of their vocal beliefs. The Attorney General's request to dismiss the case was granted, and it appears that Glenn's right to freedom of speech was not affected by the HCPA in the least, as he went on to win a seat in the Michigan House of Representatives (2015–2018) and was co-author of Michigan's constitutional ban on same-sex marriage. His political website boasted that "I'll use my god-given abilities to benefit all Michigan citizens" (Glenn n.d.) – unless, it appears, if they're gay.

Criticisms of the HCPA (and similar state laws) are not, however, limited to extremists who feel that their hateful rhetoric will be threatened. Whether good or bad, hate crime laws do raise complex definitional and judicial issues that should not be ignored (Chakraborti & Garland 2015). Perhaps the most basic academic debate is over the very term "hate crime," as some have argued that many acts that could be considered hate crimes are not necessarily committed out of hate (an *emotion*), but as the result of one's prejudiced or biased *disposition* (Garland & Chakraborti 2012). Moreover, one could easily argue that hate is an element in some crimes that would not fit under the legal rubric of "hate crimes" – for example, someone who kills their spouse's lover.

In her overview of psychology-based objections to hate crime laws, Sullaway (2004) outlines the potential difficulties of measuring bias and intent in hate crimes as distinct or different from the bias and intent found in "non-hate" related crimes. She also points out that it is impossible to prove a causal relationship between one's prejudicial attitudes and actions so, even if you use one of the psychological assessments of bias that are available to measure a defendant's disposition, it wouldn't necessarily prove the commission of a hate crime, per se.

Meyer (2014) makes a compelling argument for the rejection of hate crime laws based on the misleading message they send to the public – that is, that the criminal legal system is a solution to prejudicial violence, which, as described throughout this book, has long been meted out by the state. Hate crime laws, he points out, only serve to expand the prosecutorial power of the state, which is counter to the goals of the Queer rights movement and to the reduction of social inequality. Anti-Queer violence is often couched in intersectional issues like race and class, thus the narrow focus of hate crime laws ignores the gamut of variables that determines who is at greatest risk of being a victim of such crimes. Moreover, it is the people most at risk of being a hate crime victim – that is, impoverished Queer (especially transgender) people of color – who will be disproportionately affected by the expansion of surveillance powers police are afforded through the HCPA. These worries echo trepidation regarding changes to hate crime legislation in the United States. Buist and Stone (2014) highlight Strout's (2012) research that turned attention to the concern of two prominent transgender rights groups, *Black and Pink* and the *Sylvia Rivera Law Project*, who have both contended that changing legislation will do little to combat a change in behavior or attitudes. In other words, "what the law says will not change the condition of vulnerability" (Strout 2012, as cited in Buist & Stone 2014: 39).

Regardless of the utility of hate crime statutes, it is clear that something must be done. Between 2013 and 2019 the Human Rights Campaign recorded the murders of at least 157 transgender or gender non-conforming individuals, nearly all (81 percent) of whom were transgender women of color (Human Rights Campaign 2019). These numbers, of course, do not include murders unidentified by the Human Rights Campaign, and do not include the murders of gay men, lesbians, or other sexual minorities. Hate crime statutes are at best symbolic, and serve in no way to prevent violence against the Queer community. Laws do not deter crime and, as described in the cases above, only sometimes serve to punish those who commit them.

Activities and discussion questions

- Choose one of the cases mentioned in the chapter and conduct your own research to see what else you can learn about the victim, the offender, or related legal proceedings.
- What impact has the media played on the public's perception of Queer people as victims and offenders of crime?
- What can be done to better ensure equal treatment of Queer people in the court systems?

Recommended viewing

A Girl Like Me: The Gwen Araujo Story, 2006. [Film] Directed by Agnieszka Holland. USA: Braun Entertainment Group.

Aileen: Life and Death of a Serial Killer, 2003. [Film] Directed by Nick Broomfield and Joan Churchill. USA: Lafayette Films.

Licensed to Kill, 1997. [Film] Directed by Arthur Dong. USA: Deep Focus Productions.

Monster, 2003. [Film] Directed by Patty Jenkins. USA: Media 8 Entertainment.

Out in the Night, 2014. [Film] Directed by Blair Doroshwalther. USA: ITVS.

Outrage, 2009. [Film] Directed by Kirby Dick. USA: Chain Camera Pictures.

The Case Against 8, 2014. [Film] Directed by Ben Cotner and Ryan White. USA: HBO.

The New Black, 2013. [Film] Directed by Yoruba Richen. USA: Promised Land Film.

Valentine Road, 2013. [Film] Directed by Marta Cunningham. USA: BMP Films.

References

ACLU. 2005. *Limon v. Kansas: Case background.* Accessed from www.aclu.org/lgbt-rights_hiv-aids/limon-v-kansas-case-background.

Associated Press. 2020. Washington passes ban on gay and trans panic defenses for homicide. NBC News, February 28. Accessed from www.nbcnews.com/feature/nbc-out/washington-passes-ban-gay-trans-panic-defenses-homicide-n1144931.

Barlow, Z. 2011. Brandon McInerney sentenced to 21 years in prison for killing Larry King. *Ventura County Star,* December 19. Accessed from www.vcstar.com/news/local-news/crime/judge-sentences-brandon-mcinerney-to-21-years-in.

Brower, Todd. 2011. Twelve angry – and sometimes alienated – men: The experiences and treatment of lesbians and gay men during jury service. *Drake Law Review, 59*: 669–706.

Buist, C.L. & Stone, C. 2014. Transgender victims and offenders: Failures of the United States criminal justice system and the necessity of a queer criminology. *Critical Criminology, 22,* (1): 35–47.

Burdge, H., Licona, A.C., & Hyemingway, Z.T. 2014. *LGBTQ youth of color: Discipline disparities, school push-out, and the school-to-prison pipeline.* San Francisco, CA: Gay-Straight Alliance Network.

Chakraborti, N. & Garland, J. 2015. *Hate crime: Impact, causes, and responses,* 2nd edition. London: Sage.

Chesney-Lind, M. & Eliason, M. 2006. From invisible to incorrigible: The demonization and marginalization of women and girls. *Crime, Media, Culture, 2,* (1): 29–47.

Collins, Jeffery. 2014. Latta, South Carolina rallies for fired lesbian police chief Crystal Moore. *Huffington Post*, July 13. Accessed from www.huffingtonp ost.com/2014/07/13/latta-fired-lesbian-police-chief-_n_5583048.html.

Cramer, A.C. 2002. Discovering and addressing sexual orientation bias in Arizona's legal system. *Journal of Gender, Social Policy & the Law*, 11, (1): 25–37.

Daly, F. 2018. *The global state of LGBTIQ organizing: The right to register.* New York: OutRight Action International.

Ellin, A. 2019. Is sex by deception a form of rape? Laws seeking to elucidate the problem of "rape by fraud." *The New York Times*, April 23. Accessed from www.nytimes.com/2019/04/23/well/mind/is-sex-by-deception-a-form-of-rape.html.

Erderly, S.R. 2014. The transgender crucible. *Rolling Stone*, July 30. Accessed from www.rollingstone.com/culture/news/the-transgender-crucible-20140730.

Erlanger, S. & Sayare, S. 2013. Protests against same-sex marriage bill intensify in France. *The New York Times*, April 22. Accessed from www.nytimes.com/2013/04/23/world/europe/in-france-opposition-to-same-sex-marri age-bill-S

Espinoza, R. 2007. *A global gaze: Lesbian, gay, bisexual, transgender and intersex grantmaking in the global south and east.* New York, NY: Funders for Lesbian and Gay Issues.

Farr, K.A. 2000. Defeminizing and dehumanizing female murderers: Depictions of lesbians on death row. *Women & Criminal Justice*, 11, (1): 49–66.

Ferrigno, L. 2014. Attack after same-sex marriage shines light on Michigan hate crime law. CNN, April 7. Accessed from www.cnn.com/2014/04/05/us/michigan-hate-crime-attack/.

Garland, J. & Chakraborti, N. 2012. Divided by a common concept? Assessing the implications of different conceptualizations of hate crime in the European Union. *European Journal of Criminology, 9*, (10): 38–51.

Glenn, G. n.d. Gary's Pledge. Accessed from www.garyglenn.us/pledge.

Glenn v. Holder. 690 F. 3d 417 (2012).

Himmelstein, K.E.W. & Bruckner, H. 2011. Criminal-justice and school sanctions against nonheterosexual youth: A national longitudinal study. *Pediatrics, 127*, (1): 49–57.

Holroyd, M. 2020. Hungary passes bill ending legal gender recognition for trans citizens. *Euronews*, April 20. Accessed from www.euronews.com/2020/05/20/hungary-passes-bill-ending-legal-gender-recognition-for-trans-citizens

Human Rights Campaign. 2019. A national epidemic: Fatal anti-transgender violence in the United States in 2019. Accessed from www.hrc.org/resources/a-national-epidemic-fatal-anti-trans-violence-in-the-united-sta tes-in-2019.

Human Rights Campaign. 2020. Maps of state laws and policies: State hate crimes. Accessed from www.hrc.org/state_maps.

Human Rights Watch. 2019. "A really high hurdle": Japan's abusive transgender legal recognition process. Accessed from www.hrw.org/report/2019/03/19/really-high-hurdle/japans-abusive-transgender-legal-recognition-process.

Hunt, E. 2013. Satanic lesbian vampire killer Tracey Wigginton terrified Australians in gruesome 1990s trial. *Herald Sun*, March 5. Accessed from www.heraldsun.com.au/news/law-order/evil-act-of-a-satanic-lesbian-vampire-killer/story-fnat7jnn-1226590831480.

Itaborahy, L.P. & Zhu, J. 2014. *State-sponsored homophobia. A world survey of laws: Criminalization, protection & recognition of same-sex love.* Geneva: International Lesbian Gay Bisexual Trans and Intersex Association.

Italiano, L. 2007. Attack of the killer lesbians. *New York Post*, April 12. Accessed from http://nypost.com/2007/04/12/attack-of-the-killer-lesbians/.

James, S.E., Herman, J.L., Rankin, S., Keisling, M., Mottet, L., & Anafi, M., 2016. *The report of the 2015 U.S. transgender survey.* Washington, DC: National Center for Transgender Equality.

Keck, T.M. 2009. Beyond backlash: Assessing the impact of judicial decisions on LGBT rights. *Law & Society Review, 43*, (1): 151–185.

Knight, K. 2019. India's transgender rights law isn't worth celebrating. *The Advocate*, December 5. Accessed from www.advocate.com/commentary/2019/12/05/indias-transgender-rights-law-isnt-worth-celebrating.

Kosciw, J.G., Clark, C.M., Truong, N.L., & Zongrone, A.D. 2020. *The 2019 national school climate survey: The experiences of lesbian, gay, bisexual and transgender youth in our nation's schools.* New York, NY: Gay, Lesbian and Straight Education Network

Lee, C. 2013. Masculinity on Trial: Gay Panic in the Criminal Courtroom. *Southwestern Law Review, 42*: 817–831.

Meidinger, M.H. 2012. Peeking under the covers: Taking a closer look at prosecutorial decision-making involving queer youth and statutory rape. *Boston College Journal of Law & Social Justice, 32*, (2): 421–451.

Mendos, L.R. 2019. *State-sponsored homophobia 2019: Global legislation overview update.* Geneva: International Lesbian, Gay, Bisexual, Trans and Intersex Association (IGLA World).

Mendos, L.R., Botha, K., Lelis, R.C., de la Pena, E.L., Savalev, I., & Tan, D. 2020. *State-sponsored homophobia 2020: Global legislation overview update.* Geneva: International Lesbian, Gay, Bisexual, Trans and Intersex Association (IGLA World).

Meyer, D. 2014. Resisting hate crime discourse: Queer and intersectional challenges to neoliberal hate crime laws. *Critical Criminology, 22*: 113–125.

Mogul, J.L. 2005. The dykier, the butcher, the better: The state's use of homophobia and sexism to execute women in the United States. *New York City Law Review, 8*: 473–493.

Mogul, J.L., Ritchie, A.J., & Whitlock, K. 2011. *Queer (in)justice: The criminalization of LGBT people in the United States*. Boston, MA: Beacon Press.

People v. Rodriguez. 256 Cal. App. 2d 663 (1967).

Perkiss, D.A. 2013. A new strategy for neutralizing the gay panic defense at trial: Lessons from the Lawrence King case. *UCLA Law Review, 60*, (3): 778–824.

Pew Research Center. 2013. Gay marriage around the world. December 19. Accessed from www.pewforum.org/2013/12/19/gay-marriage-around-the-world-2013/.

Potts, A. 2014. France had 78% rise in anti-gay incidents in the year it legalized gay marriage. *Gay Star News*, May 14. Accessed from www.gaystarnews. com/article/france-had-78-rise-anti-gay-incidents-year-it-legalized-gay-marriage140514.

Prunas, A., Clerici, C.A., Gentile, G., Muccino, E., Veneroni, L., & Zoja, R. 2014. Transphobic murders in Italy: An overview of homicides in Milan (Italy) in the past two decades (1993–2012). *Journal of Interpersonal Violence*: 1–14.

Schilt, K. & Westbrook, L. 2009. Doing gender, doing heteronormativity: "Gender normals," transgender people, and the social maintenance of heterosexuality. *Gender & Society, 23*, (4): 440–464.

Sears, B. & Mallory, C. 2011. *Documented evidence of employment discrimination and its effects on LGBT people*. California: The William Institute.

Sexual Orientation Fairness Subcommittee. 2001. *Sexual orientation fairness in the California courts: Final report of the Sexual Orientation Fairness Subcommittee of the Judicial Council's Access and Fairness Advisory Committee*. Published in California.

Sharpe, A. 2015. Sexual intimacy, gender variance, and criminal law. *Nordic Journal of Human Rights, 33*, (4): 380–391.

Sharpe, A. 2017. Queering judgement: The case of gender identity fraud. *The Journal of Criminal Law, 81*, (5): 417–435.

Shay, G. 2014. In the box: Voir dire on LGBT issues in changing times. *Harvard Journal of Law & Gender, 37*: 407–457.

Shortnacy, M.B. 2001. Guilty and gay, a recipe for execution in American courtrooms: Sexual orientation as a tool for prosecutorial misconduct in death penalty cases. *American University Law Review, 51*, (2): 309–365.

Signorile, M. 2014. CeCe McDonald, transgender activist, recalls hate attack, manslaughter case. *Huffington Post*, February 22. Accessed from www.huffingtonpost.com/2014/02/22/cece-mcdonald-manslaughter-case_n_4831677.html.

Smith, A. 2002. The complex uses of sexual orientation in criminal court. *Journal of Gender, Social Policy & the Law, 11*, (1): 101–115.

Snapp, S.D., Hoenig, J.M., Fields, A., & Russell, S.T. 2014. Messy, butch, and queer: LGBTQ youth and the school-to-prison pipeline. *Journal of Adolescent Research, 30*, (1): 57–82.

Strout, J. 2012. The *Massachusetts transgender equal rights bill: Formal legal equality in a transphobic system*. Harvard Journal of Law & Gender, *35*: 515–521.

Sullaway, M. 2004. Psychological perspectives on hate crime laws. *Psychology, Public Policy, and Law, 10*, (3): 250–292.

Tillery, B., Ray, A., Cruz, E., & Waters, E. 2018. *Lesbian, gay, bisexual, transgender, queer, and HIV-affected hate and intimate partner violence in 2017*. New York: National Coalition of Anti-Violence Programs.

Valentine Road, 2013. [Film] Directed by Marta Cunningham. USA: BMP Films

Wallace, A., Nepon, E., & Postic, J. 2020. *2017-2018 Global resources report: Government philanthropic support for LGBTI communities*. New York: Funders for LGBTQ Issues.

Weinstein, H. 2003. Inmate in Texas sleeping-lawyer case pleads guilty. *Los Angeles Times*, June 20. Accessed from http://articles.latimes.com/2003/jun/20/nation/na-sleep20.

Wodda, A. & Panfil, V. 2015. "Don't talk to me about deception": The necessary erosion of the trans * panic defense. *Albany Law Review, 78*, (3): 927–971.

Woods, J.B. 2019. LGBTQ in the courtroom: How gender and sexuality impacts the jury system. In C.J. Najdowski & M.C. Stevenson (eds.). *Criminal juries in the 21st century: Contemporary issues, psychological science, and the law*. New York: Oxford University Press.

Yurcaba, J. 2021. Arizona legislator compares transgender people to farm animals. NBC News, February 13. Accessed from www.nbcnews.com/feature/nbc-out/arizona-legislator-compares-transgender-people-farm-animals-n1257763?fbclid=IwAR3B71VqJJ6zXIdVGfHEEvtQJSy63nVm HZfYfzWzJgFcDCqQtmDqYfy9dLo.

6

QUEER CRIMINOLOGY AND CORRECTIONS

While incarcerated, Queer people face additional barriers that must be addressed. Much like any person who is serving time in jail or prison, Queer inmates are often forgotten and their needs ignored. The explanation for this is often couched within an argument for punishment – the individual has committed a crime and broken the social contract, therefore the offender must be punished. Law-abiding citizens may contend that they are not obligated to concern themselves with the rights of an offender when the assumption is that the offender's behavior failed to respect the boundaries of society. This argument is problematic for several reasons. Theoretically speaking, the correctional literature has paid special attention to four major theories of punishment: retribution, deterrence, rehabilitation, and incapacitation. It can be argued that each of these theories is applied in tandem and in varying degrees when courts punish convicted offenders, but make no mistake, especially since the 1970s and the war on drugs, the United States primarily incapacitates its offenders – incarcerate them and forget them is the prevailing sentiment. So, it should come as no surprise that to the

DOI: 10.4324/9781003165163-6

majority of citizens, the incarcerated are easy to forget, no matter what injustices they face while under the control of the state.

There is little to no information on the specific crimes that Queer people commit, but we contend that Queer people commit the same crimes as any non-Queer-identifying person. However, there should be special consideration given to the social impact that Queer youth and adults experience based solely on their sexual and/or gender identities, such as being kicked out of their homes and/or schools, fired from their jobs, evicted by their landlords, denied health care, and so on that may have a significant impact on Queer offenders. For instance, as we touched on earlier, LGBTQ youth face being kicked out of their homes by bigoted family members; without any alternative housing, these young people often find themselves on the streets (see Holsinger & Hodge 2014; Majd, Marksamer, & Reyes 2009; Moodie-Mills & Gilbert 2014; Movement Advancement Project 2017). Street life can lead to a broad range of criminal acts, from minor vagrancy offenses all the way up to felonious behavior such as prostitution or theft. Once in the system, the likelihood that one will remain in the system increases exponentially. Further, because Queer people may lack the assistance and resources at home and within their communities, this lack of support could contribute to higher recidivism rates than heterosexual or cisgender offenders or in general, offenders who have greater social support.

Before we turn our attention to Queer folks in corrections, we want to take a moment to address other correctional topics that must not be overlooked. First, although most of the research focuses on punishment *behind bars*, this is not to say, of course, that Queer people are not found in all stages of the correctional process – as offenders they certainly may be punished by serving their sentences in the community. If this is the case, probation officers who are already tirelessly overworked would require the appropriate training in order to understand, at the very least, the unique experiences of Queer people under their correctional supervision. For instance, and perhaps especially salient for younger Queer people in the system, they may have more difficulty obtaining housing not only because of their minority status, but because they have been kicked out of their family home. Simply put, Queer people may have heightened difficulty in having familial and/or community support because they are sexual or gender minorities.

Alexi Jones (2021) of the Prison Policy Initiative gathered existing data and research on the unequal treatment of Queer folks in the criminal legal system and the compiled findings provide important insight into the Queer experience within the system. Using the National Survey on Drug Use and Health (NSDUH) data from 2019, and general population data from The Williams Institute, (Jones 2021 n.p.) indicates that the NSDUH data "reveals that [GLB] people on probation and parole are almost twice as likely to be lesbian, gay, or bisexual than people not on probation and parole." The other findings include: men on probation are somewhat more likely to be gay or bisexual (5.7 percent) as men not on probation (4.1 percent), women on probation are nearly three times as likely to be lesbian or bisexual (16.7 percent) as women not on probation (6.3 percent), men on parole are nearly twice as likely to be gay or bisexual (7.9 percent) as men not on parole (4.1 percent). Finally, women on parole are nearly three times as likely to be lesbian or bisexual (17.6 percent) as women not on parole (6.4 percent) (Jones 2021). Before we turn our attention to the experiences of Queer folks who are incarcerated or under correctional supervision, we highlight the Queer correctional officers and their experiences with and within the correctional system.

Queer correctional officers

Much like our discussion on Queer law enforcement officers in Chapter 4's section on "Queer and blue," Queer correctional officers face the same difficulties on the job, and in essence, as officers of the law, they too, are law enforcement officials. However, here we mention specific research and incidents regarding Queer-identified correctional officers only. First, it should be noted that there is little research that has been conducted specifically on prison guards who are Queer. What information that is available has highlighted court proceedings of gay-identified correctional officers who have sued their departments for having been terminated from their jobs because of their sexual orientation, or who have quit their jobs because of the profound amount of harassment they have faced and lack of support that has been offered to them. Two cases in particular are those of Robert Ranger in Canada and Kristin King in the United States.

Correctional officer Robert Ranger, who spent four years working in the Ottawa-Carleton Detention Centre, filed suit based on his continued harassment at the hands of fellow officers. Ranger told the Grievance Settlement Board that during his tenure at the facility he was taunted and the focus of anti-gay jokes and slurs. Facing such harassment led to depression and anxiety. Although the board awarded him nearly $100,000 in compensation, the psychological impact of the experiences remained. During this time, he was offered employment in other areas in corrections, but he felt as though he was being set up for failure because they were jobs that he had little to no knowledge of or skill for (Canadian Press 2013).

In the United States, former Maine correctional officer Kristin King, the only out lesbian guard working the night shift at Downeast Correctional Facility, filed suit noting that she was differentially disciplined and that the "old boy culture of disrespect for women" was pervasive in the prison and therefore made it increasingly difficult for King to perform her duties. Much like Ranger's lawsuit, King cited growing anxiety and panic attacks, migraine headaches, and sleeplessness brought on by stress from her mistreatment (Mack 2013).

In addition to the discrimination and harassment that Ranger and King identified experiencing, it is important to draw attention to the story of Mandi Camille Hauwert, a former controlman in the Navy, who became a correctional officer at San Quentin prison and underwent gender affirmation surgery while on the job. In an opinion editorial in *The Advocate*, she tells her story, indicating that her transition was slow going, but that for the most part her supervisor and prison administrators were supportive. However, there was still a fear and anxiety that Hauwert faced as she wondered how the inmates and her fellow officers would respond. She admits, "I thought I would be fired or dead within a month" (Hauwert 2015: n.p.). Interestingly, Hauwert revealed that it has not been the inmates who have had issues with her transition, even noting that the inmates continue to show her respect. Instead, it had been her fellow officers who were the most intolerant of her transition, commenting that one officer told her that he could not recognize her as a woman because of his religious beliefs. In addition, she continues to deal with some officers calling her by incorrect pronouns and others who refer to her as "it" and "tranny."

Some may argue that it is a given that inmates respect the officer because, regardless of sex or gender presentation, the guard is still their primary agent of social control. Of course, we know this is not always the case. Ask any correctional officer who has been verbally or physically attacked – they are not necessarily automatically respected because of their position of power within the prison. The administration, in this case, was supportive of Hauwert's transition, but her peers were her biggest source of anxiety; and, as indicated in the King case, the old boys network (read: patriarchal, hierarchical, and masculinist) reinforces stereotypes about gender presentation and, in turn, breeds misunderstanding, malcontent, and mistreatment.

Another example of abuse at work was reported in 2021 by Paul Egan of the *Detroit Free Press*, who details the experiences of Bridget Cadena, an officer at Parnall Correctional facility in Jackson, Michigan. Now a former officer, Cadena states that a co-worker outed her as lesbian in front of inmates in the prison, which she argues put her life at risk. In a lawsuit against the Michigan Department of Corrections, Cadena also notes that the same officer who outed her used derogatory language against lesbians and in turn their comments led to threats from some of the incarcerated population. The former officer stated that she was forced to resign because of the mental health issues she experienced not only after the incident and proceeding comments from prisoners, but because she believed the department did not thoroughly investigate the case, although the department argued that they did and in turn did not find sufficient evidence (Egan 2021).

Moving forward, we turn the focus to specific issues associated with the experiences of Queer people in jails and prisons – some of whom are offenders and some of whom are detained yet not considered criminals – namely immigrant asylum seekers. There is a real concern regarding the human rights and civil liberties of Queer people, and prejudiced attitudes and discriminatory behavior is heightened when countries have legal bans and, in turn, legal sanctions up to and including death for "homosexuality." For instance, to revisit Cameroon's "anti-homosexuality law," participants in the Human Rights Watch (2013) report noted that prison guards (warders) beat them while in custody. One victim, "G.M." reported being stripped naked, having their head shaved, and being water-boarded while correctional authorities sang anti-gay songs (Human Rights Watch 2013). Unfortunately, even in more "progressive" countries like the United States, Queer people are targeted based on their sexual orientation and gender identity as well.

First, we will begin with how Queer people are housed and classified in prisons and how the current policies continue to be problematic and damaging to Queer-identified people who are incarcerated. We will then discuss medical issues and the right to transition, followed by an account of rapes and sexual assaults committed against Queer offenders.

Housing and classification

The American Bar Association's (ABA) *Standards on Treatment of Prisoners* states in section 23, 2.2 Part C that "classification and housing decisions, including assignment to particular cells and cellmates, take account of a prisoner's *gender*, age, offense, criminal history, institutional behavior, escape history, *vulnerability*, mental health, and *special needs*, and whether the prisoner is a pretrial detainee" (American Bar Association 2010, emphasis added). As indicated in the emphasized portions of this statement on prisoner classification, the ABA denotes the importance of considering gender in prisoner classification – this is an extremely important point and brings us back to the importance of language as discussed in Chapter 1. First, as you may recall, there is a tendency to conflate the terms sex and gender by incorrectly assuming that these two things are one and the same. However, we know that they are indeed *not* one and the same – remember, sex is a biological distinction, while gender is a social construction. When you are asked to fill out a form that instructs you to identify your gender, then that form has likely conflated the terms sex and gender. The credit card company is not interested in whether or not your gender expression is consistent with your biological sex, they simply want to know if you are legally male or female (we understand that this concept is addressing binaries rather than a sex continuum, but, for this example, the binary examples are necessary).

Therefore, when the ABA states that classification should be based on *gender*, they have conflated the terms in a manner that should be to the benefit of transgender inmates. Today, transgender inmates are most often classified based on their sex assigned at birth or their genitalia, *not* their gender identity, but, according to the ABA, they should in fact be classified by their gender identity. Regardless of the intentionality of the suggested standard, language does matter. The argument here, if this statement is interpreted literally, is that transgender inmates should be classified (and therefore housed) in a prison that represents their gender, not their sex assigned at birth. Conversely, the Bureau of Prisons (BOP) (Bureau of Prisons 2017) does clearly ask for sex on forms, thus there needs to be more education and clarity with regards to how inmates will be classified, and in general a better overall understanding of the differences between the two terms. Various online searches of the BOP did not yield a clear picture of what is required information on the plethora of intake forms, but one search did find a Case Management Activity (CMA) SENTRY[1] Assignment Form for Transgender Inmates which states the following:

> I agree that Bureau of Prisons staff may enter a CMA assignment on SENTRY concerning my gender identity.
> I understand that this CMA assignment will identify me as transgender to all staff members.
> I understand that the purpose of the CMA assignment is to assist staff members in providing programs and taking measures as described in the Program Statement Transgender Offender Manual.
> I understand that specific medical and mental health information will not be disclosed to all staff using the CMA assignment; specific medical and mental health information is maintained separately.
>
> Case Management Activity (CMA)
> SENTRY Assignment Form

One of the major concerns within the corrections branch of the criminal legal system regarding Queer offenders is how to house and classify them once they are in the institution. In general, correctional agencies have a problematic history of prisoner housing and classification with other populations as well, namely the elderly and those who have mental health concerns or are differently abled. The majority of jails and prisons are ill equipped to deal with special populations. Health care is available, but often sparse and lacking specialization, outside staffing are often volunteers who, even when qualified, are not readily available, and corrections officers and administrators lack the training necessary to communicate with and understand the needs of incarcerated men and women who require specialized care. What's more, Queer-identified prisoners often require additional protection while incarcerated and indeed are at a higher risk for victimization. All of this is to say that incarcerated individuals are still considered a protected population (as they should be) in research, and even when granted access, often correctional facilities are not receptive or willing to welcome researchers, even though one of the most effective strategies for implementing positive change in the system would be bridging the gap between researchers and practitioners.

For example, transgender prisoners face unique challenges that other incarcerated people do not experience. Therefore, in addition to the same concerns that most if not all prisoners experience, such as alienation, isolation, and fear, trans prisoners may experience these emotions at a heightened level. In many prisons within the United States, the Department of Corrections (DOC) classifies prisoners based on their sex assigned at birth plus their stage of transition – meaning that regardless of how someone may present or how long they have taken hormones, if the individual has not had gender confirmation surgery, they will be placed in a prison that mirrors their sex assigned at birth. Psychologically, this can be damaging to the incarcerated person as well as being problematic for them regarding both physical safety as well as overall health, depending on the approved prescription of hormones they are allowed and/or counseling that is provided to them. Further, many prisons choose to isolate trans inmates under the guise of protection, yet this seclusion, which is essentially administrative segregation, is problematic because this is often regarded as a punishment for inmates rather than protection (Colopy 2012).

In September 2020, California passed "The Transgender Respect, Agency, and Dignity Act" which details the importance and mandatory use of gender affirming language and overall policy improvements, perhaps the most important being that those who are incarcerated should "Be housed at a correctional facility designated for men or women based on the individual's preference, including, if eligible, at a residential program for individuals under the jurisdiction of the department." (SEC. 4. 2606 (3)).

This legislation may have been passed in part because of the growing number of transgender victimizations in prison, the catalyst perhaps the 2013 murder of Carmen Guerrero by her cellmate, who told prison guards that he would kill Guerrero if she was housed with him. Reports indicate that her murderer strangled her to death after only nine hours of sharing the cell (see Leitsinger 2020). The tragic murder of Carmen Guerrero speaks to the overall lack of policy protecting transgender and gender non-conforming people in corrections. As mentioned, while California's change is a win, at least symbolically, the lack of uniformity in policy across the United States and abroad is another major loss. For instance, in 2018, Connecticut was the first in the United States to house inmates based on their gender identity. Again, while it seems like a victory and in part it is, the 2018 law required individuals to be diagnosed with gender dysphoria or have legal identification that affirms their gender (see Eaton-Robb 2018).

Internationally, there has been some movement towards inclusive policy – England and Wales, some parts of Australia, Canada, Scotland, and elsewhere – but these are not sweeping changes and almost always have a caveat that allows for case-by-case decisions, which we often see in all prisons as decisions are made with security and safety in mind. However decisions made with the concern of safety and security for LGBTQ people, especially transgender and non-binary people, are lacking or missing altogether. In the United States, states began to implement their own changes, but at a federal level, the Bureau of Prisons under former president Trump changed policy to require housing prisoners based solely on sex assigned at birth. When President Joe Biden took office after Trump, he promised to require placement based on gender identity in correctional institutions across the country (see Bali 2020; The Fenway Institute 2019; Human Rights Campaign 2020; Patrickson 2020).

As some institutions are moving towards housing based on gender identity, others have implemented wards or areas in the prison where transgender inmates are placed, including facilities in countries such as Italy, Brazil, and England (see Patrickson 2020). However, more common and dangerous, both physically and mentally, is what we would argue most facilities do, and that is segregate LGBTQ inmates. Although the explanation is often protection of the individual from violence, research has shown prolonged isolation in prison has numerous psychological effects including, but not limited to, paranoia, inability to control emotions, increased risk of suicide, and hallucinations. In most prisons, solitary confinement or segregation isolates the incarcerated in their single cells for up to 23 hours per day. In fact, research on segregation has spawned the development of what is referred to as Security or Special Housing Unit (SHU) Syndrome. Perkinson's (1994) article on California's supermax prison, Pelican Bay, highlighted Grassian's (1983) findings that 80 percent of inmates suffered from some form of SHU syndrome, "in which they become mentally ill or their preexisting conditions are severely exacerbated" (Perkinson 1994: 120). Collins (2004: 16) drew attention to the difficulty of assessing symptoms related to prisoner segregation, but commented "that at least two courts have recognized that conditions of confinement in an ECU [Extended Control Unit] can lead to serious mental injury for some inmates."

Conversely, some research has argued that solitary confinement and segregation may not lead to the long-term psychological damage that others have purported. For example, in a one-year longitudinal study of restrictive housing in the Colorado DOC, O'Keefe, Klebe, Stucker, Sturm, and Leggett (2011) found that while participants did experience symptoms that were consistent with SHU syndrome, some of those symptoms were present before their isolation, and that, in other cases, symptoms improved over time. Hanson (2011) noted that these findings were consistent with her belief that many of the people who are housed in segregated units have psychological problems before they are placed there. What must be considered and made perfectly clear is that transgender inmates are not being placed in isolation because they have displayed harmful behavior or have been diagnosed with a mental illness; rather they are being placed there simply because of their gender identity. Thus, the broader literature on the effects of solitary confinement may not be directly applicable to our understanding of its effects on transgender inmates. Moreover, Hanssens, Moodie-Mills, Ritchie, Spade, and Vaid (2014: 21) argue that, beyond the detrimental emotional and physical effects, protective custody also limits an inmate's "access to education, work, and program opportunities … essential for mental health as well as achieving good time credit and being paroled." Further still, the Prison Rape Elimination Act (PREA) of 2003 restricts segregating an inmate in order to keep them safe, even if officials believe that segregating an individual will keep them safe from the risk of being sexually abused (Browne, Hastings, Kall, & diZerega 2015; Moodie-Mills & Gilbert 2014).

Quite simply, correctional officials have little to no idea what to do with incarcerated Queer folks. This is in some ways understandable as the incarcerated population of self-identified LGBTQ offenders is significantly smaller than heterosexual and cisgender offenders. As of 2018, there were just under seven million people under correctional supervision in the United States (Jones 2021). If we were to approximate that Queer people make up 10 percent of that population, then that would equate to less than 700,000 LGBTQ people who are serving sentences either in the community, in jails, or in state or federal prisons. This statistic, 700,000 people, is no number to scoff at, but we must remember a few things: (1) If we are to enumerate this as it relates to cisgender males and females, we could estimate that over 90 percent of the 700,000 are male. (2) We cannot assume that all of these estimated offenders are open about their sexuality. Certainly, we can also assume that even if they were out in their personal lives, once they are in jail or prison it would most likely behoove them to hide their sexuality, as research has already evidenced the increased likelihood that Queer people will be victimized in prison – we also recognize that this is easier said than done for some. (3) The prison population in the United States alone is approximately 2.3 million men and women, which would decrease the possible number of Queer people in our jails and prisons to approximately 230,000. (4) There are over 3,000 jails in the United States and over 1,800 prisons in the United States that house offenders – therefore, on any given day, thousands of prisoners are held in thousands of institutions ranging from over 2,000 prisoners in the entire state of Wyoming (a sparsely populated state), to over 130,000 in California. Therefore, one would expect that California would be more equipped to address the special needs of Queer inmates than Wyoming would. However, regardless of size, or the inability to accurately assess just how many Queer inmates we have in the United States (especially transgender inmates) it is the responsibility of correctional officials to protect vulnerable populations while incarcerated.[2]

We must also note that, given the examples in the preceding chapters, research strongly suggests that Queer people are disproportionately represented in the criminal legal system and their population in prison may indeed surpass their percentage in society more broadly. However, because of the poor or entirely non-existent record keeping regarding Queer offenders and, subsequently, Queer inmates, this is difficult if not impossible to determine with complete certainty.

Other susceptible populations

In addition to Queer people being a population who are particularly susceptible to victimization in jails and prisons, the disproportionate population of juvenile offenders may be the most vulnerable to this victimization. For instance, Majd et al. (2009) highlighted the 2006 case of *R.G. v. Koller* where three Queer youth petitioned the federal district court for abuses they experienced while under the custody of the Hawai'i Youth Correctional Facility. The court found in the plaintiffs' favor and indicated that correctional authorities failed to protect the juveniles from physical and psychological abuse, isolated the juveniles under the guise of protecting them, did not adequately train officials in order to protect the juveniles, failed to provide appropriate numbers of staff, supervisors, or an acceptable grievance system, and did not have an accurate classification system in place that protected vulnerable juveniles in their facility.

This returns us to the discussion of segregation and isolation as a means of protecting Queer inmates. While the debate will continue regarding segregation's long-term effect on inmates, there is no denying that some inmates do indeed suffer long after they have been released from segregation and released from prison. In their study on LGBT girls in the juvenile justice system, Holsinger and Hodge (2014: 5) contend that we should punish the attackers, and not the victims, by putting them in isolation. They, along with others such as Moodie-Mills and Gilbert (2014), reaffirm PREA standards that express that juveniles should not be isolated as protection. Further, they report on the girls who participated in their study feeling as though they were targeted by officials based solely on their sexual orientation, and, in turn, they were differentially punished by officers and singled out in group sessions about their relationships.

With the disproportionate numbers of Queer youth in the juvenile justice system, it is imperative to develop and implement regulations and safety standards to decrease and eliminate the victimization they experience because of their sexual and/or gender identity. Moodie-Mills and Gilbert (2014) in their report, *Restoring justice: A blueprint for ensuring fairness, safety, and supportive treatment of LGBT youth in the juvenile justice system*, note that 80 percent of juvenile justice officials believe that safety for LGBT juveniles is a major problem and more than half of correctional officials were aware of Queer youth being mistreated based on their sexual orientation or gender identity. Based on their findings, Moodie-Mills and Gilbert (2014: 7) suggest that considerations be made based on sexual orientation and/or gender identity and that housing and classifying "decisions based on placement should be individualized based on youth's physical and emotional well-being and their own perspective about where they will be most secure." We are slowly seeing a move in some institutions towards this sort of classification and housing, but the trauma that Queer youth experience at home, on the streets, and often eventually in detention centers, jails, or prisons is undeniable. Multiple sources continue to report that Queer youth are overrepresented in the juvenile legal system and their pathways to incarceration are often attributed to their experiences with family members and other authority figures such as teachers, medical personal, and police to name only a few. The lack of acceptance and affirmation often contribute to homelessness, school truancy, and survival crimes (see The Fenway Institute 2019; Irvine & Canfield 2016; Jones, J.J. 2021; MAP 2017).

Recalling what was briefly mentioned earlier, one's pathway(s) to crime is vitally important to understand as related to future criminal offending. This is perhaps one of the most important ways to examine not only youth offending but specifically Queer youth, including but not limited to school bullying and how one is treated in school (Semprevivo 2020). Further, the lack of support at home and in general may contribute to the cycle of offending – keeping in mind that once an individual enters the criminal legal system it is nearly impossible to exit, especially for individuals with minority status, be that LGBTQ identity, or the heightened discrimination, fear, and violence experienced by Queer youth of color. These are points that cannot be stressed enough – the intersections of race, class, gender, and sexuality – which in turn have a major impact on violence or other victimization (Kahle, Rosenbaum, & King 2018).

One of the ongoing problems is that departments continue to vary by location and as we have mentioned ad nauseam, the lack of data on Queer youth is surprising, if by "surprising" one means, not-at-all-surprising. In a 2018 commentary from *The Advocate*, Sean Cahill draws attention to the many ways in which LGBT youth are particularly vulnerable in the system and in segregation. The author notes that LGBT youth are almost twice as likely to experience "sexual victimization" in juvenile corrections facilities or detention centers – further the lack of data speaks to the barriers to services for LGBT folks. For example, in

> … some states, such as North Carolina keep no data on LGBT youth in the custody of their juvenile justice systems and have done little to no research on LGBT incarceration, putting this group at a greater risk for physical and sexual assault and ignoring a possible root cause of their delinquent behavior.
>
> Cahill 2018 n.p.

What is even more upsetting is that the director of North Carolina's clinical programs for juvenile detention and juvenile prisons "contends that no transgender youth have come into the facility in the past 15 years – even though nearly 5,000 youth were committed to a state juvenile facility between 2003 and 2016" (Cahill 2018 n.p.). Take a moment to challenge and engage in critical thinking which requires asking questions. The first of these questions must be "who does this benefit?"[3] The "this" often varies, and in this instance the question is: who benefits from keeping information about LGBTQ+ youth from researchers and the general public? Further questions to consider may include the location – the conservative South is often not as apt to cover themselves in rainbows, both literally and figuratively, and North Carolina specifically has a tarnished past in regards to race, class, gender identity, and sexuality. Finally, clearly, the odds of there having been zero transgender youth detained is laughable at best. So, who benefits from these decisions? Certainly not Queer kids.

On a more global scale, migrants who are in immigration detention centers also face issues proving their sexual orientation or gender identity if they choose to undergo what are referred to as "credibility assessments" that are used for LGBTI asylum seekers to ascertain one's sexual orientation and/or gender identity (Tabak & Levitan 2014). Credibility assessments used in this exploration were also considered stereotypical and also relied on "Westernized" ideas of what constitutes being gay. For example, in 2004, the U.S. Board of Immigration Appeals affirmed an immigration judge who found that even though a Mexican man identified as gay, his appearance was not stereotypically gay enough to warrant protection (Tabak & Levitan 2014).

> When detention authorities either engage in or fail to make appropriate measures to respond to physical and sexual violence directed at LGBTI detainees, their actions clearly violate the prohibition of torture or cruel, inhuman, or degrading treatment as defined by applicable human rights instruments.

An example of abuse at a detention center is the case of Laura Monterrosa, a Queer asylum seeker from El Salvador who fled her country because of the homophobic gang violence she feared, so much so that her life had been threatened. The detention center she was placed in, run by CoreCivic, the largest private prison corporation in the country with revenue nearing $2 billion, ignored Monterrosa's report that she had been sexually assaulted by a guard working for U.S. Immigration and Customs Enforcement (ICE) on multiple occasions (see Gruberg 2018). Reporter Sharita Gruberg (2018) included that ICE closed her case for essentially a lack of evidence. The FBI then picked up the case, but Monterrosa remained in ICE custody under the surveillance of the officer who she reported. Monterrosa then attempted suicide and was later placed in isolation where she stated that ICE tried to get her to recant her accusation. Eventually, Monterrosa was released, and ICE was ordered to provide mental health care for her. One of the most evident take-aways from Gruberg's (2018) reporting is that ICE continues to house LGBTQ immigrants and, in doing so, they are susceptible to ongoing victimization including sexual assault and abuse. These ongoing practices, ones that we are aware of and surely countless others we will never know, are not only basic human rights violations but are clear violations of PREA standards.

Medical care and the right to transition

The rights and safety of trans-identified prisoners are real issues within the United States criminal legal system as it can be (and has been) argued that denial of treatment up to and including gender affirming surgery is a violation of the Eighth Amendment's protection from cruel and unusual punishment. Colopy (2012) indeed has noted that the World Professional Association of Transgender Health's (WPATH) Standards of Care argues for what is referred to as the full treatment series for trans inmates that includes psychotherapy, hormone therapy, and gender affirmation surgery. However, what remains especially problematic when researching trans inmates is that we are simply unaware of the number of trans inmates that are in our system. Estimates have been anywhere from 2 inmates to 400 in any given state prison not including trans populations in jails. Certainly, states with higher rates of incarcerations, such as California or New York, would most likely see greater numbers of trans prisoners (Brown 2009).

Before we go into more detail about medical concerns and transitioning in the Department of Corrections in the United States, let us first discuss the Eighth Amendment and unpack how denial of treatment and, as previously mentioned, specialized classification can violate prisoners' rights. It is oft forgotten that when an individual is sentenced, whether that is probation or incarceration, the *sentence* is the punishment. There should be *no additional punishment* that the offender faces while serving the sentence – therefore any pains of punishment that are in addition to the original sentence may in fact violate human rights protections against cruel and unusual punishment as stated in the Constitution. These additional punishments do not include punishments that are meted out based on the behavior of the offender. For instance, if an incarcerated person has broken rules within the prison or while on probation, correctional authorities are within their rights to punish them based on established approved protocol, but even still those punishments should never inflict additional harms against the person that are "grossly disproportionate" to the crime; that are "totally without penalogical justification," that "involve the unnecessary and wanton infliction of pain," and that are "inconsistent with 'evolving standards of decency'" (Dolovich 2009: 884, citing several cases. See *Coker v. Georgia* (1977); *Furman v. Georgia* (1972); *Gregg v. Georgia* (1976); *Kennedy v. Louisiana* (2008); *Trop v. Dulles* (1958)).

What's more, the actual punishment that is imposed also cannot be cruel and unusual. Take for example the death penalty – although we agree that the death penalty is cruel and unusual punishment in and of itself – there are ways by which to enforce this penalty that use the least invasive and the most humane methods (Dolovich 2009). Dolovich (2009: 885) continues by noting: "Indeed any harm prisoners suffer at the hands of the state while incarcerated is typically wholly unrelated to their original offense." Therefore, we absolutely must consider how denial of proper housing, classification, medical treatment, and transition can be considered Eighth Amendment violations.

First, as discussed earlier, by denying proper housing and classification once in prison, this allows for an already vulnerable inmate to be additionally susceptible to violent victimization. Next, instead of addressing the needs of this unique population, many institutions choose to isolate Queer inmates under the guise of protection. Again, this may have detrimental and long-lasting psychological effects on them. Finally, denial of medical treatment or medicine can also result in cruel and unusual punishment because lack of proper medical attention or prescriptions can be both physically and mentally damaging. We must also consider that because there is a class issue within our prisons, there is a distinct possibility that trans folks may not have been medically diagnosed with gender dysphoria (discussed below) or have been medically prescribed hormones or other drugs necessary for their transition prior to their incarceration. Indeed, many trans people obtain their drugs illegally because they do not have the means to seek a professional or afford the proper medication (Lenning & Buist 2012).

This problem is illuminated by the case of Dee Farmer, an incarcerated transgender woman who petitioned the court because, although she presented as a woman, underwent estrogen treatment, and had breast implants prior to her sentencing, she was sent to a maximum-security men's prison in Indiana. Upon arrival, Farmer was held at knifepoint and raped. Responding to her assault, Farmer filed a lawsuit against the "Bureau of Prisons director, the regional director, and other officials, alleging that they knew she would be sexually assaulted at USP-Terre Haute due to her feminine appearance" (Margolin 2014). Eventually, Farmer's suit was selected by the Supreme Court to be one of the less than 1 percent of indigent cases they would hear in 1994 and found in her favor, indicating that prison officials demonstrate "deliberate indifference" if she or he "recklessly disregards a substantial risk of to the prisoner" (ACLU 2012; *Farmer v. Brennan* 1984).

> The core of the mistreatment, harassment, and violence facing transgender people stems from this fundamental theme in the way the public doubts and denies us our true selves.
>
> *Mara Keisling, National Center for*
> *Transgender Equality, Bell 2014*

Another major issue is that in most prisons, transgender inmates must be diagnosed with gender dysphoria before they are allowed any medical care or to maintain a drug protocol (Brown 2009), but as mentioned this may vary depending on the institution itself and based on "individual medical need" (National Commission on Correctional Health Care 2020). Again, this may be an additional fence to jump for trans inmates, as we could contend that many are unable to access or maintain legal and/or medically supervised hormone treatments. The issue of diagnoses highlights a distinct double standard that only trans inmates seem to face. If, for example, a diabetic inmate was unable to afford insulin prior to incarceration, we do not deny that medication to them once incarcerated. Why? Because correctional institutions have a legal obligation to provide reasonable medical care to inmates. Thus, trans inmates are clearly facing discriminatory medical care and, as such, are facing cruel and unusual punishment.

Medical care for trans inmates will continue to be a major issue; however, there have been modest victories for incarcerated transgender folks in the United States within recent years. For instance, in 2011, Wisconsin's anti-trans law, the Inmate Sex Change Prevention Act, was found to be unconstitutional in *Fields v. Smith* (2011) on the grounds that preventing transgender prisoners from accessing transition-related care violated the Eighth Amendment's prohibition against cruel and unusual punishment (Glezer, McNeil, & Binder 2013). Also in 2011, *Adams v. Bureau of Prisons* (2010) reversed the federal "freeze frame" policy that had prevented transgender prisoners from beginning transition-related care unless they could prove that they had already started it prior to incarceration (Glezer et al. 2013). Indeed, *Adams v. BOP* (2010) is an important victory for trans inmates as it prompted a major policy reversal for federal prisons, forcing government to begin guaranteeing access to hormone therapy and other care deemed medically necessary by doctors. Transgender BOP prisoners must now have access to "individualized assessment and evaluation." Also, "current, accepted standards of care will be used as a reference for developing the treatment plan," as outlined in the *Standards of Care* published by the World Professional Association for Transgender Health (2012). Finally, "treatment options will not be precluded solely due to level of services received, or lack of services, prior to incarceration." This tosses out the BOP's former "freeze frame" policy, whereby officials could refuse transition-related care for prisoners who could not prove they had started such treatment before being incarcerated. Such arbitrary, blanket bans of health care have been repeatedly found to be unconstitutional (Colopy 2012; Glezer et al. 2013).

One of the most noteworthy victories in recent years was the 2012 ruling that Massachusetts inmate Michelle Kosilek would receive gender affirmation surgery because the "state's failure to provide it … violate[d] the Eighth Amendment protection against cruel and unusual punishment" (Ellement & Anderson 2014). However, this was a short-lived victory. As of December 2014, the court's ruling had been overturned and now Kosilek will not be granted gender affirmation surgery. Although correctional authorities have conceded to the legitimacy of Kosilek's gender identity, providing her with medical care, women's clothing, facial hair removal, hormones, and other personal property, the higher court found that this was adequate. Judge Thompson's dissent attacked the antiquated and often inaccurate ways in which society views sex and gender, stating that "the precedent the majority creates is damaging … it … aggrieves an already marginalized community, and enables correctional systems to further postpone their adjustment to the crumbling gender binary" (as cited in Ellement & Anderson 2014).

Judge Thompson's comments speak volumes to the problems associated with how detrimental to trans inmates this decision may be. Yes, it does matter that prison officials recognized Kosilek's gender identity and have acted in ways that respect and reaffirm that identity, but not to the extent by which it should. To force a woman to live out the rest of her life (Kosilek is serving a life sentence) in an all-male institution is the definition of deliberate indifference to the harm that has been done to Kosilek and the potential harm that may further be inflicted. This is something that must be considered for all transgender prisoners who wish to complete gender affirming surgery.

As of 2018, Kosilek was still fighting for transfer to a women's prison and potentially gender affirming surgery, although no new information is found. In general, however, there have been cases of gender affirming surgeries of incarcerated individuals across the United States but the numbers are small and appear to have gained only minimal momentum since 2017. California, which was the first state to approve gender confirmation surgeries for transgender inmates, has received 205 requests for surgery since 2015 (Miller 2021). Of those requests 65 have been approved, but so far only nine surgeries have actually been completed. Two hundred and sixty-one prisoners have submitted requests to transfer to facilities that align with their gender identity.

As decisions change throughout the world regarding gender affirming surgery for those who are incarcerated, the argument, as mentioned, often goes back to the Eighth Amendment with the focus on cruel and unusual punishment. As we will discuss below, and we cannot reiterate it enough – one's sentence should be the only punishment they receive – denying surgery can lead to violence including suicide, body mutilation, and mental health crisis.

Rape and sexual assault in prison

Prisoners in the United States and abroad face additional punishment and pains of imprisonment in addition to their original sentencing – one such abuse that those incarcerated experience is sexual violence. Just Detention International (JDI) reports that approximately 200,000 prisoners (including children) have been the victims of sexual abuse while held in United States prisons, with half of the assaults occurring at the hands of prison staff (Beck, Berzofsky, & Krebs 2013; Beck & Johnson 2012; JDI 2015). While being raped in prison is often the punch-line to pop culture's sick joke ("Don't drop the soap!"), this is a very real problem, so much so that PREA was enacted specifically to "provide for the analysis of the incidence and effects of prison rape in Federal, State, and local institutions and to provide information, resources, recommendations, and funding to protect individuals from prison rape" (Prison Rape Elimination Act 2003). Passing PREA was a step in the right direction, but it can be argued that little if any change has occurred since 2003. For example, the Bureau of Justice Statistics report on sexual victimization in adult correctional facilities from 2012 to 2018, reports 1,673 *substantiated* incidents of sexual victimization, although prison administrators reported nearly 19,000 *allegations* of sexual victimizations – up from just over 7,500 in 2012 (Maruschak and Buehler 2021 n.p.) Whether rates of rape are increasing or reporting is improving remains to be seen. What is known is that the assaults that do occur, reported or not, have devastating consequences.

> The degrading experience caused damage to my self-esteem for many years … I definitely felt that I did not own my own body. It was enough to convince me that my life did not belong to me and I was robbed of every single drop of dignity of a human being.
>
> *Cecilia Chung, transgender inmate, San Francisco County Jail*
> *Just Detention International 2005*

Incarcerated Queer-identified persons experience sexual violence in prison at devastatingly higher rates, up to ten times higher, than heterosexual inmates (Beck et al. 2013; JDI 2015). Additionally, according to Colopy (2012), in California prisons, nearly 60 percent of trans inmates reported being sexually assaulted as opposed to only 4 percent of the general population. The rape problem in the U.S. correctional system is pervasive and impacts anyone who is incarcerated. As CeCe McDonald, a formerly incarcerated trans woman, remarked: "Prisons aren't safe for anyone, and that's the key issue" (as cited in Hanssens et al. 2014).

Comparatively speaking, we remind you of the victimization faced in places like Cameroon as mentioned earlier. We also would like to draw special attention to the treatment of Queer-identified immigrants who are often seeking asylum from countries where they face violence based on their sexual and/or gender identity. Tabak and Levitan (2014) highlight the harms that are done to migrants who are being detained and indicate that this vulnerable population of LGBTI detainees oftentimes faces increased challenges and violence. Much like PREA, the European Court of Human Rights has found that forced segregation for protection should also be considered a violation of human rights. As evidenced, incarcerated Queer people experience pains of punishment well beyond their sentences. We must remember that correctional practices, while a means of social control, can have, at times, unintended and collateral consequences that further punish those who are especially vulnerable while incarcerated.

Activities and discussion questions

- Investigate the Department of Corrections in your state, or the agency that oversees corrections wherever you live. Are there policies and procedures in place that address the unique needs of incarcerated LGBTQ folks?
- List and discuss the benefits and drawbacks to housing LGBTQ inmates in special areas of the facility separate from other inmates.
- Explore the Prison Policy Initiative at www.prisonpolicy.org and explore their publications and visual materials. What information can you find about LGBTQ folks under correctional supervision?

Recommended viewing

Cruel and Unusual, 2006 [Film] Directed by Janet Baus, Dan Hunt and Reid Williams. USA: Reid Productions.

Free CeCe!, 2016 [Film] Directed by Jacqueline Gares. USA: Jac Gares Media.

Notes

1 "SENTRY is a real-time information system consisting of various applications for processing sensitive but unclassified (SBU) inmate information and for property management. Data collected and stored in the system includes information relating to the care, classification, subsistence, protection, discipline, and programs of federal inmates. SENTRY was developed and implemented in 1981 and continues to be updated to reflect new requirements. SENTRY has also been modernized to take advantage of web-based technologies.

Bureau of Prisons 2012

2 For further reading, visit the Prison Policy Initiative at www.prisonpol icy.org

3 For a full critical thinking worksheet, see: https://blog.education.nationa lgeographic.org/2017/01/20/12-things-we-learned-this-week-8/ultim ate-critical-thinking-worksheet/

References

Adams v. Bureau of Prisons. 716 F. Supp. 2d 107 (2010).

American Bar Association. 2010. *Standards on treatment of prisoners*. Accessed from www.americanbar.org/publications/criminal_justice_section_arch ive/crimjust_standards_treatmentprisoners.html#23–2.2.

American Civil Liberties Union. 2012. Know your rights: Medical, dental and mental health care. *ACLU National Prison Project*. Accessed from www.aclu. org/files/assets/know_your_rights_—_medical_mental_health_and_denta l_july_2012.pdf.

Bali, M. 2020. Why are transgender women jailed in men's prisons around Australia? ABC, July 2. Accessed from www.abc.net.au/news/2020-07-03/why-are-transgender-women-jailed-in-mens-prisons-in-australia/ 12416562.

Beck, A.J., Berzofsky, M., & Krebs, C. 2013. *Sexual victimization in prisons and jails reported by inmates, 2011–2012*. Washington, DC: Bureau of Justice Statistics.

Beck, A.J. & Johnson, C. 2012. *Sexual victimization reported by former inmates, 2008.* Washington, DC: Bureau of Justice Statistics.

Bell, B. 2014. Six questions for transgender rights advocate Mara Keisling. ABC News, August 16. Accessed from http://abcnews.go.com/blogs/politics/2014/08/6-questions-for-transgender-rights-advocate-mara-keisling/.

Brown, G.R. 2009. Recommended revisions to the World Professional Association for Transgender Health's Standards of Care Section on Medical Care for Incarcerated Persons with Gender Identity Disorder. *International Journal of Transgenderism, 11*, (2): 133–139.

Browne, A., Hastings, A., Kall, K., & diZerega, M. 2015. *Keeping vulnerable populations safe under PREA: Alternative strategies to the use of segregation in prisons and jails.* New York, NY: Vera Institute of Justice.

Bureau of Prisons. 2012 July 02. *Privacy Impact Assessment for the SENTRY Inmate Management System.* Accessed from www.bop.gov/foia/docs/sentry.pdf.

Bureau of Prisons. 2017 January. *Case Management Activity (CMA) SENTRY Assignment Form for Transgender Inmates.* Accessed from www.bop.gov/policy/forms/bp_a1110.pdf.

Cahill, S. 2018. How the Juvenile Justice System in Failing LGBTQ Youth. *The Advocate,* October 29. Accessed from www.advocate.com/commentary/2018/10/29/how-juvenile-justice-system-failing-lgbtq-youth.

Canadian Press. 2013. Gay former Ottawa jail guard gets $98K in homophobia suit: Robert Ranger endured "profoundly humiliating" homophobic harassment. CBC, July 26. Accessed from www.cbc.ca/news/canada/ottawa/gay-former-ottawa-jail-guard-gets-98k-in-homophobia-suit-1.1321771.

Coker v. Georgia. 433 U.S. 584 (1977).

Collins, W.C. 2004. *Supermax prisons and the constitution: Liability concerns in the extended control unit.* Washington, DC: National Institute of Corrections.

Colopy, T.W. 2012. Setting gender identity free: Expanding treatment for transsexual inmates. *Health Matrix: Journal of Law Medicine, 22*: 262–271.

Dolovich, S. 2009. Cruelty, prison conditions, and the Eighth Amendment. *New York University Law Review, 84*, (4): 881–972.

Eaton-Robb, P. 2018. Law: Trans Connecticut inmates will be housed appropriately. AP News, May 26. Accessed from https://apnews.com/article/fc5861ef1924494481bc2840f28afe12.

Egan, P. 2021. Lesbian officer at Michigan prison: I was outed in front of inmates, put my life at risk. *Detroit Free Press,* June 23. Accessed from www.freep.com/story/news/local/michigan/2021/06/23/michigan-prison-officer-gay-bridget-cadena-lawsuit-parnall-correctional-facility/5313252001/.

Ellement, J.R. & Anderson, T. 2014. Court denies inmate's sex-change surgery. Reverses ruling in 2012 Kosilek case; Sex-change surgery funding is at issue. *The Boston Globe*, December 16. Accessed from www.bostonglobe. com/metro/2014/12/16/federal-appeals-court-overturns-ruling-order ing-sex-change-surgery-for-mass-prison-inmate/WqBuLuGI14yZ6nV oFCIfjK/story.html.

Farmer v. Brennan. 511. U.S. 825 (1984).

Fenway Institute, The. 2019. Emerging Best Practices for the Management and Treatment of Incarcerated Lesbian, Gay, Bisexual, Transgender, and Intersex (LGBTI) Individuals. Accessed from https://fenwayhealth.org/wp-cont ent/uploads/TFIP-33_Best-Practices-for-LGBTI-Incarcerated-People-Brief_web.pdf.

Fields v. Smith. 653 F. 3d. 550 (2011).

Furman v. Georgia. 408 U.S. 238 (1972).

Glezer, A., McNeil, D.E., & Binder, R.L. 2013. Transgendered and incarcer ated: A review of the literature, current policies and laws, and ethics. *Journal of American Academy Psychiatry Law, 41*: 551–559.

Grassian, S. 1983. Psychopathological effects of solitary confinement. *American Journal of Psychiatry, 140,* (11): 1450–1454.

Gregg v. Georgia. 438 U.S. 153 (1976).

Gruberg, S. 2018. ICE's rejection of its own rules is placing LGBT immigrants at severe risk of sexual abuse. *American Progress*, May 30. Accessed from www.americanprogress.org/article/ices-rejection-rules-placing-lgbt-imm igrants-severe-risk-sexual-abuse/.

Hanson, A. 2011. Solitary confinement: Rumor or reality? Solitary confine ment: Does it provoke mental illness? *Psychology Today*, August 25. Accessed from www.psychologytoday.com/blog/shrink-rap-today/201108/solitary-confinement-rumor-and-reality.

Hanssens, C., Moodie-Mills, A., Ritchie, A.J., Spade, D., & Vaid, U. 2014. *A road map for change: Federal policy recommendations for addressing the criminalization of LGBT people and people living with HIV*. New York, NY: Center for Gender & Sexuality Law at Columbia Law School.

Hauwert, M.C. 2015. Op-ed: Transitioning as a guard at San Quentin State Prison. *The Advocate*, March 3. Accessed from www.advocate.com/comment ary/2015/03/03/op-ed-transitioning-guard-san-quentin-state-prison.

Holsinger, K. & Hodge, J.P. 2014. The experiences of lesbian, gay, bisexual, and transgender girls in juvenile justice systems. *Feminist Criminology*: 1–25.

Human Rights Campaign. 2020. Trump's Timeline of Hate. Accessed from www.hrc.org/resources/trumps-timeline-of-hate.

Human Rights Watch. 2013. *Guilty by association: Human rights violations in the enforcements of Cameroon's anti-homosexuality law*. United States of America: Human Rights Watch.

Irvine, Angela Ph.D. and Canfield, Aisha M.P.P. 2016. The overrepresentation of lesbian, gay, bisexual, questioning, gender nonconforming and transgender youth within the child welfare to juvenile justice crossover population, *Journal of Gender, Social Policy & the Law, 24*: (2): Article 2. Accessed from http://digitalcommons.wcl.american.edu/jgspl/vol24/iss2/2.

Jones, A. 2021. Visualizing the unequal treatment of LGBTQ people in the criminal justice system. *Prison Policy Initiative*, December. Accessed from www.prisonpolicy.org/blog/2021/03/02/lgbtq/.

Jones, J.J. 2021. LGBT Identification Rises to 5.6% in Latest U.S. Estimate. Gallup, February 24. Accessed from https://news.gallup.com/poll/329708/lgbt-identification-rises-latest-estimate.aspx.

Just Detention International. 2005. National prison rape elimination commission testimony of Cecilia Chung. Accessed from www.justdetention.org/en/NPREC/ceciliachung.aspx.

Just Detention International. 2015. The basics about abuse in U.S. detention. Accessed from www.justdetention.org/en/fact_sheets.aspx.

Kahle, L., Rosenbaum, J, & King, S. 2018. Examining the intersections of gender and sexual orientation within the discipline: A case for feminist and queer criminology. In R. Martinez, M. Hollis, & J. Stowell (eds.), *The Handbook of Race, Ethnicity, Crime, and Justice*. Oxford: Wiley.

Kennedy v. Louisiana. 554 U.S. 407 (2008

Leitsinger, M. 2020. Transgender prisoners say they "never feel safe." Could a proposed law help? *KQED*, January 8. Accessed from www.kqed.org/news/11794221/could-changing-how-transgender-inmates-are-housed-make-prison-safer-for-them.

Lenning, E. & Buist, C.L. 2012. Social, psychological and economic challenges faced by transgender individuals and their significant others: Gaining insight through personal narratives. *Culture, Health & Sexuality: An International Journal for Research, Intervention and Care, 15*, (1): 44–57.

Mack, S.K. 2013. Gay former prison guard files discrimination lawsuit against state. *Bangor Daily News*, May 7. Accessed from http://bangordailynews.com/2013/05/07/news/down-east/gay-former-prison-guard-files-discrimination-lawsuit-against-state/.

Majd, K., Marksamer, J., & Reyes, C. 2009. *Hidden injustice: Lesbian, gay, bisexual, and transgender youth in juvenile courts.* Washington, DC: Legal Services of Children, National Juvenile Defender Center and National Center for Lesbian Rights.

Margolin, E. 2014. Does the LGBT movement ignore inmates? MSNBC, November 14. Accessed from www.msnbc.com/msnbc/lgbt-prisoners-abuse.

Maruschak, L.M. and Buehler, E.D. 2021. *Survey of Sexual Victimization in Adult Correctional Facilities, 2012–2018 – Statistical Tables.* Washington, DC: Bureau of Justice Statistics.

Miller, L. 2021. California prisons grapple with hundreds of transgender inmates requesting new housing. *Los Angeles Times*, April 5. Accessed from www.latimes.com/california/story/2021-04-05/california-prisons-consi der-gender-identity-housing-requests.

Moodie-Mills, A. & Gilbert, C. 2014. *Restoring justice: A blueprint for ensuring fairness, safety, and supportive treatment of LGBT youth in the juvenile justice system.* Center for American Progress.

Movement Advancement Project, Center for American Progress, and Youth First. June 2017. Unjust: LGBTQ Youth Incarcerated in the Juvenile Justice System. Accessed from www.lgbtmap.org/criminal-justice-youth-detention.

National Commission on Correctional Health Care. 2020. Transgender and Gender Diverse Health Care in Correctional Settings. www.ncchc.org/tran sgender-and-gender-diverse-health-care.

O'Keefe, M.L., Klebe, K., Stucker, A., Sturm, K., & Leggett, W. 2011. *One year longitudinal study of the psychological effects of administrative segregation.* United States Department of Justice. National Criminal Justice Statistics Service.

Patrickson, V. 2020. A "Double Punishment": Placement and protection of transgender people in prison. *Penal Reform International.* Accessed from www.penalreform.org/blog/transgender-people-in-prison-the-double-punishment/.

Perkinson, R. 1994. Shackled justice: Florence federal penitentiary and the new politics of punishment. *Social Justice, 21,* (3): 117–132.

Prison Rape Elimination Act of 2003. *PREA Public Law 108–79.* Accessed from www.gpo.gov/fdsys/pkg/PLAW-108publ79/pdf/PLAW-108publ79.pdf.

R. G. v. Koller. 415F. Supp. 2d 1129 (2006).

Semprevivo, Lindsay, K. 2020. Dating violence and sexual violence among lesbian, gay, bisexual, and questioning youth: Considering the importance of gender and sexual orientation. *Journal of Aggression, Maltreatment, and Trauma.* Available online.

Tabak, S. & Levitan, R. 2014. LGBTI migrants in immigration detention: A global perspective. *Harvard Journal of Law & Gender, 37:* 1–42.

Trop v. Dulles. 356 U.S. 86 (1958).

World Professional Association for Transgender Health. 2012. *Standards of Care.* www.wpath.org/.

7

FUTURE DIRECTIONS IN QUEER CRIMINOLOGY

The continued development of a sustainable queer criminology is paramount to examining and understanding the use of the criminal legal system as a means to control groups of people and individuals who identify outside of the gender binary and heteronormative landscape. Thus far, we have provided examples from the United States and abroad that highlight the ways in which laws and attitudes surrounding sexuality and gender are used as weapons of the state to control the behavior of those who do not fit the societal norm. These examples both demonstrate the research that has already been done and highlight areas in which the research is lacking, thus providing a roadmap for the future of queer criminology. In this chapter, we will revisit the areas of criminalizing queerness, offending and victimization, law enforcement, legal systems, and corrections by focusing on the gaps within the bodies of literature in those areas. Then, we will consider how other (non-queer) criminologies can be strengthened by the consideration of Queer communities, and discuss why queer criminology must be intersectional, interdisciplinary, public, and in constant evolution.

DOI: 10.4324/9781003165163-7

Gaps in the literature

Since the first edition, queer criminology has gained in popularity within academic circles, building on the foundations abroad, especially in the UK and Australia, and increasing interest in the U.S., evidenced in the work of scholars both seasoned and upcoming who have begun to expand the research and extend the development and application of queer criminology. The field, however, still faces challenges in a number of ways, but still perhaps the most significant challenge is the relative lack of accurate data available. Unfortunately, many of the questions that are left unanswered in the book and beyond are left as such because official information is still rarely and/or properly collected in the criminal legal system. While it is true, as we hope to have demonstrated with this book, that there is a sizeable amount of qualitative and anecdotal evidence to highlight incidents of queer (in)justice around the world, quantitative data describing even the most common criminal justice interactions (e.g., queer arrest data) is largely non-existent. While it is true that quantitative data has its own limitations, it would help to determine the magnitude of the problems exposed in the qualitative data. True, even if officers reported the sexual or gender identities of their arrestees as they do, for example, race, the picture would not be completely accurate (as officers may misidentify or individuals may not feel comfortable providing that very personal information to a state authority they likely do not trust), but it would be an improvement on our current understanding. This is not to say that no quantitative data exists at all, and we have tried to highlight what is available in the previous chapters, but that it is extremely limited in scope.

One reason for this lack of quantitative research, in addition to state negligence in data collection, is the epistemological orientation of most queer criminologists. While certainly there are strong quantitative scholars in the field, many queer criminologists are drawn to conducting qualitative work due to its powerful ability to illuminate the human experience. While quantitative data provides us with a broad understanding of any particular issue, qualitative data uncovers the nuances of the personal, interpersonal, and structural forces that shape our everyday lives, to include our interactions with the criminal legal system. As the field continues to grow and young scholars join the ranks of queer criminology, scholars in the position to mentor others must encourage both quantitative and qualitative approaches, and privilege a mixture of the two.

So, while research continues to mount, new directions continue to develop, including the importance of theory-building and practical application, and activism (Ball 2014; Buist 2019; Buist & Semprevivo 2022), queer criminology is nowhere near the end of its lifecycle. Throughout the book, we have focused on what might be considered traditional areas within the criminal legal system, such as police, courts, and corrections, and expanded the conversation to include a greater focus on experiences of victimization and offending. We have also taken care to elaborate on our discussion of intersectionality and the impacts of experiences within the criminal legal system at the intersections of, for example, race, sexuality, gender, and class, which often have what Collins (2000) refers to as multiplicative effects. These multiplicative effects exacerbate the encounters of Queer folks in the system, often with negative consequences to the individual, and collateral consequences for themselves and their relationships and the broader Queer community. Although Chapter 1 contains the first discussion of intersectionality, the concept/theory/application is highlighted throughout each chapter. Along these overall themes, language is something else that is discussed in the introductory chapter and how it is imperative to be aware of changing times and locations, and how the variety of spaces language is used and how it is applied does not jibe with everyone, everywhere in the same ways.

Chapter 2 focused on how queerness is criminalized throughout the world. The United States, for example, has religious exemption laws, by which child welfare agencies, marriage officiants, medical professionals, or private businesses can deny service to Queer people based on religious objections, in at least fourteen different states. While they do not specifically criminalize sexual orientation and/ or gender identity, they essentially allow for others to discriminate against the Queer community based on religious beliefs. While discrimination guised within freedom is not a new occurrence, we have to remind ourselves that we are well into the new millennium and still fighting for equity. The fight for equal treatment under the law is not something of the past – there are still issues that Queer people face on an everyday basis.

Certainly, trans folks face stress, anxiety, and fear that cisgender people would rarely if ever have to encounter, let alone even think about. For instance, when the first edition of this book was released, there were several states in the United States considering legislation that would not only ban trans folks from using the bathroom of their choice, but that would criminalize the behavior up to a felony, with fines and possibly jail time as a result (Brodey & Lurie 2015). Though most of the bathroom bills considered then, and those introduced more recently, failed, they were only replaced with other attempts by largely conservative lawmakers to limit trans people's full participation in social life, with 2021 seeing the greatest number of anti-trans laws introduced across the country ever (Ronan 2021). Rather than concede to an evolving public conscience, lawmakers hurled forth a flurry of laws meant to discriminate against and prohibit trans people from public spaces and services. These laws run the gamut, from banning transgender children from playing on sports teams consistent with their gender identity, to limiting insurance coverage for transition-related costs, to charging parents with felony child abuse if they medically assist their transgender child (Riemann 2021; Ronan 2021). These bills are almost always sponsored by conservative "family" organizations and backed by the Republican Party and should serve as a reminder of the ways in which queerness is criminalized and bodies are controlled by the state.

Whether or not these laws pass, and far too many of them do, they impact the Queer community simply for being introduced. They send a clear message that Queer people aren't welcome in public spaces, and that people in power will go to extreme lengths to banish them from doing the things that everyone else takes for granted, whether it be using a public restroom, playing sports with their peers, creating a family, or receiving life-saving medical care. While arguably the laws themselves affect trans people more than cisgender Queer folks, the fear they cause is no less palpable for them. In addition to the trans population impacted by bathroom legislation, for example, lesbians who self-identify as "butch," masculine, or genderqueer have addressed being bullied in the bathroom based on others' assumption about their sex and gender identity. Writing for the popular online site for lesbians,

Autostraddle, which heralds itself as "news, entertainment, opinion, community and girl-on-girl culture," one editorial contributor tells of her personal experiences in public restrooms as other women fear her because they assume that her masculine presentation means that she is a man who has wandered into the ladies room, no doubt to assault them in some way.

> Since my gender presentation is most often mistaken for a teen-age boy, the thought of using public bathrooms is anxiety-creating ... I hate the second looks, the stares ....At the same time, I feel guilty and ashamed that my presence in the women's bathroom was read by this woman as a threat ...
>
> Kate 2013: n.p.

These are real fears, and while not always deemed as criminal or law-breaking behavior, the way in which Queer folks are made to feel is often controlling and unmanageable for some who merely want to go about their daily lives in peace. Imagine how you would feel if you were so frightened that you may be arrested or, at the very least, accosted either physically or verbally because you used the restroom in a public place – how paralyzing that fear could be – so much so that it may keep you from engaging in the world around you, avoiding certain locations for fear that you might be confronted for using a facility that we all use on a daily basis. Perhaps that fear would keep you from these places, keep you in your home, out of the public purview. What these heteronormative gazes do is rob Queer people from obtaining and gaining human agency and social capital, which, criminological research has revealed, is a pathway to deviance and crime.

As we are well aware, legislation is changing every day, and there-fore the experiences of individuals and groups are likely to change as well. However, issues regarding the criminalization of queerness quite possibly will always remain problematic. One of those reasons returns us to language and identity. New perspectives will develop, new ways of gender presentation will emerge, and, beyond that, we must remind ourselves that while this book has attempted to take the most inclusive stance we could, it can be troublesome to group all LGBTQ folks together. In Chapter 1, we discussed the influence of queer theoretical approaches that have focused on the deconstruction of categories. We further highlighted the work of Sedgwick (1990), who so accurately noted that an individual will identify themselves in a myriad of ways that may in fact not align with how the public would identify someone. We must always keep this in mind when we are examining the criminalization of queerness – reminding ourselves, fellow scholars, and agents in the criminal legal field that while identity can be fixed for some, for others it is dynamic and ever changing – this is also true of sexual orientation. The possibility of this fluidity makes categorization difficult at best, although, as we have argued, categories can be empowering as well. In many ways, we still live in a monochromatic world; outsiders looking in will continue to categorize others in efforts to understand the world in which they live, and until that stops, using categories and descriptions to empower and impede continues.

Chapter 3 reminded us that these identities and categorizations – whether static or fluid – impact the ease with which Queer people can navigate through life and with which they can harness the social institutions (family, education, healthcare, work, etc.) that everyone relies on to survive. Limited access to these institutions, resulting from stigma, legal barriers, and cisheteronormative social norms, put Queer people at greater risk for victimization, offending, or both. Though a significant amount of research exists in certain areas of queer victimization and offending, there is still much to learn.

Research on hate crimes and intimate partner violence must continue to be produced, but other avenues of inquiry must be established and expanded upon. For example, there is much to learn still about Queer victims of sexual assault and rape, especially as it relates to reporting to law enforcement, treatment by healthcare professionals, and accessing post-assault support services. Among other things, these may be impacted by a victim's location, their sexual orientation or gender identity (or that of their assailant), their relationship with their assailant, or their prior experiences with practitioners.

Beyond considering queer victimization through the lens of interpersonal crimes, however, queer criminology must continue to investigate and uncover state violence, because these are the harms that most egregiously violate the social contract. So long as state actors engage in state sanctioned violence against Queer people, Queer people will never be safe at the hands of civilians, who take cues from those with power. Without a doubt,

> This violence, trauma, abuse – sanctioned by the state – serves to instill fear, which contributes to invisibility and/or 'othering,' which leads to an entire group of people being, at a minimum, controlled, and at worst, slaughtered.
>
> Lenning, Brightman, & Buist 2021: 168

While it is important to interrogate the media, and therefore understand and highlight the queer criminal archetypes that permeate the public consciousness, our research must be used to dispel (or, maybe even validate) these narratives. Without more research on Queer offenders who commit heinous crimes – like murder – there really is no way to know whether these archetypes are merely caricatures, or if they contain some modicum of truth. We know that people like Jeffrey Dahmer, Bruce McArthur, and Luka Magnotta exist – what we don't know is how they compare to Queer people who murder intimate partners or family members, or who do so in self-defense. Alas, conducting these studies does take us back to the issue that none of our official data on homicide captures sexual orientation or gender identity, so until that happens, queer criminologists will have to design small-scale studies as a starting point.

Conversely, it would be just as important to learn if Queer people offend in different ways, perhaps because of their own victimization, which may lead to victimizing others. Or, on the other end of the crime continuum, they may commit less serious criminal offenses, such as survival crimes, to mitigate the loss of legitimate employment opportunities or to counter the effects of the structural systems that work to keep Queer folks out – institutions such as education, religion, family, and more, whose rejection, discrimination, and hate all too often have a lasting impact on individual agency. Although Chapter 3 highlighted the intersections of victimization and offending, the information available is still fairly scant. One direction that could add to a better understanding of those intersections may be to further explore survival crimes related to transition, such as the receiving of black-market hormones because of the prohibitive cost of any variety of legitimate medical services.

Of each of the three arms of the criminal legal system (i.e. law enforcement, legal systems, corrections), our understanding of Queer experiences with and as law enforcement officers is perhaps the most complete. Still, the research that does exist only scratches the surface. As Chapter 4 demonstrates, there is evidence that in their interactions with police officers, Queer people (especially trans people) face selective enforcement, harassment, and brutality at significantly greater rates than the general public (e.g. Buist & Stone 2014; Dwyer 2011; Greenberg 2011; NCAVP 2012). Queer criminology should seek to contextualize these experiences beyond what we already know. In particular, the victims of police brutality can vastly improve our understanding of how multiple identities can increase or decrease risk of victimization by agents of the state. Again, expanding research to focus on victims and offenders, in this case officer–offenders who abuse members of the Queer community and people of color, must be used to develop and implement training protocols for law enforcement, especially in the area of policing diverse communities. These protocols must be enforced and there must be regulation and repercussions, up to and including termination for law enforcement personnel who are unwilling to follow inclusive policies.

Further, it is not enough to respond to reported incidents of disproportionate contact and heightened police victimization of Queer people by simply noting that within policing, just like any occupation, there are good and bad representatives of the law. This argument does not hold water in response to racist behavior conducted by law enforcement officers either. We cannot continue to allow agents of social control, who have the most interaction with the public, to abuse their powers and use their authority to brutalize citizens. We expect our officers of the law to be held to a higher standard and, in turn, we should not continue to accept these abuses of power as a means to illegally control and victimize the people – departments using the "few bad apples" analogy does nothing to implement real structural change. It is time to switch focus from those few bad apples, and start tending to the orchard. In addition to these problems between law enforcement and civilians, it is imperative that we understand that people working within the existing paramilitaristic and hyper-masculine structure of policing are also victims of harassment, discrimination, and violence because of their sexual orientation and/or gender identity, and that the abuses they face are not unlike the abuses the public faces. We should not sit back, idly by, and assume that these are only private problems when they are in fact public issues that affect all of us (Mills 1959), and therefore should concern all of us regardless of sexual orientation or gender identity.

Related to the overall application of a queer criminology, it is not enough to simply describe incidents in the criminal legal system, although we use these examples and case studies to shed light on these ongoing concerns – a queer criminology must seek to use empirical data to influence policy and practice, and that cannot be done by confining our work to academic circles. Researchers must focus on systemic problems as well, such as examining the real possibility that institutions within the criminal legal system, like patriarchal law enforcement agencies, are heteronormative and homophobic (Ball 2014) and therefore those systems must change in order for civilians to reap any benefits from policy and practice. As noted in Chapter 4, there has been some success in places like England and Wales and Canada, among others, that once departmental policy was changed and, importantly, deviations from the policy enforced, Queer citizens' as well as Queer officers' feelings of safety and acceptance increased.

Queer experiences within legal systems is perhaps where there is the most work to be done. It is true that quite a bit of research and debate exists in the areas of hate crimes and hate crime legislation (e.g. European Union Agency for Fundamental Rights 2014; Garland & Chakraborti 2012; Meyer 2014; NCAVP 2014; Ramirez, Gonzalez, & Galupo 2018; Sullaway 2004), but the reality is that hate crimes likely occur far less often than other crimes that Queer people are prone to fall victim to, thus resulting in an interaction with the legal system. For example, there must be more research centered on the courtroom experiences of Queer victims of domestic violence and sexual assault. The work that has been done on bias in the courtroom (e.g. Brower 2011; Cramer 2002; Meidinger 2012; Shay 2014; Shortnacy 2001; Woods 2019) implies that Queer victims who seek legal protections from violence would face greater barriers than non-Queer victims, and should therefore be a focus of future research.

Even less is known about the disparate sentencing of Queer offenders. We know little about whether or not Queer offenders committing more common, nonviolent crimes are sentenced with leniency or are sentenced more harshly than non-Queer offenders. Again, this is because data on sexual or gender identity is not collected in the same way that other demographic information is. An overwhelming amount of research demonstrates that race influences sentencing outcomes (see Mitchell 2005), which begs the question, what might we learn if we explore the intersection of race and actual or perceived sexual or gender identity as they relate to judicial decision making? More research on sentencing outcomes will not only tell us more about Queer experiences in the courtroom, but will reveal new avenues for research in the area of corrections, which is also in need of attention.

Further, the inequality that Queer people face in court systems throughout the world is unacceptable. In the United States, where the importance of "justice for all" is touted, it is rare to see this play out in a court of law with not only Queer folks but poor people of color as well. As research has indicated, Black people are more likely to be sentenced, and for longer periods, than whites for comparable crimes. Further, Black folks are more likely to receive the sentence of death, especially if their victims are white, and the poor are the least likely group to have capable representation. We know, as highlighted in Chapter 5, that Queer people as adults and juveniles have received harsher sentences in some cases, but the empirical data is still inadequate and thus in need of attention.

Beyond exploring the issues that play out directly in courtrooms, queer criminology must interrogate the law as it relates to issues of civil rights (or lack thereof) and their impact on Queer people. Around the world anti-LGBTQ legislation continues to be enforced and new laws are introduced on a near-daily basis, and their consequences can be explored through a criminological lens. How does the failure to legally recognize transgender people at all in Hungary, for example, impact trans people's experiences with the criminal legal system there? How does the lack of legal recognition impact data collection, and thus our understanding of crime and victimization? Given what we know about pathways to criminal behavior, and the positive impacts of young people engaging in prosocial activities, how might banning transgender youth from playing sports in the United States impact youth crime? It would be remiss not to acknowledge that even those laws not immediately seen as related to the criminal legal system, are inextricably linked to the work that we do as queer criminologists.

As pointed out in Chapter 6, there is a dearth of research in the area of community corrections. Most of what we know about Queer encounters with corrections centers around the incarceration of Queer people. While there is a mass incarceration epidemic that should not be ignored, especially in the United States, offenders more often face punishments of probation and those who are incarcerated are likely to experience some sort of post incarceration surveillance. Thus, it is necessary to understand the conditions that Queer offenders face under these types of correctional supervision. As is the case with law enforcement and legal systems, it is safe to assume that Queer offenders face unique challenges, and an understanding of those challenges would enhance what we already know about probationers, parolees, and barriers to reentry. For example, how much harder is it for a Queer parolee to gain employment than other parolees? What about Queer parolees of color? Knowing how queerness and intersectionality affects one's correctional experiences can lead us towards the development of more effective sanctions and reentry services.

Further, a majority of the research on corrections and the Queer community has been couched within the needs and the experiences of transgender offenders and inmates. Certainly, we do not disagree that this should be a major focus of the research, as we have indicated that Queer-identified inmates, but especially trans-identified inmates, face an increased likelihood of victimization. Therefore, exploring the experiences of Queer, but perhaps especially trans, offenders once they have been released from incarceration is wholly important to queer criminology. For instance, research from the National Transgender Discrimination Survey found that 16 percent of trans folks reported having lost at least one job based on their gender identity, while 23 percent had experienced on-the-job harassment based on their gender identity (James, Herman, Rankin, Keisling, Mottet, & Anafi 2016). If we focus on the percentage of trans individuals who lost their job solely because of their identity, think about the heightened impact that having a criminal record would have on trans people. Research has found that most employers would not hire the formerly incarcerated (Raphael 2008), contributing to the millions of parolees who are without legitimate work. "Ban the box" initiatives are working to help increase work opportunities for job seekers with criminal records, but this does not speak to the problems associated with being transgender *and* formerly incarcerated.

As mentioned, the literature that exists on the incarceration of Queer people appears to be the only area of LGBTQ-focused research where the transgender community is concentrated on to a greater degree than the lesbian and gay communities. While past research ignored transgender inmates and instead focused exclusively on consensual and unwanted same-sex sexual encounters, they have emerged to be a central focus. Certainly, as trans people become more visible and as the rights of transgender inmates continue to be defined by the courts, new avenues of research will be exposed. This should not, however, undermine the importance of considering the correctional experiences of all Queer people. Bisexuals, for example, are virtually invisible in all areas of criminological research, even though, as discussed in Chapter 3, they face a greater likelihood of gender-based abuse.

It is important to remember that, in large part due to the media, the general public often thinks about the criminal legal system in terms of the most sensational issues, such as police brutality and the death penalty, and/or the archetypes mentioned above, and any public debate around these issues is almost always predicated by extraordinary and (usually) rare, high-profile criminal cases. Being less interesting, issues like police training, the terms of probation, or the classification of inmates rarely get attention. As we can see from the research highlighted in this book, criminologists focusing on Queer issues also tend to gravitate towards the sensational. While the research on topics like police violence, hate crimes, and the death penalty is important and should continue, there must also be a shift in focus towards the more mundane – the everyday issues of the criminal legal system that affect greater numbers of people, such as those mentioned above.

Queer(ing) criminology

Queer criminology is more than simply adding sexuality or gender identity as a variable to research. Indeed, as described in Chapter 1, queer criminology is a criminology that investigates, criticizes, and challenges heteronormative systems of oppression in the context of the criminal legal system. The perspectives in queer criminology are as diverse as Queer people, and thus we are not limited to one "right way" to apply these perspectives to our understanding of crime and justice issues. Queer criminology can and does focus on both theoretical and practical considerations, but beyond merely the criminal legal system, there are other areas and disciplines that can benefit from queering, such as sociology, or psychology, or social work, and so on. This is to say that, ultimately, multiple areas within academia and in the professional field must increase interest in the Queer experience and consider how these experiences are often intersected with those multiple identities. Certainly, some research and professional areas are more willing to or have already begun to implement these queered changes, but with all things considered, the change, although great, is decades late.

Therefore, despite positive advances, criminology, other disciplines, and varied professional fields still often reflect stereotypes about Queer people and typical (i.e., white, middle-class, male) social constructions of queerness. Thus, we have minimal understanding of sexuality and/or gender as related to personhood. In short, researchers and practitioners often construct our hypotheses, training, and policy around preconceived notions about people.

The complicated nature of measuring and understanding the impact of sexuality and gender on crime and justice issues may be exactly why criminology has largely avoided doing so. It is also quite possible that sexuality and gender are ignored for fear of being politically incorrect. As Panfil (2013) argues, some criminologists may hesitate to recognize and investigate Queer people, especially as violent offenders, in fear of further marginalizing them. Regardless of why Queer experiences in general (and Queer offending more specifically) have not historically been a focus of criminological inquiry, it is clear that both deserve greater attention, and the responsibility of doing that should not lie only within the realm of queer criminology.

Sustaining and growing queer criminology

Relative to criminology more generally and critical criminology more specifically, queer criminology is in its infancy. Indeed, it is only in the last decade or so that queer criminology has begun to establish a presence among academic circles, been given undivided attention by scholarly journals (e.g. special issues of *Critical Criminology*, *Current Issues in Criminal Justice*, the *Journal of Contemporary Criminal Justice*, and *Criminal Justice Studies*), been the sole focus of scholarly books, and been validated through the establishment of the American Society of Criminology's Division on Queer Criminology. This means that we are in a critical moment in the history of the field, and that today's pioneers of queer criminology play a crucial role in defining and shaping its future. What this book has revealed is that queer criminology must follow a path of intersectional, interdisciplinary, and public scholarship that is designed to adapt to the changing landscape of the Queer experience.

> There is no such thing as a single-issue struggle because we do not live single-issue lives.
>
> *Audre Lorde 2007; 138*

If queer criminology is "queer" because of its focus on deconstructing and challenging the role that the criminal legal system plays in the oppression of Queer people, then it must be committed to recognizing and exploring intersectionality. "Given that racism, sexism, and social class inequality make possible many forms of anti-queer violence," both interpersonal and institutional, "challenges to these forms of abuse must not merely consider homophobia but also account for other dimensions of inequality" (Meyer 2014: 116). For example, Black, poor, transgender women are not disproportionately targets of violence just because of homophobia or transphobia. Their victimization can only be understood by examining a web of racism, classism, sexism, and homophobia (Meyer 2012). To ignore this web is reductionist, and dilutes queer criminology in the same way that essentialism diluted feminist criminology with the assumption "that all women are oppressed by all men in exactly the same ways or that there is one unified experience of dominance experienced by women" (Burgess-Proctor 2006: 34). All Queer people are not, in fact, created equal, and a common identity of Queer does not make Queer experiences homogeneous. This returns us to the ongoing debate in this book, primarily as indicated here and in Chapter 1, about these ideas surrounding deconstruction as well as the impact of categorical description. We cannot stress enough that we see the validity in both approaches and we are not willing to choose one over the other, because our goal here has been to strive for inclusion in order to expand the scope of the research. Further,

> employing an intersectional approach to examine the lives of LGBT people necessitates not only including queer people who are oppressed along multiple axes of inequality, but also moving beyond frameworks that construct homophobia as the most predominant form of oppression confronting LGBT people.
>
> Meyer 2012: 869

This is especially true as Queer people continue to win their fight for civil rights. Just as *Brown v. Board of Education* did not halt institutionalized racism, neither did *Lawrence v. Texas* end institutionalized homophobia and heterosexism. The battle for Queer civil rights (e.g. marriage) has in large part been fought by the most privileged (white, middle-class, male) Queer people, and those are the individuals that will most immediately reap the benefits. Low-income Queer people of color will continue to face discrimination in large part due to their race and class, not their sexuality or gender identity. Thus, there must be a continued focus on how the matrix of domination plays out within the criminal legal system.

That said, it should also be noted that the make-up of the academy must more closely reflect the population we are studying. At present, the majority of criminological research that might be considered "queer" is being conducted by people who arguably fit the description of the most privileged (i.e. white, middle class, and residing in the global North) – including the authors of this book. In truth, these privileges describe most scholars of popular and contemporary criminology, so "diversifying" the field is far easier said than done. Given, however, that the focus of queer criminology is to challenge systems of oppression, there must be a focus on elevating the voices that reflect those most oppressed.

Further, as the field of queer criminology grows, one area of research should be the experiences of queer criminologists themselves, especially if they identify on the Queer spectrum. An article by Walker, Valcore, Evans, and Stephens (2021) reveals that transgender scholars face unique challenges in the academy and revealing those challenges can serve to expose inequities in our field and equip young scholars for the path that lies ahead. Another avenue for understanding the experiences of Queer scholars might be to consider how vicarious trauma, meaning trauma resulting from work with traumatized people, impacts them, especially when they are studying a community with which they identify. How, for example, is a bisexual scholar uniquely impacted by their work with bisexual victims of intimate partner violence, or how do trans scholars cope when they research violence against other trans people? The findings of studies on vicarious trauma could help us to better prepare Queer scholars for the work they do – work that is vitally important. Finally, there are cisgender, heterosexual scholars engaging in queer criminological work, and their motivations and experiences are worth exploring as well. What draws cis hetero people to do queer criminological work, and how does it impact them emotionally and professionally? Understanding these motivations and experiences can perhaps inspire or prepare more cis hetero people to engage in this important work, or at least encourage them to be more open to the idea of incorporating Queer communities into their existing research.

In addition to recognizing and representing all of the possible dimensions of identity, research in queer criminology must also embrace an interdisciplinary approach. It behooves us to engage the scholarship that has been done in the realm of legal studies, psychology, social work, and others in order to improve and not reinvent the wheel, so to speak. For example, imagine the possibility of combining the legal literature on courtroom bias (e.g. Brower 2011; Cramer 2002; Shay 2014) or police brutality (e.g. Buist & Stone 2014; Dwyer 2011; Greenberg 2011; NCAVP 2012) with the psychological study of implicit (i.e. unconscious) bias towards the Queer community. Or imagine the possibility of arming social workers with everything we know, and will learn in the future, about the relationship between structural disadvantage and survival crimes. Only when we can understand and harness the myriad causes of discrimination can we subvert them, and that is a task far too great for one field.

In addition to blending disciplinary approaches, we must look outside of academia for information and knowledge. Much of what we know about Queer experiences with the criminal legal system does not come from research conducted by criminologists or, for that matter, even academics. By and large, it is journalists (most often working for LGBTQ publications), nongovernmental agencies, and other government-employed or independent groups of researchers that are uncovering and reporting them, such as those that are cited in this book. This is not necessarily a bad thing, as the academy has proven to have a rather limited audience, inasmuch as academic books are cost-prohibitive and peer-reviewed journals are not readily available to the general public as of yet and, even if they were, still wouldn't fit the definition of "accessible." Rather, this is a reminder that a transformative queer criminology must also be a public criminology, one that embraces and utilizes the power of technology and global interconnectivity, such as that found in new media. Queer criminologists must continue to engage in media studies, as they can help us understand offending, such as the use of social media apps for the commission of violent crimes, victimization, such as when those crimes go viral, and resilience, such as when people around the globe harness the power of social media to memorialize victims and collectively grieve, as they did in the aftermath of the Pulse nightclub shooting.

> TWEET: Roommate asked for the room till midnight. I went into molly's room and turned on my webcam. I saw him making out with a dude. Yay.
> *Dharun Ravi, September 19, 2010, three days before his roommate jumped off of the George Washington Bridge, Foderaro 2010*

Though the deaths of white Queer people more often make it to the mainstream media, it is still often on the heels of a social media firestorm. The suicide of 17-year-old Leelah Alcorn, a young, transgender teenager from Ohio, did make national headlines, but only after she posted her suicide note to the social media site Tumblr. In her note, Leelah wrote, "the only way I will rest in peace is if one day transgender people aren't treated the way I was, they're treated like humans, with valid feelings and human rights …. My death needs to mean something" (Corcoran & Spargo 2015). Tyler Clementi, a college freshman, likely would not have taken his own life by jumping off of the George Washington Bridge had his roommate not tweeted about and livestreamed video of him having an intimate encounter with another man in his dorm room. Thus, queer criminology would be incomplete if we did not take social media seriously as both a vehicle for victimization and offending, and as a tool for exploration, exposure, and transformation. New media must be recognized as an accessible forum for queer engagement and as central to making queer criminology a public criminology (Uggen & Inderbitzin 2010).

What new media reveals distinctly is that the inconsistent evolution of Queer rights is another complication to queer criminological research, inasmuch as Queer rights are changing (both for the better and the worse) on a daily basis. Indeed, by the time you are reading this book, it is entirely likely that some (if not many) of the laws that we highlight will have changed, so an ongoing challenge for queer criminologists is the constantly changing landscape of the Queer experience. Thus, queer criminology must be in constant evolution – in concert with and in reaction to the advancement of Queer rights (both within and outside of the criminal legal system) and the resulting backlash.

> Fix society. Please.
>
> *Leelah Alcorn, December 28, 2014,*
> *suicide note, Corcoran & Spargo 2015*

The sheer magnitude of the Queer struggle broadly – and with the criminal legal system narrowly – is, in and of itself, a roadblock to timely change. As we hope to have demonstrated here, the struggle is complex and changing, and manifests differently based on a variety of factors, including individual identities and presentations, geography, culture, history, and political climate. Not only does this present a daunting task to queer criminologists, it creates a challenge to local, state, national, and global criminal legal systems. While queer criminologists should

focus their immediate attention on throwing "bricks through establishment or mainstream criminology's windows" in the spirit of critical
criminology (DeKeseredy & Dragiewicz 2011: 2), citizens and criminal
legal professionals alike must commit to a more egalitarian world and
to the development of a criminal *justice* system, and to do so will mean
tearing down the suffocating walls of (in)justice that have been built
around us, one brick at a time.

Activities and discussion questions

* Now that the book has come to an end, it is time for you to form
  your own questions and identify what activities *you* can engage in
  to aid in the quest for a more egalitarian world and a *just* criminal
  legal system. You are now the builder, so take the bricks that others have torn down, and start building a new foundation. Now the
  real work begins.

References

Ball, M. 2014. What's queer about queer criminology? In D. Peterson & V.
 Panfil (eds.), *Handbook of LGBT communities, crime, and justice* (pp. 531–555).
 New York, NY: Springer.
Brodey, S. & Lurie, J. 2015. Get ready for the conservative assault on where
 transgender Americans pee. *Mother Jones*, March 9. Accessed from www.
 motherjones.com/politics/2015/03/transgender-bathroom-discriminat
 ion-bills.
Brower, T. 2011. Twelve angry – and sometimes alienated – men: The experi-
 ences and treatment of lesbians and gay men during jury service. *Drake Law
 Review, 59*: 669–706.
Buist, C.L. 2019. LGBTQ rights in the fields of criminal law and law enforce-
 ment. *University of Richmond Law Review, 54*, (3): 877–900.
Buist, C.L. & Semprevivo, L.K. (eds.). 2022. *Queering criminology in theory and
 praxis: Re-imagining justice in the criminal legal system and beyond.* Bristol: Bristol
 University Press.
Buist, C.L. & Stone, C. 2014. Transgender victims and offenders: Failures of the
 United States criminal justice system and the necessity of queer criminol-
 ogy. *Critical Criminology, 22*, (1): 35–47.
Burgess-Proctor, A. 2006. Intersections of race, class, gender, and crime: Future
 directions for feminist criminology. *Feminist Criminology, 1*, (1): 27–47.

Collins, P. 2000. *Black feminist thought: Knowledge, consciousness, and the politics of empowerment.* New York, NY: Routledge.

Corcoran, K. & Spargo, C. 2015. Suicide note of 17-year-old transgender girl is DELETED from her Tumblr page after her Christian parents demand message blaming them for her death be removed. *Daily Mail,* January 3. Accessed from www.dailymail.co.uk/news/article-2895534/Heartbreak ing-suicide-note-17-year-old-transgender-girl-DELETED-Tumblr-page-candlelit-vigils-held-honor.html.

Cramer, A.C. 2002. Discovering and addressing sexual orientation bias in Arizona's legal system. *Journal of Gender, Social Policy & the Law, 11,* (1): 25–37.

DeKeseredy, W. & Dragiewicz, M. (eds.) 2011. *Handbook of critical criminology.* New York, NY: Routledge.

Dwyer, A. 2011. "It's not like we're going to jump them": How transgressing heteronormativity shapes police interactions with LGBT young people. *Youth Justice, 11,* (3): 203–220.

European Union Agency for Fundamental Rights. 2014. *EU LGBT survey: European Union lesbian, gay, bisexual and transgender survey.* Luxembourg: Publications Office of the European Union.

Foderaro, L. 2010. Private moment made public, then a fatal jump. *New York Times,* September 29. Accessed from www.nytimes.com/2010/09/30/nyregion/30suicide.html?_r=0.

Garland, Jon & Chakraborti, Neil. 2012. Divided by a common concept? Assessing the implications of different conceptualizations of hate crime in the European Union. *European Journal of Criminology, 9,* (10): 38–51.

Greenberg, K. 2011. Still hidden in the closet: Trans women and domestic violence. *Berkeley Journal of Gender, Law & Justice, 27,* (2): 198–251.

James, S.E., Herman, J.L., Rankin, S., Keisling, M., Mottet, L. & Anafi, M. 2016. *The report of the 2015 U.S. transgender survey.* Washington, DC: National Center for Transgender Equality.

Kate. 2013. Butch please: Butch in the bathroom. *Autostraddle.* May 3. Accessed from www.autostraddle.com/butch-please-butch-in-the-bat hroom175366/.

Lenning, E., Brightman, S., & Buist, C.L. 2021. The trifecta of violence: A socio-historical comparison of lynching and violence against transgender women. *Critical Criminology, 29,* (1): 151–172.

Lorde, A. 2007. Sister Outsider: Essays & Speeches. Berkeley, CA: Crossing Press

Meidinger, M.H. 2012. Peeking under the covers: Taking a closer look at prosecutorial decision-making involving queer youth and statutory rape. *Boston College Journal of Law & Social Justice, 32,* (2): 421–451.

Meyer, D. 2012. An intersectional analysis of lesbian, gay, bisexual, and transgender (LGBT) people's evaluations of anti-queer violence. *Gender & Society, 26,* (6): 849–873.

Meyer, D. 2014. Resisting hate crime discourse: Queer and intersectional challenges to neoliberal hate crime laws. *Critical Criminology, 22*: 113–125.

Mills, C.W. 1959. *The sociological imagination.* New York, NY: Oxford University Press.

Mitchell, O. 2005. A meta-analysis of race and sentencing research: explaining the inconsistencies. *Journal of Quantitative Criminology, 21*, (4): 439–466.

National Coalition of Anti-Violence Programs. 2012. *Lesbian, gay, bisexual, transgender, queer and HIV-affected hate violence in 2012.* New York, NY: National Coalition of Anti-Violence Programs.

National Coalition of Anti-Violence Programs. 2014. *Lesbian, gay, bisexual, transgender, queer, and HIV-affected hate violence in 2013.* New York, NY: National Coalition of Anti-Violence Programs.

Panfil, V. 2013. Better left unsaid? The role of agency in queer criminological research. *Critical Criminology, 22*, (1): 99–111.

Ramirez, J.L., Gonzalez, K.A., & Galupo, M.P. 2018. "Invisibility during my own crisis": Responses of LGBT people of color to the Orlando shooting. *Journal of Homosexuality, 65*, (5): 579–599.

Raphael, S. 2008. The employment prospects of ex-offenders. *Focus, 25*, (2): 21–26.

Reimann, N. 2021. 2021 will become record-breaking year for anti-LGBTQ laws, advocacy group warns. *Forbes*, April 22. Accessed from www.forbes.com/sites/nicholasreimann/2021/04/22/2021-will-become-record-breaking-year-for-anti-lgbtq-laws-advocacy-group-warns/?sh=629232a77549.

Ronan, W. 2021. Breaking: 2021 becomes record year for anti-transgender legislation. Human Rights Campaign, March 13. Accessed from www.hrc.org/press-releases/breaking-2021-becomes-record-year-for-anti-transgender-legislation.

Sedgwick, E. 1990. *Epistemology of the closet.* Berkeley, CA: University of California Press.

Shay, G. 2014. In the box: Voir dire on LGBT issues in changing times. *Harvard Journal of Law & Gender, 37*: 407–457.

Shortnacy, M.B. 2001. Guilty and gay, a recipe for execution in American courtrooms: Sexual orientation as a tool for prosecutorial misconduct in death penalty cases. *American University Law Review, 51*, (2): 309–365.

Sullaway, M. 2004. Psychological perspectives on hate crime laws. *Psychology, Public Policy, and Law, 10*, (3): 250–292.

Uggen, C. & Inderbitzin, M. 2010. Public criminologies. *Criminology & Public Policy, 9*, (4): 725–749.

Walker, A., Valcore, J., Evans, B., & Stephens, A. 2021. Experiences of trans scholars in criminology and criminal justice. *Critical Criminology, 29*: 37–56.

Woods, J.B. 2019. LGBTQ in the courtroom: How gender and sexuality impacts the jury system. In C.J. Najdowski & M.C. Stevenson (eds.). *Criminal juries in the 21st century: Contemporary issues, psychological science, and the law.* New York: Oxford University Press.

ADDITIONAL RESOURCES

American Civil Liberties Union www.aclu.org/
American Society of Criminology Division on Queer Criminology
    https://queercrim.com/
Amnesty International www.amnestyusa.org/
Black & Pink www.blackandpink.org/
Center for Victim Research Repository https://ncvc.dspacedirect.org
Forge https://forge-forward.org/
GLBT Historical Society www.glbthistory.org/
GLSEN www.glsen.org/
Human Dignity Trust www.humandignitytrust.org/
Human Rights Campaign www.hrc.org/
Human Rights Watch www.hrw.org/
International Gay, Lesbian, Bisexual, Trans and Intersex Organization
    https://ilga.org/
Intersex Society of North America https://isna.org/
Lambda Legal www.lambdalegal.org/
Movement Advancement Project www.lgbtmap.org/
National Black Justice Coalition http://new.nbjc.org/
National Center for Transgender Equality https://transequality.org/
National LGBTQ Institute on IPV https://lgbtqipv.org/
National LGBTQ Task Force www.thetaskforce.org/
OutRight Action International https://outrightinternational.org/
PFLAG https://pflag.org/
Prison Policy Initiative www.prisonpolicy.org/

The Trevor Project www.thetrevorproject.org/
Transgender Europe https://tgeu.org/
Transgender Law Center https://transgenderlawcenter.org/
Urban Institute www.urban.org/
Williams Institute https://williamsinstitute.law.ucla.edu/
Witness Media Lab https://lab.witness.org/

INDEX